Newspaper
Layout and Design

★ ★ **SECOND EDITION**

Newspaper
Layout and Design

BY DARYL R. MOEN

IOWA STATE UNIVERSITY PRESS / AMES

DARYL R. MOEN is Director of Professional Programs and professor in the School of Journalism, University of Missouri, Columbia.

© 1989, 1984 Iowa State University Press, Ames, Iowa 50010
All rights reserved

Composed by Iowa State University Press in 10 on 12 English Times
Printed in the United States of America

First edition, 1984
Second printing, 1985
Third printing, 1986
Second edition, 1989

Library of Congress Cataloging-in-Publication Data

Moen, Daryl R.
     Newspaper layout and design / by Daryl R. Moen. — 2nd ed.
          p.   cm.
     Bibliography: p.
     Includes index.
     ISBN 0-8138-1227-5
     1. Newspaper layout and typography.   2. Printing, Practical —
Layout.   I. Title.
 Z253.5.M63 1989   88-9021
     686.2′252 — dc19   CIP

Contents

III

NEWSPAPER DESIGN

Preface

"No longer are people satisfied with pages that are dull, gray, and hard to read. They want their news presented so they can find it quickly and get a summary of important stories in a hurry."

THAT COMMENT SOUNDS as if it came from a market researcher in the late 1980s. It didn't. Albert Sutton wrote it in his 1948 book *Design and Makeup of the Newspaper* (Prentice-Hall). Does this mean that we have not made much progress in the last 30 years? Possibly. It is always hard to tell the difference between change and progress without the benefit of hindsight. That we are still complaining about dull, gray, and hard-to-read pages does not mean that the industry has not tried to improve.

Take headline formats, for example. With gusto, the industry embraced one-line horizontal headlines and threw away old-fashioned decks in the early 1960s. Well, almost the entire industry. The *New York Times* and the *Wall Street Journal* clung stubbornly to the decks, and in hindsight, correctly so. We have discovered that our new headline styles represented change but not progress. Our modern, spare headline formats forced us to strip context away and made it harder to tell and sell with fairness and flair. Now we look to papers such as the *Portland Oregonian* for a headline format that preserves the strengths of the deck in a modern look.

Whether it is change or progress, there has been enormous activity in the field of newspaper design in the 1980s. Much of it is attributable to the Society of Newspaper Design, through its journal, convention, and contest, all of which have served to educate designers, editors, and publishers. Other periodicals, such as *U & lc* and *Ligature,* have a wider visibility among newspaper designers. *USA Today,* born of an entreprenuer's dream and nurtured on the milk of research, has demonstrated that there is a market for innovation and that newspaper quality printing is not an oxymoron. Yet a negative factor drives much of the change. Penetration at many newspapers continues to decline. Publishers are looking for answers.

This book offers some of them. This second edition reflects and, I hope, contributes to the improvement of newspaper design. Much is different from the first edition. There are two new chapters. One is devoted to information graphics. Because information graphics is so new to so much of our industry, I have compiled a unique list of checkpoints to help students, designers, and editors evaluate the graphics. The other new chapter is devoted to special problems and opportunities within each section of the newspaper.

I have also changed most other chapters significantly. Three-quarters of the illustrations are new; the results of the latest design research have been integrated into the text. The ethical considerations of photographic manipulation is expanded. The impact of new technology, from pagination to color scanners, is reflected in these pages. The chapter on color, of course, has been expanded as has its use in American newspapers. Finally, the most visible change is the format. The larger size permits us to display the many illustrations better. And each illustration now has a caption to help students understand its significance.

What has not changed is the organization of the book. The first half is still devoted to the mechanics of laying out pages because all teachers understand that you have to know how to do something before you explore how to do it well. The second half concentrates on the more complicated aspects such as color and publication design and the conceptual process needed to produce papers that are informative and easy to read.

Also, for the first time there is a workbook to accompany this textbook. Teachers will find it useful for classes ranging from editing and layout to newspaper design.

No book is the work of one person. I have been fortunate in my teaching, consulting, and workshop activities to come in contact with hundreds of journalists from around the country, all of whom have helped me in some way shape my ideas and clarify my message. A special thanks to Alan Jacobson of the *Norfolk* (Va.) *Ledger-Star,* Pegie Stark, formerly of the *Detroit News;* Jackie Combs of the *Chicago Tribune;* Christian Anderson of the *Register* in Orange County; and Jim Jennings of the *Lexington* (Ky.) *Herald-Leader.* I have benefited in many ways from my conversations with fellow authors Mario Garcia of The Poynter Institute and Robert Bohle of Virginia Commonwealth University. I have also benefited from the wisdom of several of my fellow faculty members at the Missouri School of Journalism, particularly Bill Kuykendall, Dr. Birgit Wassmuth, and Dr. Paul Fisher.

I especially wish to gratefully acknowledge permission to reprint materials used as examples throughout. A complete list of credits appears at the back of the book.

Most of all, I thank my wife Nancy and our children for their loving support.

I

Introduction

1

Evolution of design

NO MATTER how great the author's wisdom or how vital the message or how remarkable the printer's skill, unread print is merely a lot of paper and little ink. The true economics of printing must be measured by how much is read and understood and not by how much is produced.

Herbert Spencer
PHILOSOPHER

TECHNOLOGY advances geometrically. Employees who started their careers laboriously setting headlines letter by letter on a Ludlow machine are likely to be bouncing signals off satellites so that newspaper editions can be printed simultaneously around the world. That dizzying progress is in sharp contrast to the snail's pace in the post-Gutenberg years. Nearly 400 years passed before there was a significant improvement in Gutenberg's press. Then the pace quickened. In the next 150 years, several generations of presses and composition machinery were invented and discarded as obsolete. Less than 40 years after the first color photograph moved on a wire service, color photographs were commonplace in newspapers.

The evolution of American newspaper design in the nearly 300 years since *Publick Occurrences* was first published on September 25, 1690, includes stories of economic courage, improved technology, and responses to competitive pressures. Gutenberg borrowed money to print the Mazarin Bible, was unable to repay it, and lost his press and type. He may have been the first publisher to go bankrupt, but he was not the last. In 1964, two years after becoming the first competitive metropolitan daily to try offset printing, the Phoenix *Arizona Journal* folded.

Technical developments will have a continuing influence on our ability to meld words and visuals; they expand our opportunities when we control them but hinder us when they limit our ability to perform the necessary journalistic functions. That is why it is necessary for us to study four areas of the production system: paper, presses, type and typesetting, and photographs.

3

Paper

The supply and cost of paper have a direct effect on newspaper size and quality. For example, colonial journalists increased page size in response to a tax levied on the number of pages. The revolutionary war eliminated the tax but reduced the supply of newsprint, which was made from rags. Some papers shrank to approximately 8½ by 11 inches. Newsprint was rough in texture and often blotched or gray (Mott 1945). By 1800, with the war over, the supply of newsprint had returned to normal and newspaper pages began increasing in size. Although most newspapers enlarged their pages to 15 to 16 inches in width, in 1853 the New York *Journal of Commerce* was 3 by 5 feet, which was unusually large and undoubtedly impossible to handle. Newspaper pages usually contained 6 or 7 columns of type set 15 to 17 picas wide.

The Civil War again interrupted the supply of newsprint, and the price soared to $440 a ton (Emery and Emery 1978). Soon after the war ended, wood pulp replaced rags as the raw material in newsprint and changed the economics of printing. With new mills and cheap forestland, the price of paper declined to $42 a ton in 1899. It was only $8 a ton higher 40 years later. Cheap newsprint, much of it supplied from Canada, continued to aid the development and growth of the newspaper industry until the late 1960s and early 1970s when increasing demand and labor strikes in the newsprint manufacturing industry collided. Newsprint, hard to obtain for about two years, shot up in price. Newspapers lowered the percentage of the paper devoted to news, reduced type size and pictures, dropped syndicated services, and reduced or eliminated some comics. Coming soon after editors had realized the value of white space, the newsprint shortage was a setback to design because material had to be shoehorned into the paper. The newsprint industry gradually caught up to demand, but the new pricing structure made many publishers wary. As they incorporated the new costs into the newspaper's pricing system, publishers eased up slightly. However, they continued to maintain tight papers, and design had to respond to this need.

Already reeling from increasing newsprint prices, publishers in the 1960s and 1970s faced the additional threat of declining circulation. The industry responded with special-interest sections, most of which had open covers. Design flourished in these sections, and the experimentation done there had an effect on the news sections of many newspapers.

The pressures of price continue to exist. Studies show that a significant portion of potential subscribers cannot read a newspaper because of the small type size, but editors are reluctant to use larger text type because an increase from 9- to 10-pt. type means an 11 percent loss of expensive newshole.

One way to slow the rate of increase of newsprint prices is to decrease the weight of the paper. A lower weight, however, means a flimsier newsprint and lower printing quality. Consequently, there is more show-through from one side of the page to the other as well as more paper breaks during printing. Most newspapers use 30-pound paper, down from 32-pound in 1974. Next stop: 28-pound paper.

Researchers are trying to determine if the use of kenaf, a fibrous plant, can lower newsprint prices as dramatically as wood pulp did more than 100 years ago. In an Arizona test, kenaf grew to a height of 14 feet in four months. Unlike trees, which require years of growth, kenaf is harvested annually. Although newsprint made from kenaf has been tested successfully in several newspaper plants, it is not yet known whether farmers can make enough profit to justify substituting it for their other crops or if newsprint mills can buy it cheaply enough to justify changeover costs. If the economics prove favorable for both farmers and newsprint producers, kenaf may soon start replacing wood pulp.

Regardless of whether newsprint is made from wood pulp or kenaf, the size of the newspaper page will shrink. In the late 1970s, with newsprint at $500 a metric ton, most newspapers were 30 to 32 inches wide. An industry effort to standardize page sizes to accommodate national advertisers and cut paper costs has resulted in a standard 28-inch width. Although this size is easier for readers to handle, legibility is decreased slightly because of narrower column widths.

Presses

Journalism historian Frank Luther Mott described how newspapers were produced in the 1700s: "The type was inked by a sheepskin ball filled with wool and attached to a hickory stick; a boy wielded two such balls, transferring the ink from the slab on which it was spread to the form and often bedaubing himself" (Mott 1945, p. 46). Printing was slow, and the quality poor. In 1980, that boy with the hickory stick would have been awed by the giant contraptions spewing out newspapers at speeds up to 70,000 impressions an hour. But this progress has its price. It takes a letterpress unit that weighs more than 400 tons and consumes about 750 horsepower to put one-fifth of an ounce of ink on 64 pages of newsprint (Puncekar 1980). Enormous amounts of space are required to house these presses. Today, researchers are working on smaller, lighter presses with better reproduction quality. If history is any guide, smaller presses will be developed to meet the needs of increased speed and quality. That is the way it has been ever since 1825 when the *New York Daily Advertiser* installed America's first steam-driven cylinder press and forced the boy with the hickory stick out of a job.

Steam-powered presses printed 2,000 papers an hour and increased production to 4,000 an hour less than 10 years later. The next breakthrough came in 1847 when the revolving printing surface was invented. Curved type forms were locked on the cylinder and fastened with wedged or V-shaped column rules. Speed reached 20,000 copies an hour, but editors could not use headlines more than 1 column wide because the type had to be locked in. Stereotype plates solved that problem in 1861. Instead of locking the actual type into a form, a metal impression (stereotype or metal plate) was made of the type, curved to fit the rollers, and put on the press. Vertical makeup continued out of habit, and probably preference, for many years, but the mechanical justification for it was gone.

Further press developments came rapidly. In 1863, the first web-perfecting press was installed in an American newspaper. It was called web because the paper was fed onto the press from a roll rather than in sheets and perfecting because the paper was printed on both sides as it passed through the press. By 1890, a Hoe press could print 48,000 twelve-page papers an hour. By 1920, improved presses increased production to 60,000.

Until 1940, all papers were printed on letterpress units. This is a direct printing method in which paper and ink are brought together under pressure to make an impression. Unfortunately, the reproduction quality, especially of photographs, is not good on such presses. The problem was solved in 1939 by offset printing, a method in which the inked image is transferred from the plate to a rubber blanket and then to the paper. With a finer halftone screen, a little higher grade of paper and ink, and less plate pressure, offset produces better tones. This method of printing became popular with small newspapers and was usually accompanied by cold type composition, a photographic process that does not require metal type. As manufacturers increased press speed, papers with larger circulation went offset. In 1965, the Dubuque (Iowa) *Telegraph Herald* installed an offset press (Goss Metro) that printed 50,000 papers an hour. To show off the printing quality, offset papers increased the size and number of photographs, and photographers flocked to them. Photojournalism—reporting with a camera—had existed ever since the Spanish-American War, but it was refined on the small- to medium-sized dailies during the 1960s and 1970s, and the photographer began to be integrated into the newsroom.

While editors and photographers were changing the face of smaller papers, publishers of metropolitan papers were looking for ways to improve the quality of their letterpress printing without investing several million dollars for new presses and changeover costs. Research spearheaded by the American Newspaper Publishers Association Research Institute produced a photo-imaged relief plate that permitted letterpress papers to use cold type of photocomposition techniques and eliminate stereotype plates. This breakthrough improved reproduction at the big dailies.

In 1968, the Research Institute produced the DiLitho system that used aluminum offset plates on a specially altered letterpress unit. Eighty dailies had adopted DiLitho by 1980 and achieved nearly offset-quality reproduction. By 1980, 99 percent of American dailies were printed by offset, DiLitho, or a refinement of DiLitho.

Today, nearly three-quarters of the nation's dailies are offset. A number of larger newspapers, including *Newsday,* the *Chicago Tribune, Houston Post,* and *Free Press* and *News* in Detroit, have switched to offset. Speed is up to 70,000 impressions per hour, and some of the larger newspapers have bought two complete units to double their output.

Just as offset printing excited the industry with its promises of improved reproduction, as the 1990s approached, a new printing process called flexography was capturing the attention of publishers. Although flexography is like letterpress in that it is a form of direct-relief printing, in flexography the contact is lighter. Flexography, according to its supporters, reduces newsprint waste, decreases the amount of show-through, which in turn might permit use of lighter paper; produces halftones at least as good as offset if not better; reduces the amount of maintenance needed on the press; and eliminates most ink rub-off on readers' hands.

That last advantage is a most important one. A common complaint about newspapers is that they leave ink smudges on readers' hands and clothes. Newspapers using other printing systems can switch to more expensive ink. The Orlando (Fla.) *Sentinel* found that low—rub-off ink reduces rub-off 71 percent. Flexography decreases rub-off because it uses water-based instead of oil-based inks.

Another encouraging development is ink made from soy oil. In 1987 the Cedar Rapids (Iowa) *Gazette* became the first newspaper to use ink with an oil base squeezed from soybeans. This ink has little rub-off. It also has other benefits. It prints more impressions per pound than petroleum-based ink, the supply is plentiful, and it is less hazardous to the environment in the pressroom and at the disposal site.

Publishers care about press speed and cost, editors care about reproduction, and readers care about rub-off. We may be looking at a time when all these concerns are solved in a single printing method.

Type and typesetting

The necessity to cut type from wood by hand inhibited the development and use of type for the first 150 years of American newspapering. Wood type was followed by metal type that was cast by hand at first but produced by machine in 1822.

Even though display type was more readily available, editors did not use headlines consistently until the Mexican War in 1846 when heads often appeared with several decks. Until stereotype plates were introduced in 1861, headlines were restricted to 1 column to keep the type from flying from the form during printing. Makeup remained vertical for a long time, even after the advent of stereotype plates. During the Civil War, headlines were still 1 column with 6 to 12 decks descending from them. Often six different kinds of type were used. The yellow journalism practiced in the 1890s brought with it big, black Gothic headlines. It was the first time that headlines were consistently used wider than 1 column. Historian Mott commented, "There was, however, so much lawless variety in front-page makeup that it amounted to monstrous confusion" (Mott 1945, p. 544). The type was crudely hand drawn because none was available in the several-inch-high sizes that were used.

About that time, the Linotype was introduced. Until then, all the text type was set by hand. Several people, including Mark Twain who went broke in the effort in the 1890s, had been trying to produce such a machine. Ottmar Merganthaler finally succeeded where the others had failed. Type quality improved, and the setting speed increased dramatically. That in turn improved newspaper typography. As Mott commented, "Better taste of both type founders and makers of Linotype faces made for greatly improved typography in the newspapers" (Mott 1945, p. 602).

In 1892, 22 typefounders consolidated to become the American Type Founders, a company that improved type and type use. Cheltenham was designed in 1902 and immediately joined the ranks of other popular typefaces such as Bodoni and Goudy. Ionic, Excelsior, and Ideal were introduced for text use in the 1920s and 1930s. All were highly legible and held up under the punishment of rotary presses. With Corona, they remain among the most popular newspaper text faces today. Futura and Times New Roman were cut after World War I and have also lasted in newspapers. In the 1940s, Univers, Helvetica, Optima, and Palatino were introduced. Few new typefaces were designed in the 1960s and 1970s because photocomposition was being introduced and companies were too busy converting their type stocks to film to meet the requirements of the new production process.

Another deterrent to new typeface design was the lack of copyright

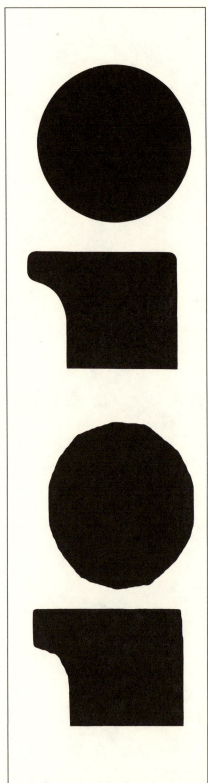

1.1. The quality of digitally produced type depends on the number of lines per inch.

protection. In 1970, the International Typeface Corporation (ITC) was formed. When ITC buys the rights to a typeface, it licenses that face to any company that wants to produce it under its own name. In its first ten years, ITC produced 23 new typefaces, including Avant Garde Gothic, Franklin Gothic, Zapf Book, and Tiffany, all of which appear regularly in newspapers but not necessarily as the basic display face.

Photocomposition has improved the use of type even though it slightly damaged the design of individual letters. When type was produced in metal, each size had its own proportions; when it is produced for photocomposition, one size, approximately 5 points, is stored on film. When 10-pt. type is desired, the image is magnified by a factor of two; for 30-pt. type, the magnification factor is six. Consequently, subtle changes cut into metal type as it increased in size were lost in photocomposition. That shortcoming was rectified with the introduction of digitized cathode ray tube typesetting, in which each character in a font is stored as computer information and broken down into overlapping strokes. The more the type is broken down, the better it looks when reproduced. Autologic, which breaks type down up to 2,880 lines per inch, produces a high-quality letter (Fig. 1.1).

Laser typesetting is another step forward. Laser printers capture the precise, uniform beam of light. A laser typesetter will print one point at a time across the length of the line; that is, it begins at the top of the letters in a sentence and works down in consecutive rapid passes back and forth. Laser typesetters produce a high-quality letterform that does not show rough edges when enlarged as much as photocomposition or digitally set type does.

Photocomposition, digital, and laser typesetting equipment also permit designers to control the amount of space between letters, between lines, and between headlines and copy. Control of the spacing between letters was not possible with metal type, and the designer had to accept the spacing built into the typeface. Kerning (setting type so letters touch each other) can be done more easily by adjusting computer programs. This is especially useful for correcting the optically incorrect amount of space that occurs, for instance, when a capital T precedes a lowercase letter. Because of the cross stroke (top of the T), the next letter looks like it is too far removed from the stem (Ti). Using the computer, such letters can now be moved closer to the stem to be more pleasing optically (Ti).

Typesetting machines that produce both display type and text copy at the same time can be programmed to provide the correct amount of space between headline and copy. Because that space should change as the size of the headline changes, today's typesetters offer time-saving flexibility as well as improved quality of reproduction. (Specifics of handling type are treated in detail in Chapter 11, 12, and 13.)

Photographs

The newspaper's potential as a visual medium began modestly in America on January 26, 1707, when the New York *News-Letter* printed a drawing that had been cut in wood. Other publishers did not rush to emulate the leader because they were too busy trying to get type on paper and did not have time to worry about developing the medium visually. The New

York *Evening Telegram* started using cartoons regularly in 1867, even though the process of making them into woodcuts was time-consuming and cumbersome. In the 1870s and 1880s, zinc etchings (zinc plates etched with acid) were introduced, and the reproduction quality improved. There was no rush to develop a method for using halftones in newspapers because the photographic process was still in its infancy. A Frenchman had discovered a way of producing a positive from an exposure in the early 1820s, but despite further developments, the lengthy exposure time inhibited use of a camera for anything but landscapes for nearly 30 years. Matthew Brady made thousands of pictures of the Civil War; then, as for years after, "pictures" in newspapers consisted of artists' renderings of photographic images.

The first photograph to appear in a newspaper showed some of the New York Shantytown dwellings. It appeared in the *New York Daily Graphic* on March 4, 1880. Public reaction was a resounding silence. Meanwhile, Joseph Pulitzer, who was caught up in the yellow journalism circulation battles, ordered his editors to reduce the number of woodcuts because he was afraid they hurt the dignity of his paper. Circulation fell. Pulitzer responded by reinstating pictures and increasing their size. When the halftone process was perfected in 1886, Pulitzer was one of the first to use it (Kobre 1980).

The development of the halftone process was to newspaper photography what steam-driven presses were to mass circulation. The process involves the use of a screen that breaks the image into thousands of tiny dots of varying sizes on a film. The larger the dot, the darker the tone. The dots transfer the ink to the paper as it runs through the press. The result is a picture (halftone) that has all the tones between black and white. Reproduction improves as the screen becomes finer. Newspapers today commonly use a screen of 85 to 100 lines. A 133-line screen is often used in high-quality commercial work.

Reproduction may not have been as good in the 1890s when Pulitzer finally embraced photography, but it was exciting. On May 4, 1890, Pulitzer's *World* used 39 2-column photos of a clergyman who was the subject of a 4-page supplement.

The first news photography developed during the Spanish-American War in 1898 but was still considered a curiosity. Melville Stone, a great editor of the *Chicago Daily News,* said, "Newspaper pictures are just a temporary fad, but we're going to get the benefit of the fad while it lasts." The *Daily News* went out of existence in 1978, but newspaper photography is stronger than ever.

To realize photography's potential, camera size had to be reduced, film speed increased, and artificial lighting developed. Dangerous flash powder was replaced by flash bulbs, which were followed by electrically charged flashes in the late 1930s. The 4 by 5 Speed Graphic was the standard camera until the 1950s, even though the smaller and faster 35-mm camera had been introduced by Leica in 1924.

The impact of news photography was stunning. It brought home the Spanish-American War (even promoted it), proved that the Wright brothers had invented the airplane, and complemented the works of the muckrakers. Slums were shown to people who did not know they existed, and child labor laws were enacted after stories and pictures appeared of little children working in the coal mines and farm fields.

Picture syndication began in the early 1900s, and by 1927 the Associated Press News Photo Service was inaugurated.

On June 7, 1939, the Associated Press distributed the first spot news color picture (President Roosevelt welcoming King George VI in Washington, D.C.) for the daily press. Because of the time needed to process the film and make separations and the extra press capacity required, color photographs did not commonly appear in American newspapers until the 1960s, although they were frequently used on special occasions and in special sections before that. In the 1970s, laser scanners were introduced to make the separations, and computers were used to enhance the color.

In less than a century, the industry had advanced from illustrations to color photography. The next technological advance is expected to be a startling new development — a filmless camera that stores images digitally in a waferlike sensor and then transmits them to a computer where they can be examined, enhanced, and cropped. The Associated Press and United Press International already handle most of their photographs in a computer.

In 1987, the Honolulu *Advertiser* became the first newspaper to install an electronic darkroom. When enough newspapers can receive photographs directly into computers, the news syndicates will begin offering the service. And when that happens, the industry will see the first significant improvement in syndicate picture quality since they first started sending pictures in the 1930s.

Development of the filmless camera will speed processing time, cut development costs, and improve the quality of the pictures.

The continued development of photographic technology and photographic techniques has had a substantial effect on newspaper design. Better reproduction quality has brought about more frequent use and larger sizes, which in turn has encouraged horizontal formats. The increased use of pictures has had yet another benefit; communication improved as photographers and reporters learned to work together. Even Melville Stone of the *Chicago Daily News* would admit today that pictures are here to stay.

The future

Predictions for the future would be considered science fiction if it were not for the rapid advances in newspaper production technology since 1965. Developments are now occurring so rapidly that new equipment is often obsolete within a year.

In 1960, typesetters at most newspapers, as they had done for 100 years, set the copy on a metal-casting machine such as a Linotype. Headlines were set separately in the composing room and pages were made up by putting the metal type in a form. Engravings were made of the photographs and locked into the form with the type. An impression of the page was made on a metal plate, and the plate was placed on a letterpress unit to be printed.

By 1970, reporters at most newspapers typed their stories directly into video display terminals (VDTs), from which the material was sent electronically to a photocomposition machine that produced the type on paper through a photographic process. That type; the headlines, which were also produced photographically; and any prescreened pictures were pasted on the page. The completed page was photographed, and a negative was prepared. If halftone negatives were used, they were spliced into the page negative. After the page negative was transferred to an aluminum plate by exposing it to a bright light source, the plate was placed on an offset press or a letterpress converted to use offset-type plates. The introduction of cold type composition and video display terminals eliminated human typesetters and saved publishers 30 to 50 percent of previous production costs.

By 1975, newspapers were eliminating not only the typesetters but also many of the pasteup employees because the text and headlines could be set together on photocomposition machines. Because cutting and pasting was reduced, pages were produced faster. In addition, lasers were being used to burn the impressions on plates, sometimes at far-flung printing plants.

Now composing rooms are being eliminated altogether. In the late 1970s, a group of 40 newspapers and IBM teamed up to produce a pagination system that would permit composition of an entire page on a video display terminal and printing by photocomposition equipment. After seven years and $25 million without success, the effort was disbanded, but similar research was continued by private companies and pagination has become a reality.

Now pictures are stored on a computer chip in a 35-mm camera instead of film. They are transmitted by phone lines to a personal computer, where they are edited and cropped. They are then sent to the typesetter through a pagination system.

In each of these steps, the editorial department gained more control over the product because there were fewer people between the journalist and the reader. The new systems also permitted more flexibility with type and white space, better standardization, and more opportunity to experiment with design.

At present, the industry is working feverishly on a system that would take the editorial department's work directly to the plate-making stage. Instead of producing type and headlines on paper in photocomposition machines, the editors would position the elements on the page electronically, and the computer would direct a laser beam to burn a plate with that information. Such a system would improve the quality of reproduction, a necessary step considering the deteriorating quality of newsprint and newspaper inks.

Even as this system is being developed, newspapers are investing in electronic home delivery systems. Most analysts believe that the newspaper will survive for many years to come, but the number of pages and its content will probably change as the home delivery systems siphon off the content most easily digested on a screen, such as calendar items, classified advertising, and news briefs. The newspaper of the future will continue to be an information disseminator, but the information will be distributed electronically as well as on newsprint. For both systems, the industry needs journalists who can report, edit, and bring words and visuals together to help the reader understand the message and increase the impact of the story.

Layout and design research

Legibility has been studied by researchers in several fields (see Chapter 12), but design research is rare. As a result, many journalists are looking for help in designing pages. Most of the academic research has been confined to classroom experiments, and the results may not apply to the general audience. Much of the significant research on design characteristics is being conducted by newspapers or their corporate headquarters. Even if the generalized results are made public, the methodology and specific findings are seldom revealed.

Yet by reviewing the literature that is available, we can reach some conclusions about the direction, if not the goal, toward which newspapers should be heading.

Click and Stempel (1974) reported on research based on the response of readers in four cities to different page formats. The study is significant because it was done among a general newspaper audience of men and women of various ages in cities with different characteristics (Louisville, Ky.; Loveland, Colo.; Lansing, Mich.; and Hattiesburg, Miss.). Front pages of six newspapers were selected for the study; three were traditional (as Fig. 1.2), and three modern (as in Fig. 1.3). The modern formats had 6 columns with a low story count and were horizontal and modular (wraps of equal depth). Two of the traditional formats had 8 columns, but all three had a high story count and were vertical, not modular. Respondents were asked to rate the pages on a scale of 1 to 10 (semantic differential scale) using a variety of factors such as interesting, boring; fair, unfair; exciting, dull; bold, timid; and active, passive. The authors concluded, "Our respondents gave an overwhelming endorsement to modern-format pages. The exceptions to the preference for those pages are relatively minor." Even

1.2. Traditional format, 1974.

1.3. Modern layout, 1974.

1.4. Contemporary layout, 1979 study.

1.5. Traditional layout, 1979 study.

respondents who were over 40 years old preferred the modern pages. Contrary to an earlier study, the researchers also found that readers did not consider the modern formats sensational or unethical.

Siskind (1979) did a study on contemporary versus traditional designs and well-designed pages versus those of average design. The audience was college students, and the pages were designed specifically for the study; all had the same name, but each had a different style (Figs. 1.4, 1.5). Again, a semantic differential scale was used to test the same kind of factors Click and Stempel had measured. Siskind found that the respondents rated the contemporary well-designed page and the contemporary page of average design as more informative and interesting than either of the traditional models, even though they did not appear to define the designs in the same way as the researcher.

Repeating a study that had been done 10 years earlier with Northwestern University students, James Stanton found that students prefer contemporary or ultramodern styles over the conservative or moderately conservative styles. The papers he used in the test were the Little Rock *Arkansas Gazette,* conservative; Jonesboro (Ark.) *Sun,* moderately conservative; the Memphis (Tenn.) *Commercial Appeal,* contemporary; and the *St. Petersburg* (Fla.) *Times,* ultramodern (Stanton, 1986).

After its redesign, the Orlando *Sentinel* tested its readers' reactions. The newspaper found that approval of the look and design of the paper rose 25 percent and approval of its new organization rose 37 percent (Orlando *Sentinel* 1984).

Christine Urban, president of Urban & Associates, reported to the International Newspaper Marketing Association that, based on her company's research, newspapers need better display and more stylish packaging to attract young readers. She said young readers regard dull graphics, badly printed color, and writing and headline styles as boring. She also recommended that editors provide more innovative display of stories to attract scanners (Gersh 1987).

A doctoral student at Syracuse University tested reader reaction to the redesign of a North Dakota newspaper. He found that beyond content the most important elements to readers were, in order, organization, typography, attractiveness, photography, and color (Pipps 1985).

Mario Garcia of the Poynter Institute and Robert Bohle of Virginia Commonwealth University conducted a test of the impact of color on reader perceptions. They found that readers preferred color to black and white and that color was regarded as more credible and more ethical. They also found that readers preferred some colors over others, that color shows relationships, and that it influences reader eye movement (Garcia and Fry 1986).

Media General of Richmond, Va., tested the impact of color on sales by placing the same issue, one printed in black and white and the other with a color photo and color bars above the fold, in adjacent rack boxes in seven locations. After a paper was purchased, interviewers approached and asked the buyer questions. The first finding was somewhat of a surprise: three-fourths of the purchasers bought out of habit rather than being attracted by what was on the page. The rest bought primarily for a specific story. Color did not draw the buyer to the rack in the first place, but once there, four out of five purchasers chose the issue in color. The director of the research,

John Mauro, reported that in previous studies for Media General he found that readers want a high story count on Page 1, that they will read jumped stories even though they are irritated by them, and that they generally start with news before moving to other sections (Mauro 1985).

Another design study using college students for respondents was conducted at Indiana University (Bain 1980). Two versions of the November 13, 1978, student newspaper were printed and Bain listed these findings:

1. More readers finish a story if it is all on the same page. If the story jumps, readership falls off considerably after the midpoint. Content, however, makes a difference.

2. More of the story is read if it does not jump.

3. Readers do not necessarily drop off in increasing numbers on longer stories. About the same number of readers complete the story as those who stop after the lead paragraphs. The pattern is even more pronounced if the story does not jump.

4. Most readers say they read jumps; in actuality, most did not.

5. Readers liked headlines that had bold and light type or a variety of type sizes better than roman-italic combinations.

6. Large pictures attract readers to an accompanying story better than small pictures and also hold the readers' attention deeper into the tie-in story.

7. Type is readable whether it is presented in columns of equal depth or in irregular wraps, but readers prefer the modular format.

In 1979, using focus-group sessions in which researchers lead respondents through an in-depth discussion of newspapers, Clark (1979) of Yankelovich, Skelly & White produced a wide-ranging report for the American Society of Newspaper Editors. Because her study was qualitative rather than quantitative, the findings were not given in percentages and cannot be generalized for all audiences. However, she did find a strong preference for well-organized newspapers. Said one reader, "I wonder what the editors would think if they could see me reading the paper. . . . I'm dropping it all over. The pages fall out. It's hard to fold. Either the baby is on my lap or I'm drinking coffee—and sitting here hunting and searching." The respondents also objected to blurred pictures, poor color reproduction, graphs that were difficult to read, and maps that did not show what was beyond the boundary.

In 1978, the Gannett Company interviewed 5,000 readers in four cities (Curley 1979) and found that:

1. Production, packaging graphics, and appearance are important in determining satisfaction with the newspaper in general.

2. Graphics and packaging are especially important to younger and occasional readers.

3. A significant minority of readers, especially younger ones, want color pictures.

4. Type should be larger or more readable.

Using the newly developed mini-video camera, the Gallup Applied Science Partnership has started photographing readers' eye movements around pages. The researchers and editors can then view a video tape of the route readers take and how much time they spend on each item.

Sharon Polansky (1988), who has conducted much of the Eye-Trac Research, has reported the preliminary findings. They include:

1. Where the reader begins often dictates the route on the rest of the page. This means we can lead readers away from stories as well as to them.

2. Bigger headlines get more readership than small headlines.

3. Headlines attract a lot of attention, sometimes more than photographs.

4. The typical pattern for a reader begins with the dominant photograph.

5. On inside pages with ads, increasing the size of the photograph beyond 2 columns does not appear to increase readership.

6. Smaller photos can attract more attention in photo groups.

7. Defining "reading" as at least one sentence, only one-fifth to one-quarter of the stories on Page 1 are being read.

Finding the best way

Speaking through the researchers, readers have made a strong plea for newspapers to improve graphically. That means change. Although some newspapers are anxious to change, other resist stubbornly. All ask how.

Design is a method of solving problems. Each day, thousands of bits of information pass through the newsroom on their way to the reader. Traditionally, journalists wrote stories. Now the job description of the journalist is changing.

The essential question that all journalists should ask themselves on every assignment is, What is the best way to tell this story? It used to be that the answer was to write one or more stories. Now we know there are other ways of telling stories, and some of them are better some of the time. Journalists can tell stories with pictures, charts, maps, diagrams, illustrations, and, as always, text. In fact, text will remain the primary vehicle. But we need to use all our resources to reach an audience distracted by their children, their exercising, their recreation, and their preoccupation with watching television for entertainment. Television news is not a competitor; more TV news watchers buy newspapers than those who do not. Entertainment shows compete with newspapers for the readers' time.

Journalists working during the next decade are going to have to be information gatherers. They will have to recognize what information is best told in forms other than text and then gather what is needed for the information graphic or notify the office of picture possibilities. Those journalists are going to have to learn to sublimate their egos for the good of the publication. Not all the information they gather will appear under their bylines.

When not only reporters but also line editors are asking themselves the essential question, the newspaper has a better chance of attracting the attention of busy readers and of presenting information to them in a comprehensible form.

Fortunately, we already see the results of this transformation of the industry in many of our newspapers, large and small. The introduction of

1.6. The content and design of pages such as this from the *Seattle Times* is the product of a team approach.

design management into newspapers in the early 1980s has had as dramatic an effect on the industry as the development of the camera. Changes can be seen in the product, from the startlingly excellent color photography in the *Orange County* (Calif.) *Register* to the design management approach at the *Seattle Times* (Fig. 1.6) and from the quiet integration of graphics at the *Los Angeles Times* (Fig. 1.7) to the aggressive segmenting at the Norfolk (Va.) *Ledger-Star* (Fig. 1.8). Design has brought organization and problem solving to the *Boston Globe* (Fig. 1.9), the *Washington Post,* the *New York Times,* and hundreds of smaller newspapers.

Journalist-designers have demonstrated to management that design is a planning process (see Chapter 9) in which creative minds together decide how to cover events and tell stories. Just as good writing starts with good reporting, good design starts with an analysis of the information and proceeds to finding the best ways to transfer that information to readers.

Finally, design is the newspaper's best hope of achieving its potential as a visual medium. People do not listen to it; they look at it, scan it, and read it. When all editors start using the range of available story-telling devices and package them in an orderly, simple, and aesthetic fashion, then readers will find their newspapers more informative, entertaining, and useful. How to make that happen is what the following chapters are all about.

1.7. Even the traditional *Los Angeles Times* is using more maps and charts these days.

1.8. The Norfolk *Ledger-Star* does a good job of segmenting, breaking large stories into smaller bites.

1.9. The *Boston Globe* integrates words and pictures effectively.

II

Newspaper Layout

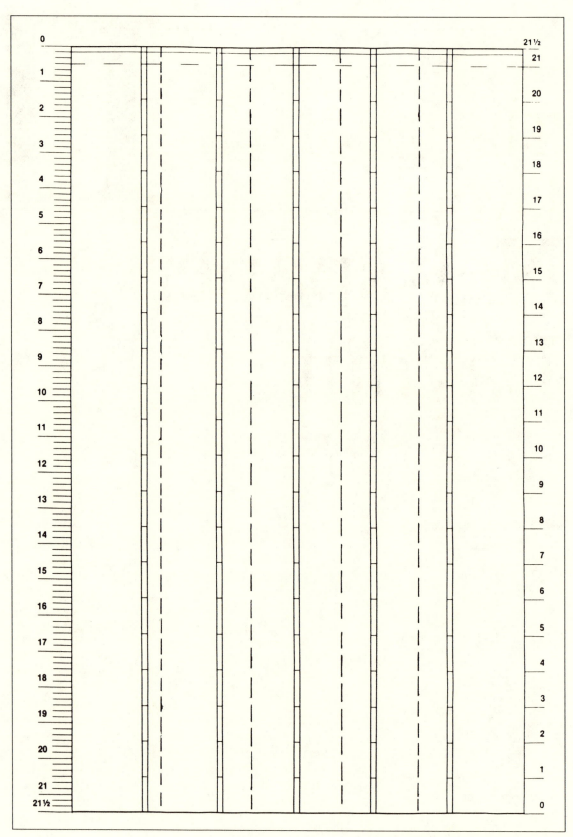

2.1. The grid, or layout sheet, defines the standard column widths. This one shows both the 5- and 6-column formats.

2

The language of
layout and design

THE main purpose of newspaper design is, of course, to improve communication—to get more people to read more of the newspaper.

Wallace Allen
ASSOCIATE EDITOR
Star Tribune
Minneapolis

GIVE ME CUTLINES for these pix, Crocker."

"I need a 3-36-2 jump head."

"Should I squeeze it or take it down a couple of points?"

"Get that Oxford rule out of there and set those heads flush left."

"This story's a couple of inches long, but we can get it all in if we change the leading from 10 to 9."

Sound Greek to you? If it does, you are not alone. This jargon is a shorthand version of the vocabulary of layout and design editors. It is sometimes logical, sometimes illogical, and often inconsistent from newspaper to newspaper. You too must become fluent in the language. When you are familiar with the vocabulary, you will be ready to begin transferring stories, illustrations, and headlines to the dummy or grid, a blueprint for the newspaper page. The dummy used by layout editors (Fig. 2.1) is usually half the size of the actual page. A good dummy sheet or grid should show the number of column inches along the margins and the pica breakdowns within the columns. It should also show other possibilities, such as running 5 columns over the basic 6. Some designers prefer to work with a full page to get a better picture of how the finished product will look. After the dummy is completed, it is sent to the composing room where employees paste up the page. At a plant using cold type, a wax coating is used to affix the type and headlines to the full-sized page according to the directions on the dummy. At the few newspapers still using hot type, the compositors place the elements into a chase, a steel rectangle.

At newspapers with pagination, the pasteup step is eliminated. Editors place the elements on a computer screen. Instead of individual stories, the typesetter produces an entire page with all the elements in place.

Regardless of the system, there is a basic layout and design vocabulary; this chapter defines these terms. Others are defined throughout the book, and all appear in the glossary.

Measurements

Although feet and inches are the basis for most measurements in the United States, editors work with picas and points. The pica, ⅙ inch, is the basic measurement and is divided into points. There are 12 points per pica and 72 points per inch. The width of copy is expressed in picas and points. A typical measurement is 13.6 or 13½ picas. The "6" refers to the number of points. The designation 13.12 would never be used because there are 12 points per pica; 13.12 would be 14 picas.

Be careful. The decimal point in math indicates tenths. The decimal point in typography represents twelfths. That is because there are 12 points in 1 pica. Thus, 13.6 is 13½, but 13.5 is slightly less than one-half. It also means that you can have 13.10 and 13.11.

Prior to computerized typesetting, editors were not concerned about points. Old production methods restricted settings to even and half-pica widths, but computerized typesetting, now common throughout the industry, offers more flexibility. Editors, who can designate exact widths in fractions of picas and points, have more control over the final product.

Picas and points are also used to measure the gutters, the white space between columns of type and between pages. The gutters between columns usually range from 1 to 2 picas. The vertical measurement of type columns is usually expressed in inches. Newspaper pages range in size from approximately 20 to 22½ inches in height. Most newspapers are 21 or 21½ inches. In the mid-1980s, most newspapers adopted a standard width of 78 picas to make it easier for national advertisers to place their ads. Before, advertisers had to make ads of many different widths or permit the newspapers to reduce or enlarge them, sometimes with disastrous results. Standard widths also make it easier to verify billings. These uniform dimensions are known as SAUs or standardized advertising units.

While the industry, especially the dailies, adopted the 78-pica width, newspapers subdivided the space differently. Most went to column widths of 12.2 or 12 picas, 2 points. Gutters, or the space between columns, are 1 pica. Some, however, went to 12.6 with 8-pt. gutters and others went to 12 with 1.4 gutters.

In layout and design, the editor must determine horizontal widths exactly. Elements that do not fit horizontally must be corrected; copy must be reset, and illustrations must be trimmed or resized. Such corrections take too much time. When fitting items vertically, however, the editor has more flexibility. Because copy that is too long can be trimmed quickly, vertical problems are solved more easily.

Ems, ens, and quads used to be familiar terms in newspaper offices. Now, outside the composing room where the pages are pasted up, the terms are not common. Some video display terminal systems still have ems, ens, and quad spaces designated on the keyboards; others have translated them into more common terms. An em is equal to the space occupied by the capital *M* in whatever type size is being used. An en is equal to half an em. In hot-metal production systems, a quad referred to a piece of metal less than type high and used for spacing. An em quad is the square of the type size.

The basic measurements at a newspaper, then, are picas, points, ems, ens, and quads. Picas and points are the most important.

The elements

The five basic tools that editors use are text, headlines, rules, photographs, and artwork. Each has its special vocabulary.

TEXT. Text is another term for the type that is used to set the stories and editorials. It is measured in points, and most newspapers use sizes of 8½ to 10 points. By comparison, books are often set in 10- to 12-pt. type. This book is set in 10-pt. type. Variations in size and legibility are discussed in more detail in Chapter 12.

The space or leading, sometimes spelled ledding, between the lines of text type is important to the legibility of the copy. Text can even be set with negative or minus leading (less than the size of the type being used). For example, the following copy block is set in 10-pt. type with 9¾ points of leading:

This is possible because type is measured from the top of the ascender (the upper parts of letters such as the *d* and *b*) to the bottom of the descender (the lower parts of letters such as *p* or *y*). Even when a descender is aligned directly over an ascender, the two do not touch at that leading, as this example, set in 10-pt. type with 9¾ points of leading, illustrates.

Most newspapers have ½ to 1 full point of leading between lines; there are 2 points in this book. The type size and amount of leading affect the number of lines that can be printed in a newspaper column. Legibility is also affected by how these factors are manipulated. When metal type is used, a slug is the combination of the type size and the leading.

Most text copy is set flush left and flush right. That is, the copy lines up evenly on both the left and right margins. To accomplish this, the type is justified by placing extra space between words and hyphenating words at the end of a line when necessary. When newspaper type was set by hand on Linotypes, the operator had to justify each line. Now the computer does it much more quickly.

Type can also be set ragged right, and this style is becoming fashionable in newspapers. Instead of hyphenating words, the computer leaves white space at the end of the line and starts a new one. Despite the irregular space at the end of the lines, ragged right does not take up more room. Some newspapers set all their text type ragged right.

Computers can also be programmed to set type in a modified ragged right. That is, the computer will hyphenate words to ensure a minimum width. An editor might want to program the computer to hyphenate only when a line of type would not exceed 50 or 60 percent of the potential line length. This eliminates inordinately short lines. Newspaper text is set in columns, legs, or wraps of type. A story that extends across five columns of a newspaper page is said to have five legs or wraps.

HEADLINES. Headlines, or heds as they are sometimes spelled, are the larger version of text type. They too are measured vertically in points. Headline type starts at 14 points and extends over 100 points. Normal headline schedules, a list of type sizes available to the editor, include 14-, 18-, 24-, 30-, 36-, 42-, 48-, 54-, 60-, 72-, and 84-pt. type. Some head schedules go even larger. Because of technological developments in computerized typesetting systems, the sizes available are now endless. Early models of phototypesetters restricted editors to the traditional headline sizes because lenses were used to magnify the type to specified sizes.

Later models, which have digitized type on computer chips, permit the editor to set type in any size desired. If a headline written to be 60 points is a letter too long, the computer can be directed to set the type in 59 points. If the headline is too short, the editor can instruct the computer to set it at 63 points. Even at plants where earlier phototypesetting machines are used, editors can have a headline enlarged or reduced in the camera room to any size desired.

The shorthand for headline instructions varies from newspaper to newspaper. One of the common systems is to designate width, size, and number of lines by writing 2-36-3. This means the headline is 2 columns wide, 36 points, and 3 lines.

Various newspapers use different rules of capitalization in headlines. The least legible (see Chapter 12) is all caps, headlines written with all the letters capitalized. Many newspapers still use the traditional or uppercase style of capitalizing the first letter of every word except articles and prepositions. The lowercase style capitalizes only the first letter of the first word of the headline and proper nouns.

Most newspapers position the headlines flush left; that is, the headline begins at the left margin of the copy. Other styles include (1) flush right, the end of the headlines is aligned with the right-hand margin of the copy and white space appears to the left of the headline; (2) centered, the headline is centered above the story; and (3) stepped down, the second and all subsequent lines of a head are written shorter than the preceding one and indented under the one above it. The stepped-down style is archaic. Although few newspapers center all heads, most use centered and flush right heads for special display packages.

Not all the vocabulary that refers to special uses of headline type is standardized. However, the following terms (see Fig. 2.2 for examples) are common:

Banner—a large headline that extends across the top of the front page above the most important story of the day.

Deck—one or more lines that are subordinate to the main headline and give the reader additional information about the story.

Kicker—three or four words that are set half the size of the main headline and usually appear flush left above the main headline. Generally, the main head is indented under the kicker, which should not be smaller than 24 points.

Hammer—a one- or two-word headline in large type. It is effective in attracting attention and adding white space to the page but needs a deck to further explain the story. The hammer usually is twice the size of the deck. Hammer heads can be set flush left or centered. They are most effective in

2- and 3-column formats. They call attention to themselves.

Sidesaddle—also called a side head, the type is placed at the left of the copy rather than over it. The headline should be aligned with the top of the text, not centered. Alignment is a key element of good design.

Readin—similar to the kicker in size and placement, the readin is a conversational approach to headline writing and needs the main headline to complete the sentence. The main head, a label or title, should be able to stand alone.

Readout (dropout)—a deck, but reads directly out of the main head. The readout is more conversational than the traditional deck and is not written to a specific count.

Blurb—also called a pullout or quoteout, it is a short piece of interesting or alluring information pulled from the body of the story and set in larger type, such as 18 points. It is either tucked under the headline or placed somewhere in the body of the copy.

The headline story
When headlines are titles or labels
they need elaboration. One way to do this
is through a readout or a dropout

Kicker head
This line is usually indented

This format can be used
to sell the story. It is
called a

Readin

Hammer head
These attract attention

This is a sidesaddle headline

Sidesaddle heads are useful devices in certain circumstances. For instance, they can be used on inside pages where the space for stories is shallow. If advertisements fill all but two or three inches at the top of the page, a sidesaddle headline can be used to good advantage. A traditional headline run over the copy would consume nearly all the space and leave room for only a couple of lines of text in each column.

Sidesaddle heads can also be used on a page with other stories above it. However, to keep from confusing the reader, the story with the sidesaddle should be boxed or a heavy rule should be placed above the story.

2.2. Examples of some common headline or title formats.

Headlines, regardless of where they are placed or their format, must fit. The writers can count the letters, but more and more, computers are doing that work quickly and accurately. However, at offices where letters must still be counted, a standardized method is needed. There are several formulas, each equally good if used consistently. In a typical formula, all lowercase letters are counted 1 except *f, i, l, t,* and *j,* which are counted ½, and *m* and *w,* which are counted 1½. All capital letters are counted 1½ except *M* and *W,* which are counted 2. Punctuation marks are usually counted 1, and the space between words is assigned a value of either ½ or 1.

A headline schedule is then established. The easiest, though not the most exact, way of making a chart is to set the headlines, using the same wording, in all the sizes you will be using. Lay the headline across a full newspaper page marked off by columns. Determine the number of counts that will fit in each column width or establish the number of counts per pica. You can check this schedule by setting another headline using different words. Sometimes a headline will count shorter because it has an unusual number of *l*'s *t*'s, or *f*'s. The following headline is marked using 1 as one count and - as a ½ count:

l- l l l - l l l - - l l - l l l - l l l l l -
President vetoes budget

There are 20½ counts in this headline.

BORDERS AND RULES. Sometimes borders and rules are used to set off headlines and are also used around illustrations and copy. A rule usually refers to a simple, plain line. Borders are more ornamental in design. The terms are often used interchangeably. A selection of both is shown in Figure 2.3. When a rule or border is used around copy, it is called a box. Different newspapers use different-sized rules for boxes, and sometimes the same newspaper uses more than one size. Most, however, use rules rather than borders to box stories. In earlier times, rules were used in the gutters to

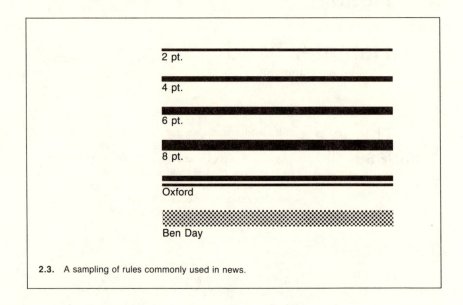

2.3.   A sampling of rules commonly used in news.

separate columns; now white space is commonly used to perform this function. A 2-pt. rule is usually used, but 4-, 6-, 8-, 10-, and even 12-pt. rules are appearing more often. Cutoff rules, lines below or alongside an illustration to separate it from unrelated copy, used to be 1 point. Now, to emphasize the cutoff and add weight to the page, 4- and 6-pt. rules are often used instead. Among the many ornamental borders available, the two most common are the Oxford and Ben Day rules. Most of the others are used only on special features on a seasonal basis or by the advertising department.

PHOTOGRAPHS. Photographs are also called cuts, pic (singular) or pix, and sometimes, mistakenly, art. Photographs come from staff photographers, wire services, and free-lancers (persons who sell pictures to a publication). Staff photographers and free-lancers provide glossies, pictures printed with a shiny surface. Photographs transmitted by the Associated Press, which has a laserphoto transmission system, are also glossy. United Press International calls its system Unifax. Regardless of the source, all have tones ranging from black to white. The text that accompanies a photograph is most commonly called a cutline, but it is also known as a caption or legend.

ARTWORK. Artwork is any illustration other than a photograph and includes serious or humorous illustrations, maps, graphs, and charts. Photographs used for special effects, such as silhouetting or screening to produce a different image (Fig. 2.4), are properly classified as art. Art that is black and white, such as a chart or a simple line drawing, is shot without a screen and is called line art. If it is the correct size, it can be affixed directly to the page from which the plate is to be burned. If it has gray tones, it must be screened (shot as a halftone).

2.4. Halftones can be shot with special-effects screens such as this one, which produces a mottled or overexposed effect.

Almost all photographs and artwork need to be reduced or enlarged before they are printed. The proportions are established by the layout editor and designer. A proportion wheel is usually used to determine the proper percentage of enlargement or reduction. Artwork shot at 100 percent will produce a duplicate the same size as the original. Anything shot at larger than 100 percent results in an enlargement; less than 100 percent provides a reduction. To size illustrations with a proportion wheel:

1. Measure the original illustration. In our example (Fig. 2.5A), the photograph is 45 by 30 picas after cropping. Always express the width first.

2. Determine the most important measurement needed to fit your dummy. Usually that is the width. In the example, the known measurement of the reproduction is 3 columns wide (42 picas in this case). While most wheels are expressed in inches, you can assign any label, including picas, to the numbers without converting them. Thus in our example, 45 inches on the wheel becomes 45 picas.

3. On the proportion wheel, place the number showing the original size (45) under the reproduction size (42) (Fig. 2.5B). Without moving the wheel, look at the window showing the reduction ratio. The arrow points to 94 (Fig. 2.5C), which means that the photograph will be shot at 94 percent and will be reduced 6 percent from its original size. When an illustration is

2.5A. The first step in sizing photographs or artwork is to measure the width and depth as you want it cropped.

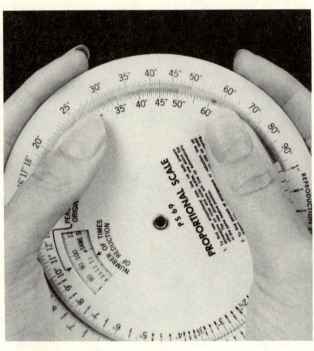

2.5B. When using the inside wheel, place the original width (45) under the new width (42).

enlarged or reduced, its size is changed proportionally in all directions. Consequently, while the width is decreasing 6 percent, from 45 to 42 picas, the depth will be shrinking by the same percentage.

4. Again, without moving the wheel, look at the 30 (depth of the present photograph) on the inside wheel, which is marked original size (Fig. 2.5D). The number above 30 is 28, the depth of the reproduced picture. In every case, you have three known measurements and one unknown. In this example, you knew the original width and depth as well as the new width. The unknown was the new depth. The same result can be achieved by working the standard proportion formula, 45:30::42:x. The original width (45) is to the original depth (30) as the new width (42) is to the new depth (x). Multiply the extremes (45 × x) and the means (30 × 42) and complete the calculation as shown.

$$45x = 30 \times 42 = 1260$$
$$x = 1260 \div 45 = 28$$

With minicalculators common at many desks, the proportion wheel may soon become a thing of the past. There are other ways to size illustrations, but the wheel and the proportion formula are the quickest and easiest.

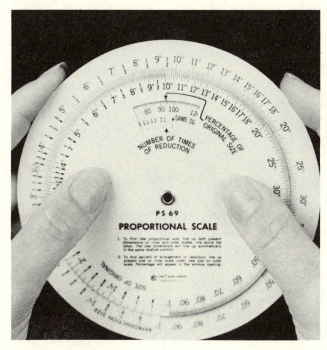

2.5C. The arrow in the window indicates that the photograph will be shot at 94 percent.

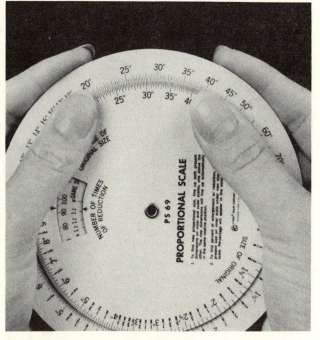

2.5D. The photograph or artwork will be reduced or enlarged by the same percentage in both length and depth. Thus 45 by 30 shot at 94 percent becomes 42 by 28.

Structures

The structure of a newspaper is its basic architecture. While there are many varieties of architecture, there are only three basic newspaper structures: vertical, horizontal, and a combination of the two. Each has its advantages and disadvantages.

The *Wall Street Journal,* which has a large circulation, is structured vertically. A vertical newspaper runs few headlines more than 2 columns wide. Stories start at the top of the page, and many run all the way to the bottom. On the inside, the vertical structure is not so pronounced because the vertical copy flow is interrupted by ads. A newspaper using a vertical structure has a personality that is conservative, reliable, and traditional. The structure of the *Wall Street Journal* contributes to its image and coincides with its content. In that sense, the *Journal* is a well-designed newspaper. Vertically structured newspapers are also quicker to lay out and compose. There is little for the layout editor to do but fit the stories in the holes vertically.

Because 1- and 2-column headlines take up less space than larger, multicolumn headlines, it is possible to get more stories on a vertically structured page. Consequently, the vertical format is the best choice for newspapers seeking a high story count on Page 1.

For some newspapers, however, the advantages of the vertical structure are also disadvantages. Newspapers that do not want a conservative, traditional image or are more concerned with the quality and length of the stories than the count on Page 1, see the vertical structure as a disadvantage. This structure also works against a page design that attempts to move the reader around the page. Vertical papers usually are top-heavy; the bottom half has little or nothing to attract the reader's attention, and it is difficult to keep the page from getting gray and dull. The *Wall Street Journal* is a special-interest publication with an unusual consumer profile. What works for it may not work for others. Some newspapers have tried to capitalize on the reliability aspects of vertical makeup while introducing a more modern look.

Few newspapers have either a purely vertical or purely horizontal structure. There are several advantages to the horizontal structure, the most prominent being that the majority of readers perceive it as more modern and pleasing (Siskind 1979). Stories laid out horizontally take advantage of the reader's inclination to read from left to right. The horizontal structure also permits the layout editor and designer to be more flexible when balancing the page. The larger, multicolumn headlines used in horizontal makeup not only attract attention but also add color and weight to the page (Click and Stempel 1974).

Another important advantage is the optical illusion that results when a story is laid out horizontally. A 20-inch vertical story would extend from the top of a page to the bottom. It would look long, and because of the limited number of things a designer can do in one column it probably would look dull. Readers who wear bifocals have difficulty reading a vertical story because they must fold or raise the paper as they proceed down the column. The same 20-inch story run horizontally across 6 columns would be 3⅓ inches deep. Consequently, it would look shorter. Not many readers want to spend the time required to read a 20-inch story, but it is the designer's job to stimulate their interest.

One of the few disadvantages of the horizontal structure is the additional time required for layout or design. Also, papers can easily become sensational in appearance with overly large headlines and cluttered graphic elements such as stars and arrows; this can affect the public's perception of the newspaper's reliability. A purely horizontal page (Fig. 2.6), however, is as dull as purely vertical makeup. What is needed is a combination of the two. A good horizontal structure needs strong vertical elements to provide contrast. Monotony is the enemy of any structure. To the editor working on a horizontal page, nothing is more welcome than a strong vertical photograph. Copy run more than the standard column width can perform the same optical function. One newspaper format features a wide column on the front page every day.

Newspaper formats

The W-format, so named because one wide column is run down the left side of the front page, has a built-in vertical element (Fig. 2.7). Newspapers most commonly use it to run news summaries or feature a popular local columnist. It is the page anchor. Used every day, it gives the page a familiar look no matter how much the rest of the page changes. The setting for the wide column is determined by the number of other columns and their width. For example, on a page 78 picas wide, the editors may decide to run 4 regular columns and 1 wide column. Using a rule of thumb that the wide column ought to be approximately one and one-half times larger than the regular columns, the editors could have 4 columns 13½ picas wide and 1 column 20 picas wide. Enough flexibility should be provided so that the wide column can start at the top left or sit at the bottom left. Such flexibility permits the use of a banner headline for important news. It also permits the editor to run copy all the way across the bottom on occasion, a pleasant variation from the usual use of space to the right of the wide column.

The W-format is one of four basic formats in use today. The others are the 8-column, optimum (6-column), and 6-on-9 columns. The 8-column format was standard in the industry for years but rapidly went out of favor in the mid-1960s when newsprint prices increased rapidly. Publishers tried to cut costs by decreasing the size of the paper. The new narrower width, in turn, forced a change in the number of columns. Legibility researchers had already suggested that newspapers should use wider columns of type for ease of reading. The 6-column width, which has come to be called optimum format because the type is near the optimum line-length range, was the logical choice of many newspapers because of the new page width and size of text type. Now that newspaper pages are becoming narrower, optimum line length is closer to 5 columns.

Design philosophies

Within these formats, the only design philosophy still in wide use is the contrast-and-balance or informal-balance approach. Editors balance the top and bottom of the page by using the contrasting weights provided by headlines, text, white space, and illustrations. Within the contrast-and-balance approach, copy can be laid out in rectangular blocks (modular), or stories can be tucked into each other in irregular shapes (brace). Almost all

2.6. While horizontal layout has many advantages, if not handled properly it can be as dull as vertical layout. This page lacks a strong vertical element for contrast.

2.7. A columnist occupies the wide column in this W-format.

newspapers use contrast and balance because it provides unlimited flexibility in layout and design. Other design philosophies have more or less been discarded.

Formal balance was popular in the late 1800s and early 1900s, but the necessity of having two of nearly everything made the approach impractical. In formal balance, it was necessary to balance one headline with another in terms of size, column width, and weight. If there was a 1-column picture in the upper right, there had to be a 1-column picture in the upper left. In formal balance, form overrode content.

Circus makeup enjoyed a spectacular but relatively brief reign, particularly among the Hearst and Pulitzer papers that were competing for circulation. Big headlines; plenty of typographical ornaments such as bullets and stars; large pictures, often in irregular shapes; and copy set in various sizes and widths were features of circus makeup. It was exciting but hard to read. It is still practiced by grocery store tabloids such as the *National Star* and *National Enquirer*.

3

Laying out pages

SO WHAT is whole journalism? It means . . . that editors will widen the view of our work so that words, illustrations and page design are thought of as one, not apart, and handled whole.

Eugene C. Patterson
CHAIRMAN, ST. PETERSBURG TIMES PUBLISHING CO.

IN TRIBAL TIMES, witch doctors protected their position in the community by hoarding knowledge. In our time, many beginning journalists in newspaper offices think there is some magical process for laying out pages that involves potions and secret formulas. It is not that experienced journalists are hoarding knowledge; it is just that most young journalists never take the time to learn the rather simple process of dummying newspaper pages.

Dummying is the technique of producing a blueprint for page makeup by placing elements on a page. Normally, it is done under deadline pressure. A designer might do one page in two or three hours, but a layout editor may need to do several. Journalism, as it refers to the reporting and writing process, has been described as literature in a hurry. Layout is design in a hurry. Journalists doing layout need to know how to work in modules, show relationships, and display photographs. They must also understand the basic principles of contrast and balance. Because speed is essential for the majority of pages in a newspaper, there is and will continue to be a need for people who know the basics of layout. Newspapers can neither afford to have an entire staff of newspaper designers nor give them the time to do the work. Designers may work on Page 1, sectional fronts, and special projects, but the majority of pages will continue to be drawn by layout editors.

Prior to preparing the dummy, some decisions must be made.

Predummy decisions

Before your pencil touches a dummy sheet (or your video cursor touches the electronic grid) the following decisions must be made within the philosophy of the publication on which you are working:

3.1. The Allentown *Morning Call* produced an unusual front page by combining related stories and using a map as an information graphic.

3.2. The weight would have been better distributed if the Hinckley story and picture had been moved to the bottom.

1. Determine the number and size of the various stories, pictures, and pieces of art that will be placed on the page.
2. Decide which elements are related and how to group them.
3. Select the major display element or elements for the page.
4. Select the second major display elements or elements for the page.
5. Identify the lead story.

For the beginner, this list is like the formula you used when learning to write an inverted pyramid story. When you began, you mechanically went through the process of identifying the who, what, where, when, and why in each story and ranking them in order of importance. For the beginner in layout, it is helpful if you use these five steps. With a little experience, the process will become second nature to you. Let us take a look at each of the steps.

The number of elements goes a long way toward determining the looks of the page. Traditionally, that decision has been made by managing editors, and the layout editors were left to to find a way to make all the pieces fit. However, this method is increasingly recognized as being unsatisfactory. The problem and a proposed solution are discussed further in Chapter 9. Regardless of who makes the decision, story count is critical to what can be done with the page.

The newspaper's jump policy is also critical. If the paper is willing to continue stories from Page 1 or from one inside page to the next, as the *Los Angeles Times* does, the story count can be higher. If the paper does not jump stories or sets a maximum number of stories that can be continued, stories will have to be shorter, there will be fewer of them, or both. Within the confines of the newspaper's policy, then, you determine the number of elements that must appear on the page and their size or length.

The second decision involves related elements. Which picture or pictures go with which story? Do any of the stories have sidebars? Is there more than one story on the same general topic, such as health or education? The process of grouping related elements forces the editor to think in terms of packages rather than individual elements. Sometimes this can result in elevating two or more less important stories to a larger package that is more significant because of its combined message, makes more sense to the reader, and is easier to handle graphically. For instance, the Allentown (Pa.) *Morning Call* found that it had several stories related to the then-developing crisis in Iran. Handled separately, they all would have been on inside pages. Grouped, with a map of the world pinpointing the trouble spots, the package became the lead story (Fig. 3.1). Grouping related stories helps the reader make sense from the news. Packaging is good journalism.

The next step is to determine which element or elements will be the major display item. This is not always the same as selecting the most important story. The major display element consists of the dominant visual element. If the lead story does not have any photographs or artwork with it, the major display element may consist of a secondary story that has visuals. However, even if the most important story does not have any visuals, it still can be the major display element. The editor can use type and other graphic devices to create a package that adds to the information in the story and attracts attention to it. This is discussed further in Chapter 13.

Usually, the major display package consists of text and illustrations. If the major display element is also the most important story, the editor's job is simplified. If it is not, the editor must lay out the page so that the most important story attracts the attention it deserves even though the page is built around the visual elements. In most cases, the page is built around the major display element, which should be placed at or near the top of the page.

The next decision is identification of the second major display element, which will anchor the bottom of the page. That package, which usually includes illustrations, is needed to balance the weight at the top of the page and attract the reader's eye. This creates motion on the page. The reader's eye will move from the major display elements at the top to those at the bottom. In the process, most readers scan the headlines on the page as they go. If the stories are interesting and the headlines are well written, they may stop or return after reading other stories. If no major display element is placed at the bottom, the editors have conceded that half of the page to dullness (Fig. 3.2).

The last step in preparing to lay out the page is to identify the lead story. If it goes with the major display element, the editor then moves on to determine how to show the proper relationship between the story and the photo or art element. If the lead story is not related to the major display element, the editor then must determine how to disassociate them while placing both at the top of the page.

When you have completed these steps, place your major display element at or near the top of the page. Then place your secondary display element at the bottom of the page. Once you have completed those two steps, you can fill in the rest of the page.

Basic principles

The following basic principles should always be kept in mind when dummying a page (note exceptions):

1. Avoid most tombstoning, the practice of bumping headlines against each other. You should not bump heads because the consumer might read from one head into the next. Tombstoning also concentrates type in one area and can create clutter and unbalance the page. However, there are ways to prevent the bad effects of tombstoning and still bump heads:

   a. Run a large, one-line, multicolumn head against a small, 1-column head. It is reasonable to assume that a consumer would not read from a one-line, 4-column, 48-pt. headline into a 1-column, two- or three-line, 24-pt. headline.

   b. Vary the typeface. Using regular type against italic or bold against a lighter weight can prevent the reader from inadvertently going from one head to the other (Fig. 3.3). Such techniques, however, may not avoid clutter or clustering of too much type in one place.

   c. Write the headline on the left intentionally short (Fig. 3.4). White space provides the buffer.

   d. Dutch wrap the copy under the related photo or artwork (Fig. 3.5) or box the stories (Fig. 3.6). A Dutch wrap refers to copy that comes out from under its headline.

3.3. The tombstone is no problem at the top of this page because of the space between heads and the different faces, roman and italic.

3.4. Although the type is the same face and even almost the same size, there is little danger the reader will go from one head into the other. There is a danger, though, in amassing too much type in one area.

3.5. The Dutch wrap can be used effectively with related visuals.

3.6. The Dutch wrap works in a box and helps avoid the tombstone. However, it must be used carefully.

2. Do not tombstone unrelated photographs or artwork. Again, there are two reasons: bumping photos or artwork concentrates too much weight in one place on the page, and the reader may think the photographs or artwork are related because they are adjacent to one another.

3. On inside pages, avoid placing art, photographs, or boxes next to advertisements because they usually have a high "noise level"; that is, they contain their own large type, photographs, or artwork. Similar editorial material placed next to ads also results in an unbalanced page. Because many inside pages have little news space, it is not always possible to avoid bumping editorial art against advertising art. As a general practice, however, it is better to speak with a softer voice on inside pages dominated by ads. The contrast is likely to attract more attention than if both the news and advertising are competing with the same type of materials. Boxed news stories on top of ads, which also are boxed, look like advertising copy (Fig. 3.7). If it is necessary to box a story adjacent to an ad, the box should extend into the news space instead of running flush with the advertising.

4. Try to avoid Dutch-wrap copy situations. Readers are not accustomed to having the text width exceed that of the headline. However, if there is no possibility that the reader will become confused by the layout, it is permissible, even advisable, to wrap the copy from underneath the head. This most often occurs on inside pages where advertising takes up all but the top few inches of the page. If there is only one story, the reader can easily follow the path of the copy (Fig. 3.8). If there are two or more stories above each other, the material must be separated. Sometimes this is done with a heavy rule such as 4 or 6 points or by wrapping copy underneath a related photograph (Fig. 3.6). A similar situation exists when editors use a

3.7. Avoid putting boxes on advertising.

3.8. The Dutch wrap works here because there is nowhere else for the reader to go after the headline ends.

sidesaddle head with a story on a tight inside page. The head sits alongside the story rather than over it.

Two design principles

The principles of design are discussed in detail in Chapter 10. Only two, contrast and balance, are dealt with here.

Contrast refers to the technique of using different typographical elements — text type, headline type, white space, photographs, and artwork — and different shapes to relieve dullness, provide visual excitement, and balance the page. Balance refers to the distribution of weights on the page. Formal balance, as practiced by newspapers years ago, meant balancing a 2-column, 48-pt., 3-line head in the upper right with the same headline specification in the upper left. This principle produced a symmetrical page. However, artists have known for centuries that symmetry is not pleasing because it is monotonous. For example, a square is symmetrical and is the least attractive shape to work with. Editors gradually realized that balance could be produced by contrasting different elements with similar weights. The weight of a headline is determined by its design, size, width, and number of lines. The weight of a photograph is determined by its size and tones. A photograph can be used to balance the weight of a headline mass. White space that is used properly around headlines and between other elements on the page also helps balance the page.

Both designers and layout editors try to balance their pages. Placing the second major display element at the bottom of the page helps balance the weight at the top. Depending on the other elements, the second element usually is placed at the corner opposite the lead visual element. Balance, then, is achieved by using contrasting elements to distribute the weights. When properly done, this draws the reader's eye around the page.

Dummying the page

Inside pages arrive at the layout desk with the advertising space already indicated on the dummy sheet. In Figure 3.9, the dummy shows three ads on the page. At some newspapers, the name of the advertiser may be shown on the dummy. Even when editors know the name, they seldom know the content of the ads. Consequently, it is best to avoid placing illustrations adjacent to the ads because there might be too much competition for the reader's attention. Because the ads are stacked in a pyramid, the editor must try to work off the ledges to create modules. Note that the editor identified the Argentina picture and story as both the lead display element and the lead story (Fig. 3.10). The editor also had a related story and picture from the Philippines. Because all the stories are from outside the United States, the page is labeled World. Figure 3.10 shows the dummy for the page and Figure 3.11 shows the completed product.

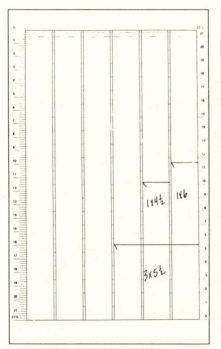

3.9.   This is what the grid or dummy looks like when it arrives in the newsroom. Advertising spaces are already designated.

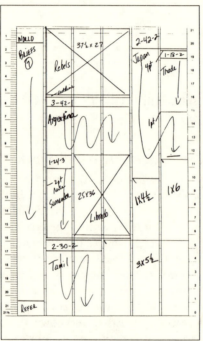

3.10.   The page might look like this when it leaves the newsroom. Grid markings are not standard in the industry.

3.11.   This is what results from the layout shown in Figure 3.10.

Notice how the editor placed the two related pictures and stories in the same module. Notice, too, how the editor worked off the ledge of the ad at the bottom right to create a module for the Tamil story. The story from Japan is not strictly in a module, but that is insignificant.

As Figure 3.10 shows, each story has a slug, the identifying name. That slug also appears at the top of the copy. At newspapers where the headline is typeset with the story, the slug usually appears over the headline in small type so that it can be trimmed easily. The pasteup person matches the slug on the story with that on the dummy to ensure proper placement.

At papers with pagination systems, there is no paper dummy. The editor places stories instead of slugs on the electronic dummy.

The story slugged "Argentina" has a 3-42-1 headline. That means the headline is 3 columns wide, is 42 points high, and has 1 line. The headline over "Surrender" is 1-24-3, which means 1 column wide, 24 points high, and 3 lines. Such a designation is common, but many newspapers do it differently. Some use numbers. A #4 head, for example, might mean a 36-pt. head over 2 columns. Others give headline directions by writing only 6-48, which indicates the number of columns and the point size. At some papers, the number of lines in the headline is indicated by marking *X*'s on the dummy. At others, the number of vertical lines underneath the type size indicates the number of lines.

Regardless of how headlines are marked on the dummy, size selection is important. For the experienced editor, this task is second nature. It is more difficult for the beginner. The best way to get a feel for it is to learn to recognize headline sizes. Go through a newspaper and try to identify the size of the type in the heads. Then take a pica ruler and measure the heads from the top of the ascender to the bottom of the descender (see Chapter 11). The headlines may not come out in traditional sizes because of the variety of type designs, since most phototypesetters can produce type in 1-pt. increments and some newspapers reduce their pages slightly before printing them, but you should be within 1 or 2 points.

The proper size for the headline depends on the type design and column width. The bolder the headline, the less size is needed. At newspapers that use the regular weight as the standard head and have column widths of 12 to 14 picas, Table 3.1 can be used as a guide.

The *X*'s indicate, for instance, that you can use a 30-pt. headline for 1- and 2-column stories, but not for 3 and larger. The chart is based on the number of characters it takes to fill the space in a given column width. Type set at 36 points in 1-column width looks large; but spread over 4 or 5 columns, it looks smaller and is difficult to read. Type set at 48 points in 2 or 3 columns looks large and makes the story look more important; however, used across 6 columns, it looks smaller and is used for softer or feature stories. Type set at 24 points looks small over 25 to 29 picas, but it will work on a 2-column news summary or as a conversational readout headline over a story that is 2 columns or wider. Even then, however, the type is usually set narrower than the copy underneath and is indented under the main head.

At newspapers where headlines are set separately from the copy, it is important to mark the depths of the headlines on the dummy. This permits the composing room employees to paste in the copy even before the headline arrives. This is not necessary where the newspaper is produced on video display systems or personal computers on line to typesetting machines because headlines and copy are produced together.

Copy flow indications on the dummy sheet vary widely among newspapers. Some depend on the dummy to indicate where the copy begins and ends. Some do not have any copy flow marks, but the person doing pasteup probably will have no trouble determining how to place the copy on the page. Other newspapers use a line as illustrated in Figure 3.10. Still others show the end of the story by drawing a horizontal line, as shown in the story slugged "Japan." Each newspaper has its own set of easily learned

Type Size	Column Width					
	1	2	3	4	5	6
18	x					
24	x	x				
30	x	x				
36	x	x	x	x		
42	x	x	x	x		
48		x	x	x	x	x
60		x	x	x	x	x
72		x	x	x	x	x

Table 3.1.   Guide for sizing headlines with a bold headline face

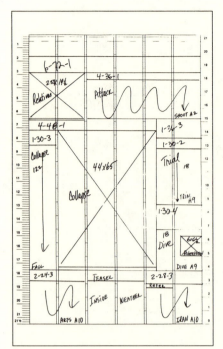

3.12. The layout editor deviated from the standard column widths to provide good display space for the picture yet allow adequate display for the two vertical stories on the right.

3.13. With two lead stories, the paper stripped one and then used the other as its dominant element.

symbols. As the industry moves toward dummying pages electronically, those symbols will be relegated to history books.

Now let us look at a dummy for the front page from the Memphis *Commercial Appeal* (Fig. 3.12). The page has been subdivided into seven modules. The dominant element is the picture from the scene of the collapsed building (Fig. 3.13). It is run 3½ columns wide, which sets up an 18-pica setting for the two stories down the right hand side of the page. The picture is marked on the dummy in picas, width by length. Width is always the first number. The photo credit appears in the upper right hand corner of the picture, an unusual placement.

All the stories continue on another page, which is indicated at the end of each story on the dummy. The story in the lower right hand corner has a refer line at its beginning, and the refer is also indicated on the dummy. The refer line, however, will come out of the typesetter with the copy rather than as a separate unit. The index, weather, and tease are standing elements. Compare the completed product (Fig. 3.13) to the dummy.

Special layout problems

In Figure 3.13, some copy was set in a width other than the newspaper's standard format. The use of a photograph larger than the standard column required the copy to change accordingly. How are the correct settings determined in cases like these?

You must know three measurements of your newspaper: the column width, the gutter width, and the space being used by your stories or package of stories. With these measurements, you can determine the correct copy settings for a boxed story by:

1. Subtracting a set amount of space for the box. For instance, some newspapers subtract 2 picas to accommodate the box and to leave a sufficient and standardized amount of space between the rule and the copy. The space between the rule and the first column, and between the rule and the last column on the right, is provided for in the 2 picas deducted for the box.

2. Subtracting the space for gutters.

3. Dividing by the number of columns or wraps of type. The result should be a copy setting adjusted for the box.

Assume that the columns are the standard 12.2 picas and the gutter is 1 pica. To put a box around a 3-column story, we must first determine the amount of horizontal space we are going to occupy. Three columns have two gutters; thus, we have 12.2 × 3 (columns) = 36.6 + 2 (gutters) = 38.6. Now subtract the standard 2 picas for the box and you have 36.6 picas. Subtract 2 more for the gutters, and you have 34.6. Divide by 3 columns, and your new copy setting in a box is 11.6.

Many people forget that the decimal refers to twelfths instead of tenths. That is why after you divide 3 into 34 and you have 1 left over, you must convert the 1 to 12 points. You cannot divide 3 into 16 as you would if you were dealing in decimals. What you have is 1 pica, 6 points. That is apples and oranges, and you must convert them to all apples. Because 1 pica equals 12 points, you change 1.6 to 18, then divide by 3 to get the 6 points in 11.6.

Let us try again. This time assume you are going to box a 4-column space, but you are going to run only 3 columns or wraps of type. Here are the steps:

1. Total space for the package: 51.8 picas.
2. Subtract 2 for the box: 49.8 picas.
3. Subtract 2 for the gutters: 47.8 picas.
4. Divide by 3: 15.10 picas.

Remember that in step 1 when we determined the amount of horizontal space, we multiplied the number of columns by 12.2 and added 3 picas because in 4 columns, there are 3 gutters. In step 3, we subtracted only 2 picas for the gutters because we will have only 2 gutters with three legs of type. In step 4, the division again forces you to convert picas to points. After you have done that, you are dividing 3 into 32, which gives you 10 with 2 points remaining. You drop the 2 points. You can always set narrower than your space but never wider. Few people would detect the 2 extra points of space.

If you wish to run a picture and story alongside each other and the picture is to be a bastard size, you must figure the text settings after you size the picture. The picture determines the text width. In a 5-column space, for example, you might have a picture that you want to run approximately 2½ columns wide. Again, with columns at 12.2, the picture might be sized to 31 picas. You would then proceed this way:

1. Total space for the package: 64.10 picas.
2. Subtract width of picture (31 picas): 33.10.
3. Determine how many columns of type you want in the remaining space. Let us use 2.
4. Subtract the gutter space (1 between columns of type and 1 between the type and the picture): 31.10
5. Divide by the number of columns: 15.11.

Again, in this example, it was necessary to convert 1 pica, 10 points to 22 points before arriving at the 11 points in the setting of 15.11.

There is one more copyfitting situation. It occurs when you wish to run copy alongside and under a photo and box the package. In the previous example, it was necessary to determine the width of the picture before you determined the copy setting. In this situation, it is necessary to determine a copy setting and then size the picture to the column widths (Fig. 3.14). Otherwise, you would have one size of column running alongside the picture and a different copy setting for the copy underneath the picture. In this example, we will use a 4-column space. Here are the steps:

1. Total space for the package: 51.8 picas.
2. Subtract 2 for the box: 49.8 picas.
3. Determine the number of columns or legs you wish to run. In this example, let us run 3.
4. Subtract the gutter space: 47.8 picas.
5. Divide by 3: 15.10 picas.

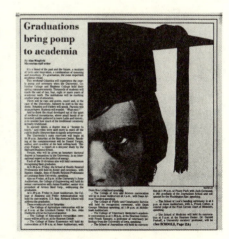

3.14. In this situation, you determine column widths first then size the picture.

Just as in the previous example when we ran 3 columns of type boxed in 4 columns of space, our setting came to 15.10. Now you size the picture to your new column settings. If you run a 2-column picture, it would be 15.10 × 2 (columns) = 31.8 + 1 (gutter) = 32.8 picas wide.

When multiplying 15 picas, 10 points by 2, you have to convert points to picas: 2 × 15.10 = 30 picas, 20 points. Because there are 12 points in 1 pica, you convert that to 31 picas, 8 points.

Electronic dummying

Pagination is a production system in which editors lay out pages on a video display terminal (VDT) or personal computer; the full page is produced from the typesetter. Because of the potential cost savings of reducing the composing room work force, publishers have eagerly awaited the arrival of this new production system. After several false starts, pagination systems appeared early in the 1980s. The most advanced was produced by Hastech, a subsidiary of Hendrix electronics. The first installation was at Gannett's Westchester-Rockland Newspapers. The system was able to do most of the editorial functions required to successfully produce a page and drastically reduced the number of composing room employees.

Hastech's Pagepro system consists of two VDT terminals, one a 23-inch screen on which copy is edited and the other a 15-inch screen on which the page is laid out (Fig. 3.15). The board has two sets of keys, one for editing and one for layout. The editor inserts instructions for size, shape, and position of the elements on the page by using the typing keys, a tablet, or a crosshair cursor controlled by what is called a joy stick, a leverlike rod at the right of the keyboard. The editor can move headlines, bylines, pictures, and copy. The screen shows the headlines in simulated type, but copy is shown only by straight lines when the full page is on the screen. However, the editor can zoom in on a portion of the page and see the actual copy. Using commands such as right-fill, left-fill, square-off, even-leg, uneven-leg, and box, the editor directs the copy flow as desired.

Photographs did not appear on the screen of the earlier systems, but the newer systems have that added capacity. Other companies have successfully produced pagination systems. Although editors appreciate the advantages of pagination, they are concerned that certain editorial functions be protected. Some believe it is important that they see the entire page, including text, on the screen. The traditional method permits some adjustments as the pages are being pasted up, but that opportunity might not exist in pagination systems after the page is sent to the typesetting machine. Looking at a page electronically on a 15-inch screen is not the same as examining the full page in pasteup form.

Some pagination systems also permit editors to program a number of preset page layouts. The material for a page is entered, and the computer is told to select an appropriate layout. If the editor cannot override the computer, there will be problems. Undoubtedly, some newspapers will use such computer functions to do inside pages. That will be an advantage if it permits editors to spend more time on open pages. If newspaper layout becomes strictly a machine function, journalism will not be served.

At newspapers where quality has never been a concern, pagination is likely to hurt the design of the paper. If the paper is concerned with quality,

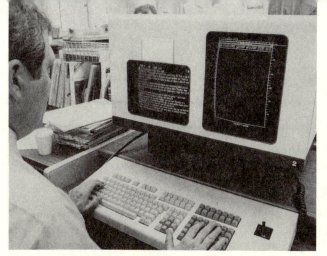

3.15A. An editor electronically strips a headline onto the page.

3.15B. Rectangles appear when the editor specifies a story shape.

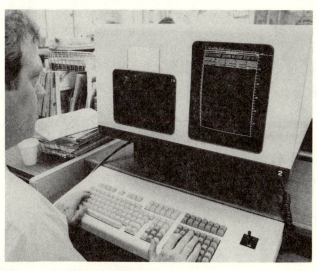

3.15C. Satisfied with the shape, he hyphenates and justifies the text.

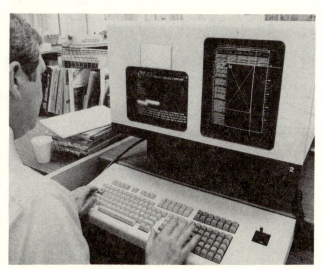

3.15D. The page continues with space reserved for the photographs and stories.

3.15E. Completed, the page can be enlarged for a final check.

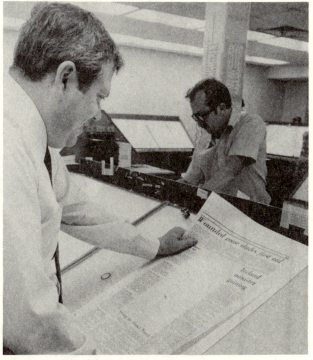

3.15F. In less than five minutes, the full page is in the composing room.

some changes must be made. For example, it may be necessary to move light tables into the newsroom so editors can make adjustments to pages, especially feature pages that are not being produced against a daily deadline.

At the same time, pagination systems will permit designers to experiment with type placement and sizing in ways not previously possible. For instance, if an editor had 48-pt. type and wanted to see how 60-pt. type would look, the new size would have to be set, a time-consuming process. With pagination, however, the editor simply types in a new command and the desired type size appears on the screen.

Any new technology creates problems. The first VDT systems, for instance, were difficult for editors to use because the keys were all labeled with printer's terms. Eventually, the names were translated to more familiar terms. VDT functions that originally required two or three commands now require only one. If history is a guide, pagination systems will be refined and become more useful as an editorial tool.

Working in modules

4.1. The *Seattle Times* pages are organized in modules.

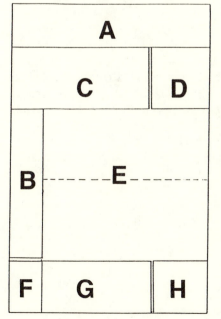

EVEN the ads in many papers make the news design look shabby. But sometimes newspapers stack up ads for a dreadful appearance.

Frank Ariss
DESIGNER

T HIS IS THE AGE of modules—modular homes, modular schools, modular furniture, modular electronics, and modular clothes. This too is the age of modular page design.

A module is a unit, a subdivision of the whole. As applied to page design, it is a rectangular unit. It contains anything from a single story to a package that includes a story, sidebar, and illustrations. Pages are formed by assembling modules. If they are put together in a pleasing arrangement, the page is well designed.

The *Seattle Times* is one of many newspapers whose editors work in modules. On the front page shown in Figure 4.1, there are eight modules and 13 elements. In module A (Fig. 4.2), the promotion items above the nameplate, there are four elements; in module E, there are two, the picture and the related story. The page is clean and organized. Most readers will look first at the large photo then move to the story underneath it. Probably before they read the story, they will move to the photo at the bottom then start to work their way to the top of the page. Photos draw the most attention, followed by headlines and pullouts. Most people scan a page before stopping to read, although a story of particular interest to them may stop them at any time.

An alternative to the modular page is one in which copy wraps irregularly around related or nonrelated stories and pictures. This type of layout is supported by the principle that readers can be led from one story to another by interlocking them like a puzzle. Some newspapers, including the *New York Times,* still subscribe to this theory. Even the *Times,* however, is largely modular.

The introduction of photocomposition and offset printing stimulated wholesale changes in the face of U.S. newspapers during the 1960s and 1970s. Better reproduction led to a desire for more attractive newspapers

4.2. This grid may help you visualize the modular spaces on the *Times* page.

43

that were easier to read. Beginning in the early 1960s, many newspapers went to the simplified modular style and eliminated column rules, fancy borders, and decorative type. By 1974, when the *Louisville* (Ky.) *Times* sponsored the watershed experimental newspaper design seminar, nearly all the proposed redesigns were modular. Newspapers did not suddenly invent the concept of working in modules. Magazines had been doing it for years with good reason. Most of them sold advertising in quarter, half, and full pages. The result was an editorial space blocked off in squares or rectangles. Most newspapers still do not have that advantage. The Standard Advertising Unit system permits 56 advertising sizes for the broadsheet page.

Advantages of modular layout

In addition to its clean, simple look, modular layout saves time in the production process, adapts quickly to technological changes, permits better packaging of related elements, provides the opportunity for contrast on the page, and has the ability to cater to reader preferences.

A pasteup person working on copy that wraps unevenly across 2 or more columns needs more time to measure, cut, and position columns of type than the person who is able to measure the depth of one wrap and cut the column of type into equal parts. Corrections are also quicker on modular layouts because lines can be added or subtracted more easily than on irregular wraps.

Production time is also saved when editors have to substitute stories on a modular page. A pasteup person can easily pull out a modular story and substitute another in its place without disturbing the entire page or a large section of it. Such changes are more difficult on a page with several uneven wraps. If the new story is shorter, the editor can insert two stories; if it is longer, the editor can eliminate two or more modules. In either case, the editor does not have to disturb a substantial portion of the page to make a change. This flexibility is especially attractive to papers with multiple editions.

People who are accustomed to working in modules will be able to adapt more quickly to pagination, the electronic method of designing pages. Although it is possible to wrap copy unevenly when using a pagination terminal, it takes more time.

Working in modules also forces the layout editor to group related stories, pictures, and artwork for the reader's benefit. (More will be said about proper packaging in Chapter 7.) The basic principle is that all related material should be in the same module. Readers want to know which stories are related and prefer to have similar stories grouped by subject matter (Clark 1979, p. 30). Proper use of modules accomplishes this in a strong visual message.

Modules also make it easier for the editor to provide balance and break up the grayness that results from unrelieved areas of textual matter. Dividing the page into modular units forces the editor to work in specified subdivisions of the page, and the final product usually has better contrast throughout. Breaking up the broadsheet into smaller, more manageable areas allows the reader's eye to deal more effectively with the space.

The last and most important advantage of the modular format is the favorable reaction of the readers. Respondents to a survey in the early 1970s told researchers they preferred newspapers with a modern design, which is characterized by modules, an optimum 6-column format, and horizontal layout. In fact, the authors concluded that the findings were a "ringing endorsement" for such newspapers (Click and Stempel 1974).

Sissors (1974) sampled young college-educated readers to determine format preferences. Reactions to the four front pages were mixed; and even though a traditional page edged out a more modern design, the clearest finding was the extremely low rating given to the only page not done in a modular format.

Until research is done using modules as the only variable, it is impossible to say flatly that modular layout is preferred over irregular wraps. It is unlikely that people in all communities will prefer one over the other. Readers on Long Island and in Miami, Minneapolis, and San Francisco may prefer newspapers with a modern appearance, but readers in other cities may like a more traditional approach. Most of the research, however, lends support to modern formats. Designers who are trying to achieve a clean, uncluttered appearance and are conscious of legibility research prefer to use the modern formats.

Advertising arrangements

It is a challenge for editors to accommodate the reader's desire for uncluttered design on pages that contain both news and advertising because some advertising formats work against good design. There are three basic advertising configurations—the well or U-shaped layout, the pyramid layout, and the modular layout.

From the readers' standpoint, the well advertising arrangement is the most annoying because news copy is stuck between overpowering advertisements. In Figure 4.3, Bob Hope and Helen Hayes are sandwiched between advertisements for a furniture store and a dishwasher. Because the well layout uses advertisements in both the upper left and upper right, it is impossible to design a page with a strong editorial focus. Seldom is there enough room to display photographs or artwork adequately. In fact, it often is preferable to use only headlines and text. Advertisements often have such large headlines and artwork that the editor may attract more attention to the stories on the page with a scaled-down design that offers a contrast.

Few newspapers still use the well arrangement; most use the pyramid layout in which ads are stacked left or right (Fig. 4.4). This permits the news department to use either the top right or left of the page for a package that will attract readers as they look through the publication.

The well and pyramid arrangements both are designed to place news copy adjacent to the advertisements. Newspaper advertising departments have long sold the idea that editorial copy that touches the advertisements brings readers into contact with them and thus increases exposure. While the intent is to serve the advertiser, the arrangement of the news and advertisements may be counterproductive. As one reader told a researcher, "I was reading this story and it was interesting, but then I turned to where it was continued and all I could find was a big ad for discount drugs or liquor or something which occupied most of the page" (Clark 1979, p. 19).

4.3. News copy is sandwiched between ads in the well format.

4.4. This is a pyramid advertising stack. It is better to have the stack go right on all pages in a broadsheet. In tabloids, better display space is created by going left on even-numbered pages and right on odd-numbered pages.

4.5. The modular ad stack contributes to better display space and less cluttered pages.

4.6. Ads should be grouped by subject matter to help the readers.

From both an economic and a readership standpoint, advertisements are important. A newspaper without advertising sells far fewer copies than a newspaper with ads. Papers that do not have a good selection of grocery ads, for instance, are harder to sell than papers that do. Classified ads attract strong readership because advertisements carry information that readers want. Consequently, it is important from a design standpoint that advertisements and editorial copy work together. While readers object to searching for copy buried among the ads, they also object to editors using space alongside large ads for uninteresting stories. A well-designed advertisement can attract readership on its own and does not need the perfume of news copy.

A modular advertising arrangement improves the looks of the paper, provides better compartmentalization, and puts fewer roadblocks before the reader. Because this arrangement requires that advertisements be stacked upon each other (Fig. 4.5), some ads will be buried, in the sense that no editorial copy will touch them. Shoppers should still be able to find them, however, when only large ads are buried and smaller ads appear at the top of the page or when several smaller ads are grouped by subject matter, such as dining guides or movie listings (Fig.4.6). Readers who want to dine out or know what movie is playing are likely to read all the ads on that topic anyway.

In the 1970s, modular advertising formats were adopted by many newspapers including *Newsday* (a tabloid), the *Chicago Tribune,* and the *Los Angeles Times*. Smaller newspapers may have trouble selling the concept to local advertisers because a purely modular advertising system restricts ad sizes to an eighth, a quarter, a half, or a full page. However, smaller papers can adopt a modified modular system by selling all the traditional sizes and stacking the ads so that they are blocked off. The publisher of a small Nebraska daily reported that he adopted a modified modular system without telling his advertisers. None of them complained. The readers, however, appreciated the more orderly inside pages and, as a result, the advertisers benefited too.

Working with advertisements

Editors of newspapers that do not use modular advertising stacks must learn to work with advertisements instead of against them. The pyramid stack poses problems, but they are not insurmountable. The editor can create modular units with the space remaining on the page by working off the corners of the ads. In Figure 4.7, lines are extended from the corner of the stacked ads. The letters A through C indicate the modular units created. Each of these units can be subdivided into more modules.

The lines represent either headlines or the edges of photographs or artwork. The number and shape of possible modules are limited only by the editor's imagination. Figure 4.8 shows a different modular arrangement with the same ad stack, and Figure 4.9 shows how one newspaper actually handled the problem and produced a clean, orderly page. The contrast between an inside modular page and one that has wraps around the corner of the ads is illustrated by Figures 4.10 and 4.11. The ads in the first illustration are pyramided right. Both the music and dance columns wrap around the corners of ads instead of breaking neatly off them, and the book

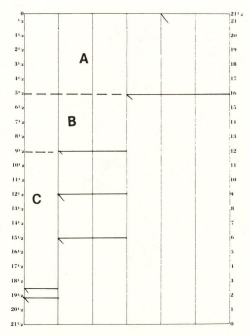

4.7. Headlines and pictures can be used at the ledges of ads to create modular units.

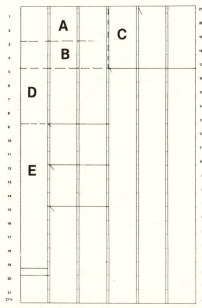

4.8. Using the same ad stack as in Figure 4.9, different modular arrangements can be created.

column wraps around the dance column. In the second illustration, the ads are stacked in a module. No copy touches the ad at the upper right, yet it has a good display space. The space remaining for news copy has been used simply and effectively.

Every reasonable designer and editor would be quick to acknowledge that the content cannot always be accommodated in a modular unit on an inside page. Often this is not possible because there is room for only one story, and the editor cannot break off the ad stack with headlines for secondary stories. In all cases, logic must temper layout decisions.

4.9. One newspaper created six modular units off the same ad stack.

4.10. When modular units are not created, the pages look cluttered.

4.11. With a modular ad stack, the copy and ads complement each other.

4.12. Although there is substantial activity on this page, it is well organized into modules.

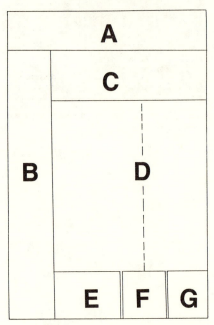

4.13. There are seven basic divisions of space on the sports page shown in Figure 4.12.

Modular open pages

Although it is much simpler to work in modules on pages with no advertisements, editors are obligated to arrange the elements on these open pages in a pattern that enhances readability.

The designers at the *Detroit News* achieve this goal consistently. The page in Figure 4.12 is active but organized. There are two elements in module C (Fig. 4.13), but there is no question that the box pullout goes with the baseball story. There are two elements in module D, but there is no question that the picture goes with the story alongside it. There is a strong vertical module in the column running down the left. The page has a variety of shapes and sizes, all stories are in modules, and all the relationships are properly established.

USA Today, serving a different market, produces an even more active paper than the *News,* one that is modern in format and high in activity. *USA Today* combines the modular look with a high story count. The result is less simplicity and focus but more activity (Fig. 4.14).

Both papers are modular and horizontal, but each has a distinct personality. The modular format does not dictate uniformity.

Working with a modular layout is relatively easy, but using modules to communicate relationships can be complicated. The effort is necessary, however, if publications are to serve the best interests of readers. Grouping stories in an orderly fashion adjacent to each other or to accompanying pictures helps the reader understand the relationships, but putting all the elements into a single module makes it easier for the reader to actually see the relationships. When related elements are not in the same module, the reader may still make the connection, but not without some effort. In Figure 4.15, the story stripped across the top has a sidebar at the lower right. The editor is depending on the content of the headline to help the reader make the connection. Sometimes that works; sometimes it does not. In Figure 4.16, the two bridal pictures at the top of the page are not packaged in the same module with the related stories to the right and left of the pictures. Unfortunately, this layout gives the visual message that the pictures go with the child-abuse story directly below them. The content and the layout are in conflict.

When multiple elements are put into the same module, a relationship is established. In Figure 4.17, two stories, a picture, and a graphic are packaged into a single module. Clutter is eliminated because each element within the larger module is a module itself, and the larger module fits into the overall page design.

Because copy laid out in a module is easier to read than columns of type that jump irregularly, it follows that an L-shaped copy block is the next best alternative to columns of equal height. Modular copy gives the reader a fixed focal point, a principle long prized by legibility experts. In Figure 4.18, even though there are four wraps of copy, readers return to the same height or focal point each time they finish a column of type. Little is lost with an L-shaped copy wrap (Fig. 4.19) where the jumps from the end of each column are the same. The L-shaped wrap also requires that the reader make less of a jump to columns B, C, and D than many other alternatives, such as a reverse L (Fig. 4.20). The jump from column A to Column B is longer, more difficult, and more time consuming. The

4.14. There is only one more module than on the sports page in Figure 4.12, but there are more elements in each module.

4.15. This layout does not show the relationship between the RS story and the disease story.

4.16. This unfortunate packaging makes it appear that the brides go with the story below them.

4.17. The module helps define the relationship between the two election stories, the picture, and the graphic.

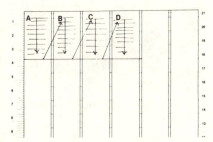

4.18. Modules bring readers to the same starting point in each column.

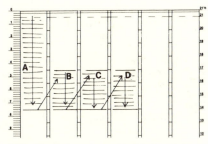

4.19. The L-shaped copy block helps relate a story and visual.

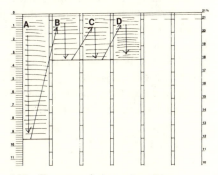

4.20. The reverse L does not create as effective a path for the eye as the regular L.

4.21. The L-shaped wrap helps relate the Reagan story to the motorcycle picture.

L-shaped wrap is particularly effective when the copy adjoins a related photograph (Fig. 4.21). The traffic flow pattern is easy to follow, and the layout has the advantage of creating a strong visual relationship between the copy and the picture.

Putting copy in a module eliminates the problems illustrated in Figures 4.22 and 4.23 in which the reader is required to make progressively higher jumps from each column. The eye flow required looks like the sales chart of a successful company. The layout, however, is not successful.

4.22. At first glance, the page looks easy to read . . .

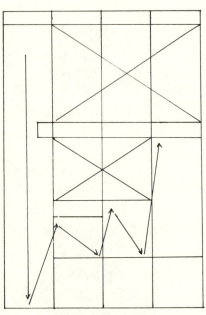

4.23. . . . but look at the copy map.

Many newspapers use the U-shaped format illustrated in Figure 4.24; even though the reader must make a long journey to the last column of type. By moving the picture to the right, the editor could relieve the monotony of the formal balance inherent in a U-shaped layout and improve the copy flow.

Editors must constantly be aware of the traffic pattern they are mapping on a page. Modular layout makes the paper easier to read, and both the reader and the publication benefit. Readers have told researchers, however, that too many newspapers are still hard to read.

4.24. U-shaped copy blocks can work if there are no other distractions.

5

Using photographs

NEWSPAPERS belong to you, as photographers, fully as much as to anyone. They are in trouble. They need your minds in all of their dimensions. So make the entire newsroom, not just the photography department, your home. And get involved.

Eugene Roberts
EDITOR
Philadelphia Inquirer

THE POTENTIAL of the photograph to attract the reader's attention, report the news, and dramatically improve the looks of our newspapers is the great untapped resource of journalism. Successful use of photographs and words in tandem is realization of the powerful potential of the newspaper as a visual medium. Photographs are the stop signs in the designer's traffic pattern. Stories with pictures command better readership and hold the reader's attention longer than stories without pictures (Bain and Weaver 1979).

We have come a long way since 1893 when the editor of the respected magazine *Nation* asserted that pictures appealed chiefly to children and were beneath the dignity of good newspapers. Even though *Look* and *Life* magazines pushed the still photograph to new limits and *National Geographic* dramatized its potential as a reporting tool, it was not until the 1960s that a significant number of newspapers started integrating the photograph into the news product instead of using it only as a decoration or to break up type.

Many editors still consider the photograph a supplement to words rather than a form of reportage. That is not surprising because most newspaper managers were trained to use words. Consequently, photographers have been second-class citizens in the newsrooms. This management structure (see Chapter 9) has stunted the growth of the newspaper as a true visual medium. As a result, a significant number of newspapers are just beginning to use photographs for their information as well as design value.

Once there is a willingness to use photographs, staff members must be trained to use them correctly. At large newspapers, a photo editor, usually a photographer by training, is responsible for the selection and display of all photographs and artwork. At small and medium papers, that job usually is done by the layout editor, who was trained as a copy editor. Editors who would be aghast at having a photographer run the copy desk think nothing of having copy editors serve as photo editors. Photographers need training to be copy editors; copy editors need training to be photo editors. Both need training to make words and pictures work together. This chapter is a start in that direction. The first step is learning the function of a photograph.

Photographic ethics

Just as the substance of a story should not be changed in the editing process, the substance of a photograph should not be changed either. Do not tamper with facts. Removing someone essential from a picture, for instance, is not unlike leaving an important name out of a story.

It used to take much time and effort to alter a photograph. All that has changed. Thanks to computers, photo editors now can retouch photos digitally. The opportunity for mischief is greater and easier than ever. Hardly had the first computerized photo systems been installed than there were celebrated cases of questionable photo manipulation.

On its February 1982 cover, *National Geographic* moved a pyramid so the photo would fit better in a vertical format. Rich Clarkson, then director of photography, explained:

"It's exactly the same as if the photographer had moved the camera's position. I have a hard time thinking that's a clear-cut issue. But people say, 'My God, you moved a pyramid! Then you can move anything!' Also in that picture was a camel train. There's suspicion that the photographer convinced them to move the camel train to that area. He also used a filter to change the sky. The scene you'd see if you were there is not the scene the photographer took. But it's a beautiful photo" (Reaves 1987).

Many in the industry were disturbed at the *Geographic*'s disclosure. But the word did not get to everyone.

In Edmonton, Canada, a staff member took pictures of a professional hockey player and his coach at a trap-shooting range. In the lab, the photos were turned and reprinted as if they were in the same frame. The coach and the player, who had been feuding, had the guns pointed at each other's heads. Only after widespread reader protest did the paper acknowledge the picture was a hoax.

National Geographic used a computer to move a pyramid; the *Edmonton Journal* performed its mischief in the photo lab. Neither method of photo alteration is acceptable to journalists such as Gary Settle, assistant managing editor for graphics at the *Seattle Times*. "It was a bad idea with scissors, and it's a bad idea now," Settle said (Reaves 1987).

Hal Buell, assistant general manager of news photos for the Associated Press, is even more plainspoken. "When it comes to news pictures, I vote for the 'no tampering' position. No tampering, not at all, of any kind, not even a little bit" (Hubbard 1987).

The question is, "What constitutes tampering?" Many newspapers used their computers to enhance the blue in the historic shot of the Challenger exploding. Is that tampering? Photographers have always used their ability to lighten or darken areas of photographs when they were printing. Should there be different standards for electronic retouching? As we have seen, this can extend far beyond anything the photo lab could do, and the computer enables us to do it quickly and with such attention to detail that it would be difficult to detect the change.

Some editors argue that they would never manipulate news photos but say they have different standards for feature photos. Some draw the line only at photo illustrations, which are a made-up situation anyway. Shiela Reaves, the University of Wisconsin adjunct professor who gathered a cross section of views on the limits of photo manipulation, concluded, "Will readers be able to make distinctions between a newspaper's handling of feature photography and news photography as easily as some editors do? If not, newspapers may risk losing the public's trust in all photography" (Reaves 1987).

Another type of manipulation is done for the sake of art, not communication. Artists use photographs for their shapes and tones. Editors use them to inform. If you can cut a picture into circles or stars, mortise its corner, or run type over it indiscriminately without interfering with the message, the picture probably was not worth publishing in the first place. Retouching, at least in news photography, should be avoided. It alters reality. In feature photography, where many photos are posed, retouching to take out a distracting telephone line, for instance, is more acceptable to some editors. Certainly, printing two pictures as one is unethical. Flopping a photo so that the subject is looking another way is also unethical, just as changing a quote or a fact in a story is. A photograph pulled from the newspaper library files and published as though it were current can be at best misleading and at worst unethical. Editors who would never consider tampering with the facts in a story have been known to stretch the bounds of propriety to illustrate it. Resist the temptation.

5.1. Readers reacted strongly against the paper that printed this photograph.

Another issue designers must be sensitive to is the use of photos showing victims grieving, bodies, and other instances of questionable taste. The profession has many examples of intense reader reaction when photos of victims or of grieving relatives have been published. More than 500 readers objected in phone calls, threats, and letters when the *Bakersfield Californian* ran a photograph on Page 1 of a family grieving over the drowning of a 5-year-old son and brother. The victim's face was visible from the half-open body bag (Fig.5.1). Managing Editor Robert Bentley said readers cited two reasons why the picture should not have been published: "They didn't want to be forced to visually intrude into what should have been a family's private time of shock and grief" and "They didn't think a newspaper photographer should have done so either" (Thornburg 1986).

Sandra Rowe, executive editor of the Norfolk *Virginian-Pilot,* reported a similar reaction from readers when her paper printed a Page 1 photograph of three young victims of a car accident (Fig. 5.2). The father, a police detective, told the paper, "Three of my children were still in hospital beds. I had no idea a picture like that was going to be in the newspaper. I was hurt. I was upset" (APME 1986).

Both photos won awards. Both photos evoked a public outcry. Journalists must be aware of public tastes. The decision may be made to print because it serves a greater public good, such as intensifying a drive for safer

5.2. The father of these children was upset when he saw the picture in the paper. Still, there are other considerations.

swimming or driving conditions. Or the decision may be made that while the photograph is exceptional, it is not suitable for a general-circulation newspaper.

Many memorable pictures are offensive. Lasting images of the Vietnam war include the photographs of a naked child running screaming down a street after she was napalmed and of a South Vietnamese general shooting a prisoner in the head. These types of photographs are always tough calls.

Here are some criteria against which to measure your decision:

1. Proximity. A picture of local people has more impact than one showing the same incident miles away. That is why so many of the war pictures were acceptable.

2. Bodies. Bodies seem to be acceptable to readers in some instances. But when the face is showing, the reaction is usually stronger and longer.

3. Death. A picture of an accident victim who will survive is accepted more readily than one of a victim who may later die. The problem is that the outcome often is not known at publication time. If the victim is in serious or critical condition, think twice about running a photograph, especially one showing the face.

4. Suffering. Many readers consider it an invasion of privacy to show the suffering of people.

5. Purpose. Is there a real or imagined public benefit to be derived from publishing the photo?

6. Size. The photos are often exceptionally good. The first impulse is to run them large. Stop and think. The larger the photo, the more people are offended. They regard the paper as being sensational.

7. Location. It is natural to put such photos on the front page. It would be less offensive anywhere else. Consider this: Would the story be on Page 1 if the picture were not exceptional?

None of these criteria are meant to suggest that such photographs should not be run. Some should; some should not. What is important is that journalists not make knee-jerk decisions. Weigh the pros and cons.

Integrity of the photograph

Changing the facts in a photograph or deciding whether to publish pictures of victims involve ethical questions. Techniques such as mortising, insetting, overprinting, and silhouetting involve the integrity of the photo.

Mortising, which is the overlapping of two or more photographs or type and a photograph, is rarely effective (Fig. 5.3). Poor placement of the close-up head shot interferes with both the copy and the dominant picture. The unequal gutters to the left and right of the head shot emphasize the misplacement. Another familiar technique is an inset that is placed entirely within another photograph. This technique is successful only when the inset adds information to the dominant photo and is effective in a small size. The inset does not work in Figure 5.4 because the background is too busy. The intention was to show the crowd watching the victory hug for golfer Scott Simpson, but the result was a cluttered background of heads sliced by the inset. This space-saving effort was not successful. In Figure 5.5, the insets and type work together, but the mortise detracts from the package. This

5.3. Avoid mortising, the overlapping of two photos or a photo and type or art.

A Sunday crowd of 30,600 raised Western Open attendance to 92,600, as Scott Simpson (hugged by wife Cheryl, inset) won the tourney.

5.4.   This inset destroys the larger photo.

5.5.   The mortise clutters this package and detracts from the message.

could be corrected by running the roller skater as an inset at the lower left and moving the copy underneath the picture or by eliminating the skater.

The use of insets in Figure 5.6 illustrates the potential and dangers of

5.6. Would you use insets to show the winners on this picture?

5.7. The inset copy works here because it does not interfere with the content of the picture.

this technique. The winners of the races are set into an excellent cross-country shot that was enlarged to 9 by 14 inches. By shooting when the runners were turning and descending a hill, the photographer was able to get a flow and feeling of motion. But do the insets work? The inset in the upper left cuts off a head and obviously interferes with the content of the photograph. Be careful with heads. Every head has a mother. Although the inset at the lower right may be in an empty space, there might have been a sign there indicating location. Even if the space was left empty, it could serve a purpose. Photographs with motion need space for the action to flow into. The space may be empty, but it serves a function. Remember this when cropping. The winners' photographs would have been more effective if they had been run next to each other at the bottom right cropped below the heads or taken out of the larger photo. By contrast, the inset copy block with the picture of Huey Lewis (Fig. 5.7) works because it is planned. Space is left in the photograph for this treatment, rather than jamming the copy into an unplanned space.

The guidelines for overprinting headlines, or occasionally text, on a photograph are similar to insetting. Type should be used only if there is an empty portion of the photograph that has a continuous tone. Black type can be printed against a light area such as the sky, or type can be reversed to run against a black background. By reversing type over a time-exposure picture of coal mining at night (Fig. 5.8), the designer was able to echo the environment of the story without interfering with the message. However, the Saturn package (Fig. 5.9), while dramatic, is too difficult to read because there is so much small text type. (See Chapter 12 for legibility considerations.) Reversed display type works when there are few words and the type is large. Text type should be larger than normal (at least 14 points) and used in small amounts, as it is in Figure 5.10.

5.8. The type does not interfere with the content, and it echoes the environment of the story—lights at night.

5.9. It is difficult if not impossible to read the text, which is set in reversed type.

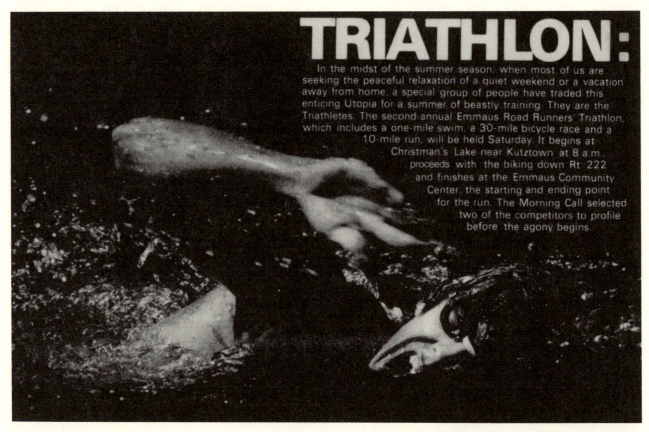

TRIATHLON:

In the midst of the summer season, when most of us are seeking the peaceful relaxation of a quiet weekend or a vacation away from home, a special group of people have traded this enticing Utopia for a summer of beastly training. They are the Triathletes. The second annual Emmaus Road Runners' Triathlon, which includes a one-mile swim, a 30-mile bicycle race and a 10-mile run, will be held Saturday. It begins at Christman's Lake near Kutztown at 8 a.m., proceeds with the biking down Rt. 222 and finishes at the Emmaus Community Center, the starting and ending point for the run. The Morning Call selected two of the competitors to profile before the agony begins.

5.10. The smaller type block and use of large type make this package work well.

Silhouettes are effective when the contrast between the silhouetted object and the background is substantial. A person wearing light clothes should never be silhouetted against a light background. Silhouettes also need an expert artist with the skill of a surgeon to cut them out and lift them off the print. Otherwise, they may have square shoulders, nicked legs, and blocked chins. A better production method is to have the photographer shoot for the silhouette and then drop out the background when the picture is printed. Publications that process photos through computers can do high-quality silhouettes.

Silhouettes can be used effectively in nonnews sections. The *Seattle Times* used the technique to highlight the size of the stomach of the man who had won the newspaper's contest to participate in a weight-loss program (Fig. 5.11).

Innovation may not always work, but it is always admired. When a photographer for a Texas newspaper was assigned to cover a men's body-building competition, the result was a dramatic play of light and darkness combined in a well-handled montage (Fig. 5.12). One reason it works is because the images do not overlap. Another is that it demonstrates the photographer's point of view; he shot it as an art exhibit.

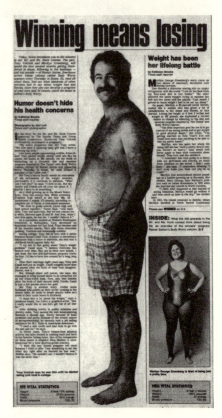

5.11. This silhouette works because it emphasizes the shape of the body, which is the point of the story.

'God gave me
this body...'

5.12. This montage is handled well. It avoids overlapping the photos.

Editors who appreciate photographs for their informational content are not likely to destroy them with artistry. We have discussed some of the potential pitfalls. Some solutions come next.

How to use two or more photographs

The one-frame mentality that dominates the thinking of many editors inhibits good photo selection and use. While a reporter can cover several disparate topics in a single story, a photographer can usually capture only one segment of a story in a single frame. Much of the drama is left in the photographer's discarded contact sheets when the editor says, "Give me your best picture to go with this story." However, the best picture may be a two-picture package. Here are some common situations:

1. Contrast. Look for dissimilarities in like subjects and subtle similarities in unlike subjects (Hurley and McDougall 1971, p. 5).
2. Close-up and context. When the photographer has to back up to show where the action is taking place, the picture makes a general statement. A second shot can give a close-up look at a small portion of the overall scene.
3. Sequence. One frame captures just one moment in the series; two or more frames permit the action to unfold. However, when displaying sequences, keep the same vantage point in the cropping.

In photography, one and one makes three. Although each photo has its own story, the message can be intensified by pairing. One and one will not equal three, however, when the pictures are not next to each other. When

Romanian gymnast Nadia Comaneci took a fall during the 1980 Moscow Olympics, it was big news in America where she had become a television personality. UPI sent pictures showing her about to fall from the uneven bars, hitting the mat, and with a dejected look on her face. The sequence was a natural. One newspaper, however, chose to use the picture of the fall on the front page as a teaser (Fig. 5.13). Besides separating an obvious sequence, the editors had the photo outlined. Because Nadia was dressed in white, the outline was so noticeable that it was distracting. Because the sequence was broken, the reader had no idea why the gymnast was on her back. On the sports page (Fig. 5.14), the moment before the fall was played with dramatic sizing, and the inset showed her disappointment. The inset sizing and the plain background were good. The use of the second picture in the sequence on Page 1 and pictures one and three in the sports section destroyed the impact and the message.

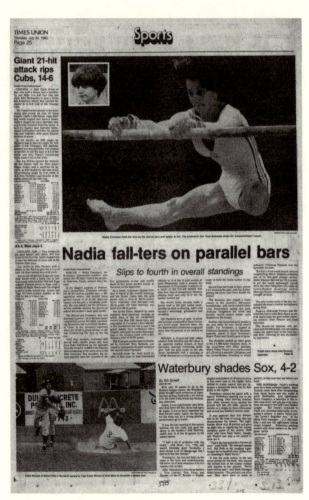

5.13.   By separating pictures in sequence . . .   **5.14.**   . . . the editors fail to capture the impact.

Properly employed, the pairing principle tells a story quickly and dramatically. However, when the words say two and there is only one picture, there is an obvious hole in the package. That was the case in the package on the woman who is both a belly dancer and a Sunday school teacher (Fig. 5.15). The story needs two pictures to show her in both roles.

A feature story on a rail transient is told through an environmental shot of the subject far down the tracks and a close-up that shows him smoking a cigarette (Fig. 5.16). The top picture communicates the loneliness and solitary nature of his life. The close-up permits readers to see him. Together, they work.

5.15. The headline immediately tells you there is a picture missing.

Lindy Burdick smokes a cigarette after a long walk down his favorite road — the railroad   Nick Lammers

Transient finds life on the move remedy for mental breakdown

By Nick Lammers
Missourian staff writer

Springfield, Ill., Memphis, Tenn., Jackson, Miss., Birmingham, Ala. — you name it, Lindy Burdick has been there by train or foot.

Lindy hops trains and rides wherever they take him. He has done so since a mental collapse he suffered in the Korean War 25 years ago.

When I met Lindy at 8 a.m. Sunday, he was near Merna, Mo., about six miles (9.6 kilometers) east of Boonville. He described how he got there:

After serving three years in World War II and enlisting to serve in the Korean War, military life inflicted unbearable pressures on Lindy.

"I had a mental breakdown in Japan," Lindy said. "Hallucinations, beating my head on walls — " His voice broke and he shook his head.

"I've got a cure for insanity in my head," Lindy said. "But beer and cigarettes don't help it any." Staying on the move does help.

"Those boxcars are hard on you," Lindy admitted. "If I keep hopping from car to car I'll become physically wrecked." That's why Lindy walks some of the distance.

"I got this cold or something," Lindy said after wiping his nose with a handkerchief. "I'm out getting some exercise today. That helps strengthen the blood," he said.

Lindy tries to average 30 miles (48 kilometers) a day to keep in shape. Sometimes he does more. Leaving Marshall, early Saturday morning, Lindy walked about 40 miles (64 kilometers) to Boonville, where he spent the night in a boxcar.

When Lindy resumed his travels eastward from Merna on the Missouri-Pacific line, I wanted to learn more about him. I drove about six miles (9.6 kilometers) to Wooldridge, Mo., where I waited for him to arrive.

After walking a half mile (0.8 kilometers) with him, he opened up.

Lindy acknowledged that the World War II was not the only cause of his depression. His family life had added to it.

Born in Utica, N.Y., Dec. 29, 1927, he lived for a while without a name until his neighbor named him "Lindy" after Charles Lindberg, the famous aviator. His father left the family when Lindy was only 4 months old.

During winter Lindy travels the southern states. He says he'll probably never stop traveling. "Gee, I've been doing this for 25 years, what else would I do. I couldn't stand myself sitting in a room with nothing to do."

Nick Lammers

5.16. This simple but strong package features proportional sizes and contrast in shapes.

62

Above, Scott Hilderbrand, 5 years old, sits in front of the recent addition to his family's 50-year-old home. Right, from the top, are a light fixture from the living room, the master bedroom in the new addition and double doorknobs on a closet on the second floor which they got from older homes.

5.17. Pictures should be sized according to their content. The small photos would waste space if run larger.

The pictures in both examples are adjacent, not redundant, and dominant-subordinate. Those three points are important to remember whether two or five pictures are being used. The adjacency guideline ensures that the relationship between the pictures is immediately grasped by the reader. The redundancy guideline ensures that the pictures complement each other and do not communicate the same message in two ways. The dominancy guideline ensures that there is focus to the package in the same way that a writer must focus on one aspect of the story.

If a package contains three or more pictures, there are four additional guidelines: Interior margins should be consistent, excess white space should bleed to the outside of the package, sizing should be proportionate, and there should be a variety of shapes. The use of these guidelines is shown in Figure 5.17 where four pictures are displayed in a space not much larger than that occupied by the dominant photo. The dominant context shot shows the outside of a remodeled house, and three interior shots complement it. The sizing is large enough to communicate the detail of the light fixture and brass doorknobs but is no larger than necessary. The interior margins are consistent, the extra white space bleeds off the top right-hand corner of the package, and the four photos are proportionate in size. The context picture is large enough to dominate the page, and the others are sized proportionately to their informational value and importance to the total package. To be dominant, a picture must be large in proportion to the page or portion of the page it occupies. For instance, in *National Geographic,* a picture 20 picas wide will dominate the page. In a tabloid newspaper, however, a dominant picture needs to be 40 picas wide, and in a broadsheet newspaper, 50 picas wide. The size of the dominant picture should be proportionate to the total space available, but the size of the subordinate pictures should be proportionate to the dominant picture. The difference in size between the dominant and subordinate pictures should be obvious to the general reader.

Experience in the use of photos permits possibilities beyond these guidelines. Some situations require two large photos of equal size. A sequence or story about a man who is a banker by day and a farmer by night might have more impact with two equal pictures. Knowing how to handle these exceptions comes with experience.

The picture page

A page of pictures does not make a story, but a page of pictures with continuity does.

Selecting and displaying a group of photographs is similar to writing a major story. When the material is selected and arranged in a coherent and entertaining manner, it has impact. If poorly done, the information is submerged in the resulting clutter.

Compare the photo editing in Figures 5.18 and 5.19. In Figure 5.18, the story is about operating room nurses, the unsung heroes. The story says that the nurse's duty is to have everything in its place for surgery, be certain that instruments and the environment are sterile, and provide the surgeon with the right instrument at the right time. The pictures do not show what the words tell. The picture at the upper left shows the nurse working on the patient herself. The picture below approaches the story; it shows an operating instrument in one set of hands, presumably the nurse's, and another set of hands, presumably the doctor's. The photo to the right is a nice head shot of an operating room nurse, but this story does not call for a portrait. The photo at the lower right is as close to the focus of the story as we get; we can see the surgeon and the nurse, but at this moment, there is no handoff of instruments as we would wish. The photo at the lower left shows a different operating room nurse comforting a patient.

5.18. See if you can find a story line in the photos.

5.19. The pictures combine to tell a story.

In Figure 5.19, the words and the photo at the upper right work in tandem. The challenge is clear; we see Chris Bryant easing himself out of his wheelchair. In the dominant photo, we see him free of the chair. At the top, we see him putting his shoes on; at the lower left, we see him soon after he has pulled himself out of the water. To the right of that photo, we see his instructor. There are a variety of shapes and sizes, which together tell the story of Bryant's challenge.

The difference between a picture story and a picture essay is like the difference between a news article and interpretive reporting (Hurley and McDougall 1971, p. 69). The picture story is a narrative. The essay expresses a point of view. Both require focus, a strong opening, and a strong closing. Unfortunately, too many groupings of pictures are just collections of related events. Such groupings are similar to stories that ramble, and they should be rejected.

When doing picture pages, remember that:

1. The telling of a story through pictures begins before the shooting when the photographer and reporter plan the project. Even if the photographer is doing both pictures and text, planning is important. It makes the difference between a story and a collection of facts.

2. The pictures and text must work together. If the text is going to tell a story by focusing on one person, the photos should too.

3. The title of the page must capture the essence of the story. The display type is essential to the success of the page because the title is the quick explanation of all the pictures and text. The title and dominant picture should hook the reader.

When selecting and displaying pictures, include these steps:

1. Select as few pictures as possible (most picture pages have too many pictures), so that the ones that survive can be sized adequately. Do not use a full page if the material is not worth it. Good photo editing saves space.

2. Edit redundancies. If the story is told with as few pictures as possible, redundancy will not be a problem. Unfortunately, there is a temptation to repeat ourselves photographically, both in full pages and lesser packages.

3. Select a dominant photo. That photo should be the dramatic moment or emotion, the essence of the story.

4. Maintain consistent interior margins. White space is trapped when the margins are not consistent, and the reader notices it for itself rather than as a feeling of airiness. Let the extra white space bleed to the outside of the package.

5. Write a cutline for each picture and place it under the picture. Ganging cutlines makes it harder for the reader to match the words and the content of the picture.

6. After you have selected the pictures and determined the length of the text, set the photos before you. The story line and the flow of action should determine the arrangement of the pictures on the page.

7. Place the copy in a modular block. The title does not necessarily have to go directly over the copy, but if it does not, a subhead over the copy is useful.

8. Write a title or headline that plays off a photograph and place the

title directly over or, preferably, under that photograph. The designer of the page on Chris Bryant did this successfully.

No list of guidelines can prescribe the proper way to produce a successful page. Such guidelines can only steer the beginner away from pitfalls that others have experienced.

Editing photos

The best photo editors have a sense of news as well as balance and flow. Like reporters, photographers often are the best judges of their own work. They do some physical editing while shooting and some mental editing on the way back to the office. However, also like reporters, they occasionally are too close to the story to see the significant or the unusual. Sometimes a second editor can catch the overlooked frame.

Picture selection depends on the space available and whether there is an accompanying story. Photos that stand alone must capture the essence of the story; photos with text can concentrate on a part of the story. The successful wedding of pictures and words sometimes requires that photos be selected to follow the text and sometimes that the text be written to focus on the dramatic angle developed by the photographers. Consequently, it is important that the photographer and reporter work together on assignments. Such teamwork can produce startlingly good journalism. For instance, consider the photographer and reporter who had been working on a story about the disagreements within an agency that repaired homes for low-income people. The journalistic team knew there was going to be a showdown at the board meeting over money for the program, and the photographer was ready. The result was a package in which editors were able to show the two principals squaring off. The pictures as well as the "Confrontation" type focused on the disagreement (Fig. 5.20).

Sometimes photo editing can be an enormous job. Two photographers can shoot hundreds of frames at a football game. Normally only two or

5.20. This visual reflection of the confrontation was planned before the shooting began.

three would be used, and they must be selected in minutes. Skeeter Hagler of the *Dallas Times Herald* shot 70 rolls of black and white and 12 rolls of color on the Texas cowboys. Editing reduced the number of photos actually used to 37, and the result won a Pulitzer Prize. Photographers at the *Lexington* (Ky.) *Herald-Leader* shot 10,300 frames of the Kentucky Derby and then used 60 of them in the final edition (Fig. 5.21). The number was that high only because the paper had a section devoted to the derby.

A former photo editor for *National Geographic* compiled the following list of questions to ask when selecting a photograph (Terry 1980):

1. Can you justify your selection on a sound editorial basis?
2. Are you looking for a record or snapshot of the event, or do you want the pictures to add depth to the story?
3. Is the photograph more than just technically acceptable and editorially useful?
4. Does the photograph have a mood?
5. Does the picture have photographic qualities that make it appealing, such as strong graphics, interesting light, and forceful composition?
6. Does the photograph tie into and reinforce the text?
7. If the photograph is unusually good, have you reconsidered the space allotted to it?

A good photo editor is like a strong city editor who can find the story line in a reporter's notes and help the reporter organize the story. A good photo editor recognizes possibilities in the photo that others may not see. Photo editors can turn tepid shots into red-hot drama by cropping tight for impact and backing off for content and form or by cropping to eliminate distractions in order to focus attention on the point of the picture. Such techniques may sometimes require close-ups; other times, context photos are needed (Figs. 5.22, 5.23).

5.21. This page was designed before the photos arrived; one layout had a vertical picture and the other, a horizontal. It is not unusual to have to lay out pages before the picture arrives.

5.22. A loose crop fails to emphasize the key subject in the photo. (Bill Sikes photo)

5.23. A tight crop emphasizes both the subject of the photo and the intensity of the discussion. (Bill Sikes photo)

Cutlines

Newspapers should have two basic cutline formats: text and one-liners. A text cutline is used when a photograph needs a longer explanation. When a picture stands alone, it often has a catchline or headline over it. Depending on the newspaper's headline style, the catchline is either flush left or centered. Cutline text type should be 10 or 11 points and should contrast with the text type. Because text type in newspapers is usually serif, sans

5.24.   Cutlines are the most useful when they are under the photo. The reader has to work too hard when they are ganged.

serif works well, but italic and boldface are also available. The designer can use all caps or all caps boldface for the first two or three words if such a style matches that of the copy.

The newspaper should have standardized text cutline settings for each width of picture. Text cutlines generally should not exceed 25 picas in width. Gutters should be the same as those used elsewhere in the paper. If the paper is gray, the designer may want to specify that cutlines be set 2 picas less than the width of the picture. This permits 1 extra pica of white space at either side of the text.

A one-line format often is a larger version of the cutline text face; 13- or 14-pt. type works well. The cutline should be written so that there is only one line of type under the picture. With this format, there are no gutters; the cutline can extend the width of the picture.

Although cutlines should appear underneath the related photo, occasionally they are placed to the right or left. In such a case, they should line up with the bottom of the photo. Cutlines set to the right can be set ragged right; cutlines set to the left should be justified left and right. If the cutline to the left is one short sentence, ragged left may be permissible. Cutlines generally should be placed underneath photographs because readers read out of the bottom of the photograph. Grouped cutlines irritate readers because they have to work much harder to match the text information with the appropriate photograph. In Figure 5.24, one cutline is used to describe the kitchen utensils. It directs the reader to follow, from top right, counterclockwise. That is hard work. The designer had two choices; one was to reverse a number in the bottom of each picture and key it to the description below, and the second was to put the identifier underneath each picture. Make your packages reader friendly.

Credit lines can appear at the end of the text cutline, but they usually look better when they are anchored at the lower right corner of the photo. When they appear at the end of a text cutline, they often dangle on an extra line. In addition, they do not fit neatly into a one-line format. Credit lines that appear at the right-hand corner of the picture should be set in type smaller than the cutline and can even be in agate type.

Photo illustrations

When a photographer cannot get a literal representation to accompany a story, a decision must be made whether to order an artist's drawing or a photo illustration. For instance, a photographer cannot always be at an undercover investigation, but an artist can effectively recreate a scene such as an exchange of drugs or money in the shadow of a doorway. Stories that discuss ideas, issues, or sensitive legal or moral subjects may lend themselves to photographic illustrations, which are pictures staged with people and/or props that represent ideas rather than literal scenes.

To produce an illustration, a photographer needs time, props, facilities, and a thorough understanding of the story being illustrated. Ideas for illustrations are often produced in conferences involving the reporter, story editor, design editor, and photographer. It is a time-consuming process, but it pays visual dividends. The photographer who received the assignment to illustrate an article on junk food (Fig. 5.25) brought two important elements to the job: a lively imagination and a casket, which she just happened to have in her van. The result was a reader-stopper.

5.25. The humorous interplay between the photo illustration and the words adds to the message that this is not a real situation.

Sometimes there is more than one way to tell a story visually, although one often works better than another. An illustration of this can be seen in Figures 5.26 and 5.27. In the first, the designer used a drawing to show the misery of math; in the second, the designer elected a photo illustration. The photo illustration appears to have the edge in impact.

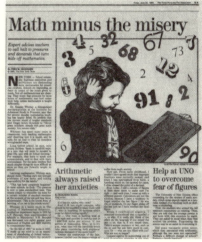

5.26. Photo or art illustration? The answer here is illustration.

5.27. The hypodermic needle full of numbers makes a statement. The words drive it home.

An illustration should not be used as a substitute for traditional photography because it lacks immediacy, spontaneity, and to some extent, credibility. It is, after all, a made-up situation. Illustrations should be obviously phony and should avoid blurring the line between real and made-up situations. On the other hand, photographic illustrations usually can communicate ideas quickly, effectively, and with more impact than pencil and ink. Figure 5.28 illustrates this.

5.28. A fowl in formal wear and a play on a well-known line. It adds up to an effective photo illustration.

6

Using information graphics

GRAPHICAL EXCELLENCE is that which gives to the viewer the greatest number of ideas in the shortest time with the least ink in the smallest space . . . and graphical excellence requires telling the truth about the data.

Edward R. Tuft
AUTHOR

WHEN the *Chicago Tribune* assembled its reporting team for the Iran-Contra hearings, one of the people who was sent to Washington, D.C., was Jackie Combs, graphics coordinator. That an information graphics specialist should be considered part of an on-site reporting team indicates how far and how quickly information graphics have risen in importance in just a few years.

Actually, it demonstrates how far back graphics have come. Artists were the first visual communicators in newsrooms, but they disappeared soon after the introduction of photography. Before they left, they did some marvelously intricate work for many papers, including the *Chicago Tribune.* By the turn of the century, newsroom artists had nearly disappeared, and it was not until Nelson Poynter, publisher of the *St. Petersburg Times,* asked his newsroom why they could not make maps and other graphics like *Time* magazine that graphics were reintroduced to daily journalism on a regular basis. That was nearly 40 years ago. Today, papers like the *Chicago Tribune* can create graphics on a daily basis to help readers understand the story better (Figs. 6.1, 6.2).

Since the early 1980s, newspapers have increased the use of graphs and maps dramatically, thanks to machines that have speeded the process, the influence of *Time* magazine's Nigel Holmes, the example of *USA Today,* and the wider appreciation of the role of graphics in communicating information.

The machine that had more to do with the introduction of information

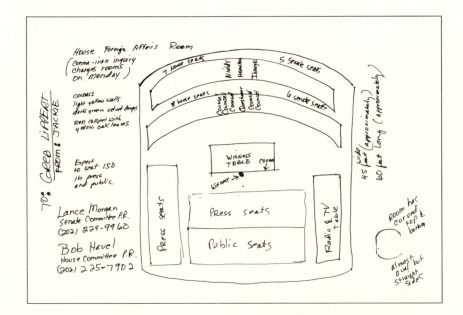

6.1. This sketch done by the graphics coordinator who was at the hearings . . .

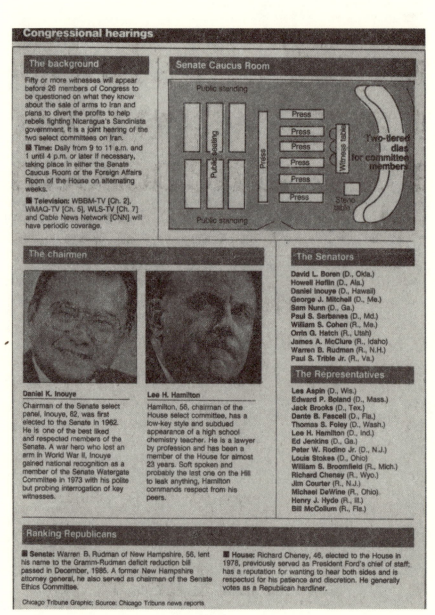

6.2. . . . led to this graphic in the *Chicago Tribune.*

graphics into newsrooms than any other is the Macintosh computer. For relatively little money, newspapers were able to buy a computer that permitted staff members without artistic ability to create charts and maps. The computer became so widely used that the Society of Newspaper Design (SND) started publishing *DeadlineMac,* a newsletter explaining how to use the Macintosh and various software programs to produce charts, maps, and diagrams (Fig. 6.3). Other companies have produced graphic computers, but Macintosh has such a head start that some syndicated services transmit their graphics to Macs.

Graphics are available from a number of sources. Both wire services provide information graphics; Gannett offers graphics to its newspapers through a Macintosh network, and Knight-Ridder and the Chicago Tribune Company offer syndicated graphics through a Macintosh network to any subscriber. One vendor sends graphics by satellite; yet others send their graphics by mail.

This sudden supply of graphics could improve newspapers or cause them to slip back into the sloppy habit of accepting someone else's work when they should at least be localizing it. The industry faces a situation similar to that back in hot-metal days when newspapers used to print large amounts of "boilerplate" (syndicated copy that came in pages already cast to put on the press). The newspaper was unable to edit the copy or even to make the typeface conform to its own. To the extent that newspapers simply run graphics from one of the services without editing or localizing, the industry will not have improved much.

But to the extent that newspapers do their own graphics or adapt syndicated graphics, they are indeed adding additional tools to the arsenal that editors can draw on to communicate clearly and simply. When editors ask themselves, What is the best way to tell the story? the answer many times is with an information graphic. Numbers are difficult to communicate meaningfully in text. Charts are visual representation of numbers. However, this relatively new form of storytelling is being thrust upon a generation of journalists who were not trained in the strengths and weaknesses of the form. Many editors do not have the background to evaluate the graphics they are running. That is a problem because just as the quality of the reporting, editing, headline writing, and photography must undergo constant scrutiny, so too should information graphics.

In addition to the evaluation function, editors must also know enough to assess whether a graphic would be more effective than text or photographs or to judge which information should be spun into graphics and which should remain in text.

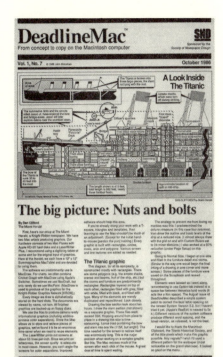

6.3. The interest in producing information graphics was so high that SND started the *DeadlineMac* newsletter for its members.

Types of information graphics

Information graphics is a generic term referring to an assortment of storytelling formats. They include charts, tables, maps, and diagrams showing process and motion and illustrations demonstrating how something works (or fails to). Each has its strengths and weaknesses.

There are three kinds of charts: bar, fever line, and pie. Both bar and fever line charts have an *X* axis, or horizontal scale, and a *Y* axis, or

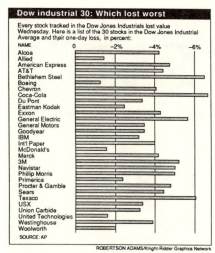

6.4. Bar charts emphasize numbers, not trends.

vertical scale. The *X* axis should contain the independent variable and the *Y* axis, the dependent variable. Thus, when charting inflation rates over time, the rates would be the dependent variable and the time would be the independent variable.

A bar chart (Fig. 6.4) consists of bars or columns representing numbers. The format emphasizes the numbers rather than a trend and is useful for comparing two sets of data. For instance, two years worth of data can be charted for each item listed along the horizontal scale. Bar charts are useful when there is missing data. With numbers along the vertical axis and time along the horizontal scale, a missing month or year would not inhibit the making of the graph the way it would stop a fever line chart. Bars can be run either vertically or horizontally (Fig. 6.5). Because the bar chart emphasizes numbers, it is useful to place the number at the end of the bar.

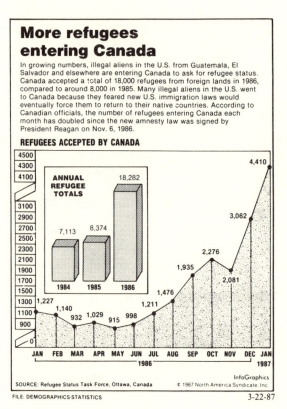

6.6. Fever line charts show trends.

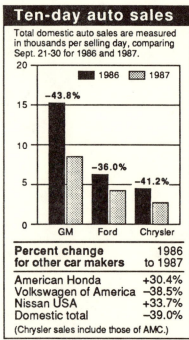

6.5. Bar charts can run vertically or horizontally.

A fever line chart (Fig. 6.6) shows trends or flows over time. This type is commonly used to chart Dow Jones averages and temperature fluctuations. The fever chart does not show the individual numbers as well as the bar chart. It does not work well when there is too little variation in the figures because the line appears flat. Sometimes when there is too much variation in the numbers, the line may jump or drop so much that too much space is required, and there are large gaps between numbers.

A pie chart is useful for one thing, showing parts of the whole (Fig. 6.7). The chart is usually, though not always, circular. The divisions are usually expressed as percentages. The circular pie chart will not work well when there are more than about eight divisions because the sections are too small to read easily. A first cousin of the pie chart would be any representation of parts of the whole. Thus, to show market share for the automobile industry, a car could be sliced into appropriate shares and labeled.

A table is simply columnar listings of names or numbers or both (Fig. 6.8). Tables should be used when there are too many numbers to chart, the data is too disparate (comparing a group of schools, for instance, by several measurements such as math and verbal scores), or it is necessary to see the exact numbers, such as in an income tax table. When there are few numbers or when the numbers show a definite trend, it would probably be better to use a chart.

Where the money went

How $30 million from sale of arms to Iran was disbursed according to Richard Secord

In millions of dollars

Unaccounted for — $2.5
Cost of arms $12
In bank accounts $8
$3.5 Diverted to contras
$3 Expenses
Other covert operations $1

Note: Secord's testimony on the amount of money diverted to the contras is contradictory; the amount could be as high as $6.5 million

Chicago Tribune Graphic; Source: Chicago Tribune news reports

6.7. A pie chart represents percentages, parts of the whole.

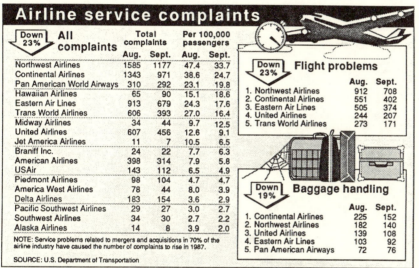

Airline service complaints				
Down 23% All complaints	Total complaints		Per 100,000 passengers	
	Aug.	Sept.	Aug.	Sept.
Northwest Airlines	1585	1177	47.4	33.7
Continental Airlines	1343	971	38.6	24.7
Pan American World Airways	310	292	23.1	19.8
Hawaiian Airlines	65	90	15.1	18.6
Eastern Air Lines	913	679	24.3	17.6
Trans World Airlines	606	393	27.0	16.4
Midway Airlines	34	44	9.7	12.5
United Airlines	607	456	12.6	9.1
Jet America Airlines	11	7	10.5	6.5
Braniff Inc.	24	22	7.7	6.3
American Airlines	398	314	7.9	5.8
USAir	143	112	6.5	4.9
Piedmont Airlines	98	104	4.7	4.7
America West Airlines	78	44	8.0	3.9
Delta Airlines	183	154	3.6	2.9
Pacific Southwest Airlines	29	27	3.0	2.7
Southwest Airlines	34	30	2.7	2.2
Alaska Airlines	14	8	3.9	2.0

NOTE: Service problems related to mergers and acquisitions in 70% of the airline industry have caused the number of complaints to rise in 1987.

SOURCE: U.S. Department of Transportation

Down 23% **Flight problems**

	Aug.	Sept.
1. Northwest Airlines	912	708
2. Continental Airlines	551	402
3. Eastern Air Lines	505	374
4. United Airlines	244	207
5. Trans World Airlines	273	171

Down 19% **Baggage handling**

	Aug.	Sept.
1. Continental Airlines	225	152
2. Northwest Airlines	182	140
3. United Airlines	139	108
4. Eastern Air Lines	103	92
5. Pan American Airways	72	76

ROBERTSON ADAMS/Knight-Ridder Graphics Network

6.8. Tables are effective when there are many numbers and it is necessary to read them exactly.

Maps should be used often. Every newspaper office ought to have a file of base maps, that is, outlines of political subdivisions such as the ward, city, county or parish, state, and nation. With base maps, you can quickly add the material needed to locate action in an accompanying story.

There are several things to remember when making maps. They include always identifying north, putting the name of the featured location in larger type than the cities around it, using a larger dot to indicate the featured location, including enough of the surrounding territory to identify the location but eliminating unnecessary detail, including a mileage scale, and in most cases, including a small secondary map window to locate the exploded area within a larger division. In Figure 6.9, the map locates the Golden Temple, and the window locates the province within the country of India. Figure 6.10 is an example from *DeadlineMac* of how *USA Today* makes its maps on the Mac.

Besides showing location, maps can show the geographical spread of data. For instance, Which states in the region or nation have the highest

76

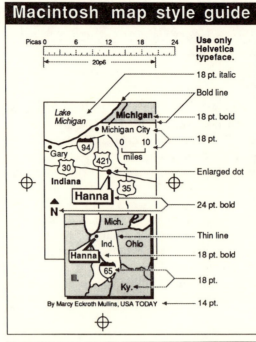

6.9. Space is used efficiently here to locate the Golden Temple in India.

6.10. Staff members from *USA Today* explained in *DeadlineMac* how they make maps.

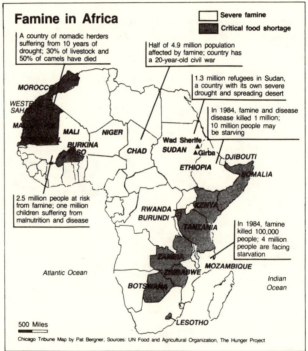

6.11. Besides location, maps can also show the geographical spread of data.

divorce or crime rates? Which states have the death penalty? Which countries in Africa are suffering from famine (Fig. 6.11)? In these instances, you are using a map as a graphic rather than a locator; thus you can usually turn them up or down or sideways without distorting the information, and you do not need a mileage scale.

Diagrams can take many forms; like pictures, they can be worth a thousand words. Nearly ever state has debated whether to require drivers to wear seat belts. Nearly every newspaper ran stories about the debate. The *Providence* (R.I.) *Sunday Journal* went a step further (Fig. 6.12). Its diagram showing how a driver was thrown from his car in an accident probably contributed more to the understanding of what happens in a collision than the hundreds of thousands of words that previously had been written about it.

A death and the seat belt debate

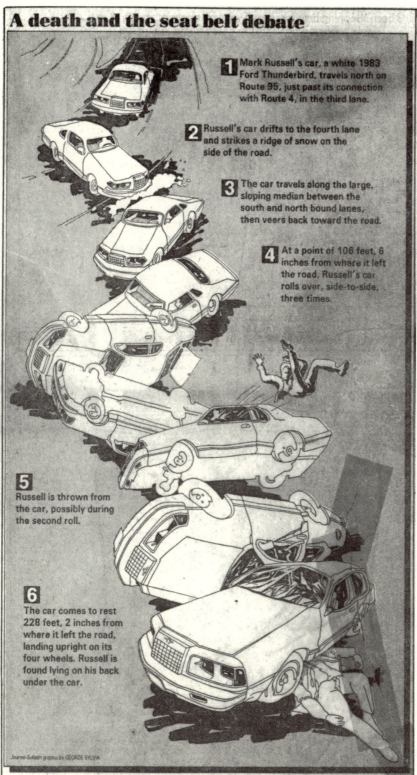

1 Mark Russell's car, a white 1983 Ford Thunderbird, travels north on Route 95, just past its connection with Route 4, in the third lane.

2 Russell's car drifts to the fourth lane and strikes a ridge of snow on the side of the road.

3 The car travels along the large, sloping median between the south and north bound lanes, then veers back toward the road.

4 At a point of 106 feet, 6 inches from where it left the road, Russell's car rolls over, side-to-side, three times.

5 Russell is thrown from the car, possibly during the second roll.

6 The car comes to rest 228 feet, 2 inches from where it left the road, landing upright on its four wheels. Russell is found lying on his back under the car.

Journal-Bulletin graphic by GEORGE SYLVIA

As R.I. debates seat belt law, crash victim's friends wonder if belts could have saved him

BRIAN C. JONES
Journal-Bulletin Staff Writer

WARWICK — Last Sunday, a 29-year-old teacher's aide, Mark Russell, died after his car drifted off Route 95 onto a wide, sloping median area and rolled over three times, throwing him out of the vehicle.

Andrew A. Kenny saw the accident happen.

pronounced dead at Kent County Memorial Hospital.

The car was badly battered. But the interior — the passenger compartment — was unscathed. The steering wheel was in place. The plush, maroon front seats were intact. The roof over the driver's seat had not caved in.

The condition of the car would catch the attention of

6.12. The diagram shows what photographs or words cannot.

Another time to think diagram is when you have chronology available for a dramatic event. The *Dallas Times Herald* used a diagram with numbered copy blocks to track the chronology of a hijacking (Fig. 6.13). Two maps set into the graphic help us place the event.

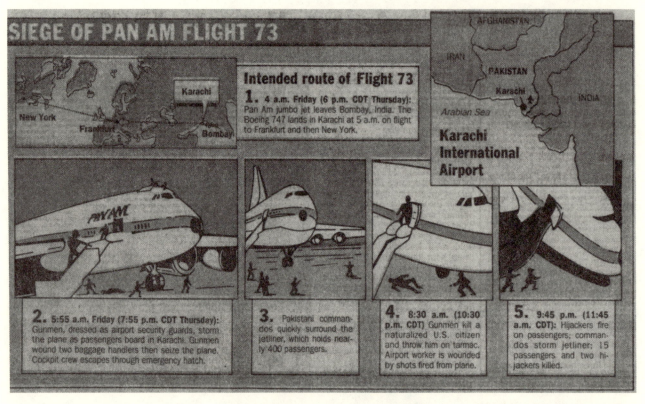

SIEGE OF PAN AM FLIGHT 73

Intended route of Flight 73

1. 4 a.m. Friday (6 p.m. CDT Thursday): Pan Am jumbo jet leaves Bombay, India. The Boeing 747 lands in Karachi at 5 a.m. on flight to Frankfurt and then New York.

Karachi International Airport

2. 5:55 a.m. Friday (7:55 p.m. CDT Thursday): Gunmen, dressed as airport security guards, storm the plane as passengers board in Karachi. Gunmen wound two baggage handlers then seize the plane. Cockpit crew escapes through emergency hatch.

3. Pakistani commandos quickly surround the jetliner, which holds nearly 400 passengers.

4. 8:30 a.m. (10:30 p.m. CDT) Gunmen kill a naturalized U.S. citizen and throw him on tarmac. Airport worker is wounded by shots fired from plane.

5. 9:45 p.m. (11:45 a.m. CDT): Hijackers fire on passengers; commandos storm jetliner; 15 passengers and two hijackers killed.

6.13.   The numbered copy blocks direct the reader through this graphic.

Chronology shows movement in time. Diagrams can also help show movement in space, often more effectively than text. A chase scene, accidents, and race routes are all candidates for diagrams.

With artists and computers, newspapers can also become almost encyclopedic. The *Tampa Tribune* explained landscaping and showed how to identify native plants (Fig. 6.14) in a comprehensible way that text alone could not accomplish. By coincidence, both the *San Diego Union* (Fig. 6.15) and the *Detroit News* (Fig. 6.16) published diagrams on myopia on the same day. That and many science subjects can be understood more easily with illustrations. The *Virginian-Pilot*'s advance story on the attempt to circle the globe without landing featured a major illustration showing everything from the route to a cutaway of the cockpit (Fig. 6.17). The story then was devoted to the takeoff and quotes from the crew.

6.14. The artist turned the page into an information graphic.

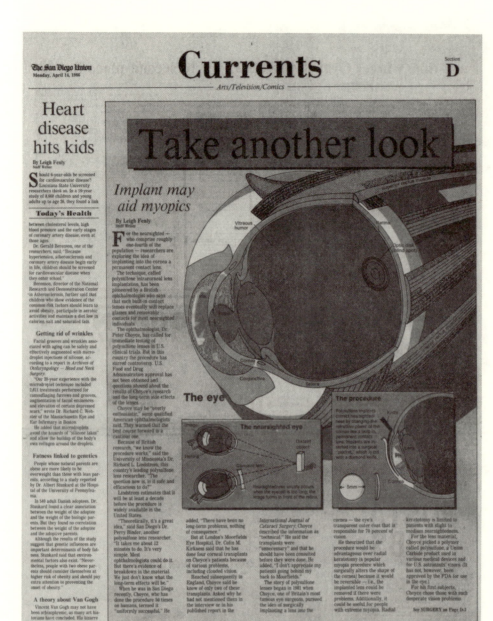

6.15. Medical illustrations make difficult subjects more easily understood.

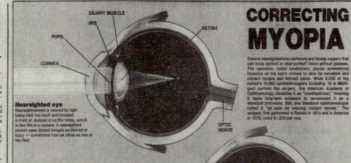

6.16. Compare this illustration with the one in Figure 6.15. Which is better?

6.17. The information graphic serves as the dominant element on Page 1. It is an appropriate choice when the graphic is the best way to tell the story.

Not every diagram has to be dramatic. In fact, the simpler and more functional it is, the better. That is why the graphic from *USA Today* on the nutritional value of the various breakfast cereals is so effective (Fig. 6.18). The reproductions of the cereal boxes immediately identify the kind; the table tells us all we need to know. The grouping under the titles "most popular," "most nutritious," and "least nutritious" organizes and evaluates the information for us. That is service journalism—giving information to readers in a format in which they can act upon it—at its best.

6.18. The categories and the presentation make the information on this page easy to grasp.

Common chart errors

Edward R. Tufte (1983), professor of political science and statistics at Yale University, finds too many inaccurate charts published today. In his excellent book, *Visual Display of Quantitative Information,* Tufte decries "chartjunk" and "data decorators." He pleads for chart makers who have the ability not only to design charts but also to understand statistics and find the substance in the numbers. "If the statistics are boring, then you've got the wrong numbers," he says. "Finding the right numbers requires as much specialized skill—statistical skill—and hard work as creating a beautiful design or covering a complex news story."

Tufte's admonition highlights a notable weakness in newsrooms. We have editors who do not know how to evaluate graphics as they do other parts of the news product, and we have artists and journalist-artists who know little or nothing about statistics. That combination of circumstances presents daily opportunities to produce misleading charts. Thus it is important that the chart makers, the copy editors, and the management editors all have some criteria by which to judge the story the chart is telling. The chart makers, the graphics editor, and the copy editors should have a more thorough understanding of these graphics. Their checklist is longer. Others, such as managing editors and executive editors, must also have some criteria by which graphs can be judged. That list need not be as technical nor as long.

Checklist for designers and editors

Here are six points designers and copy editors should keep in mind when producing and editing charts:

1. Are the right numbers used? For instance, if you were reporting on circulation of American newspapers, would you compare annual total circulation or penetration, which is circulation compared to population? When you are dealing with budget numbers, are you using actual dollars or inflation-adjusted dollars? Every newspaper ought to have the formula to convert inflation dollars to real dollars.

2. Are the measurements on the data lines spaced equally and do they represent equal amounts or time periods? A common error is to show data on an annual basis for five years and then give a quarterly or semiannual report for the last or current year (Fig. 6.19). If you do not convert the partial-year numbers to an annual rate (and tell the readers what you have done) or project the trend for the rest of the year, you have a misleading graph.

3. Do the bars and portions of the pie accurately reflect the numbers, and are they in proportion to the other numbers on the chart? Looking at the chart on football rushing records (Fig. 6.20), most people would conclude that Jim Brown is so far ahead of Franco Harris and Walter Payton that Brown's record may not be broken. It also appears as if Harris has a significant lead on Payton. The graph is inaccurate because the visual image and the numbers are not the same. At the time of this graph, Harris was only 316 yards behind Brown and Payton was 447, not much difference with 12 weeks remaining in the season. Payton is only 131 yards behind Harris. The inaccuracy resulted in the variation between graph lines. For

6.19. Beware of using charts to compare unequal time periods. This one compares one year to nine months.

Brown, one unit equaled 40 yards; for Harris, one unit equaled 66 yards and for Payton, one unit equaled 93 yards.

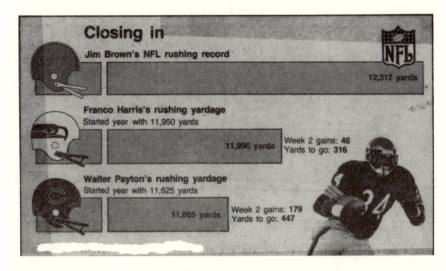

6.20. A common error in charting is not keeping proportions correct. In this version, Brown covers 40 yards per unit; Harris, 66; and Payton, 93.

The break in the bar indicates some data were left out; in this case, it is because the graph would be too long to plot 12,000 yards. But the break should represent equal amounts for all three players. Thus the corrected graph assigns a value of 10,000 yards to the bar before the break. The rest is treated equally. Now (Fig. 6.21) the visual message and the numerical message agree.

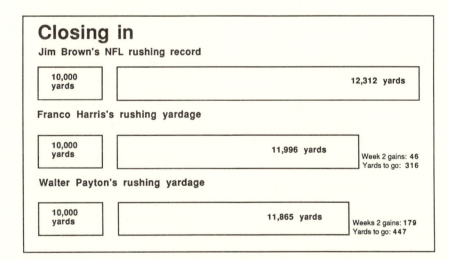

6.21. Now the graph tells a different story. The proportions are correct. Note that the bar before the split is designated as 10,000 yards. That keeps the bar from extending too far.

4. If any of the lines or shapes are canted, are the data distorted? The disturbing trend to overlay data lines on artwork often leads to a distortion of the data. When the chart is canted, it is difficult if not impossible to

maintain consistently spaced data lines, which leads to at least minor and often major inaccuracies. Should we have lesser criteria of accuracy for graphs than stories? Some graphic artists argue that the numbers are not as important as the trends the numbers show. A writer who had the numbers wrong but the trend correct would be called to task.

5. Are the data variations sufficient to be used in a chart? In Figure 6.22, the differences in categories not only are insignificant but they also vary. The first represents states with greater than 30 percent of the voting-age population over 55. Both 31 and 99 are greater than 30; the same problem exists at the lower end of the scale. In between, the difference between the top two categories is 1.4 percent; the difference between the second and third categories is 3 percent. Because the data variations are small (to the extent we can tell from the map), the data could be presented better and more accurately in a table. Which brings us to the sixth point.

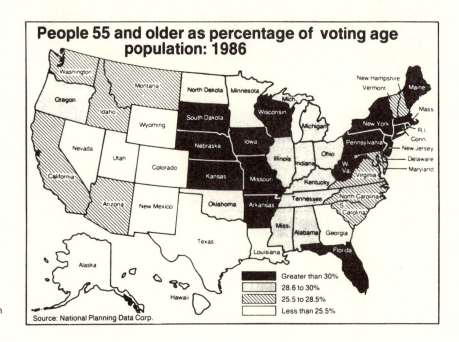

6.22.   When the data variations are slight, a table may be a better choice. The variations in two of the categories are less than 3 percent.

6. Is the choice of chart appropriate for the content? Earlier in this chapter, we listed some of the appropriate uses for bar, fever, and pie charts and tables. In Figure 6.22, we see an example of an inappropriate choice.

Sometimes we see inappropriate choices made even in diagrams. The illustration in Figure 6.23 appears to trace movement during a kidnapping. Upon closer examination, however, we discover that the kidnapper holed up in the same room for the duration of the event. Instead of his movement, the blocks are pointing out other locations where those involved in the event gathered. The format was not consistent with the content.

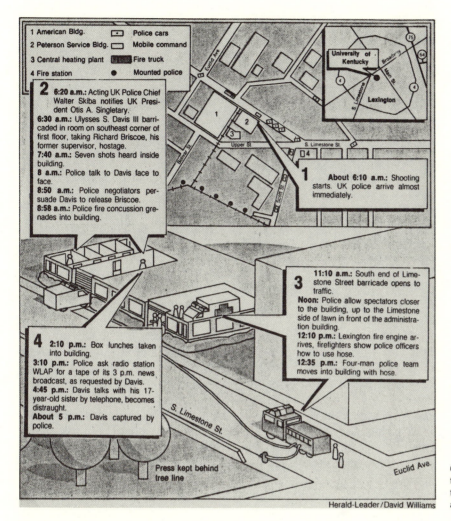

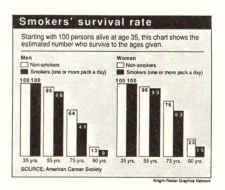

Herald-Leader/David Williams

6.23. The graphic appears to show movement through the locations. A closer look indicates that there was no movement. The graphic is ambiguous.

Management checklist

If management editors learn to evaluate graphs by any of the previous six criteria, their papers will produce more accurate stories. But even if they do not study graphs that deeply, they ought to at least make the following checks along with those for designers and copy editors:

1. Is the headline specific? The headline should tell the readers what they will see repeated in the chart. It is the continuation of the admonition to news writers, "Tell them what you are going to tell them and then tell them." Too many headlines are generic: "Retail construction" instead of "Retail construction declines" and "Growing Florida strawberries" instead of "Strawberry crop value increases." The headline in Figure 6.24 is generic; the point of the graphic is that nonsmokers live longer.

2. Is there a copy block or at least a caption that continues to explain the headline? And is the copy clear and concise? Most charts benefit from a copy block. The bar chart in Figure 6.25 has both a generic title and a copy

6.24. Headlines should report the essential information of the graphic. This one is too general. "Non-smokers live longer" is more specific.

6.25. Use the copy block to tell the essence of the graphic, that which cannot be told in the headline. This copy is too general.

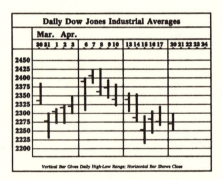

6.26. A good deal of data is packed into this small space. The chart shows the high, low, and closing Dow Jones Industrial Averages.

block that does not help explain the numbers. The following treatment would improve readers' understanding:

GNP climbs

The U.S. Gross National Product increased during the first quarter because of increases in exports and inventories.

The information currently in the copy block should appear at the bottom of the chart in smaller type. There should also be a data line for the bars to rest on. If the design of the chart does not permit space for a copy block, then use a cutline.

3. Is there a source line? We require attribution in stories; we should have the same standard for information in graphics.

4. Does it use space efficiently? Unlike photographs, charts do not get better and have more impact when they get bigger. They ought to be only large enough to maintain the legibility of the type. While the chart in Figure 6.26 may appear to be complicated, once you understand the symbols, you can see that it carries a lot of information in a small space. It is published daily at 19 by 15 picas.

5. Many charts need to be run larger than necessary because of chart-junk, the artwork that is often added. Not only does the artwork increase the need for space but it also frequently overpowers the message in the chart. All artwork is not bad, but designers should use restraint. Less is more.

6. Has the story been edited with the graphic in mind? Too often, information used in the chart appears again in the story. The story should either be shorter or the space should be used to explain the why and how.

Information graphics are a powerful tool for journalists. It is our responsibility to learn how to use them to help us transfer information to the readers.

Graphics desk books

The staff at the *Chicago Tribune* have compiled a list of books that they think are necessary for daily use at a graphics desk. Among them are:

Air Force Magazine. Monthly. Air Force Association.
All the World's Aircraft. Jan's Publishing Co.
All the World's Fighting Ships. Jan's Publishing Co.
Almanac of Seapower. Navy League of the United States.
American Demographics. Monthly. Dow Jones.
Annual Energy Review by the U.S. Department of Energy. U.S. Government Printing Office.
The Arab-Israeli Conflict. 1984. Martin Gilbert.
Barnes & Noble Thesaurus of Chemistry. 1982.
Barnes & Noble Thesaurus of Geology. 1983.
Barnes & Noble Thesaurus of Science. 1983.
Commercial Atlas and Marketing Guide. Rand McNally.
Complete Book of Sports Facts. ABC News.
Congressional Quarterly Federal Regulatory Directory. Annually. U.S. Government Printing Office.

County and City Data Book. 1983. A Statistical Abstract Supplement. U.S. Government Printing Office.

Current World Leaders. Eight times a year. International Academy, Santa Barbara.

Economic Committee by the Council of Economic Advisers. Annually. U.S. Government Printing Office.

The Economist. Weekly. Greenwood Reprint Corp.

Europa Year Book. Annually. International Publications Service.

Illustrated Science and Invention Encyclopedia. 1977. Stuttman.

Information Please Almanac. Annually. S & S Press.

Jewish History Atlas. 1985. Martin Gilbert.

McGraw-Hill Encyclopedia of Energy. 1981.

Military Balance. Annually. International Institute for Strategic Studies, London.

National Directory of Addresses and Telephone Numbers. 1986. Concord Reference Books.

Pan Am's World Guide. 1974. McGraw-Hill.

Peoples and Places of the Past. 1983. National Geographic Society.

Road Atlas. 1984. Rand McNally.

Rule Book. 1983. St. Martin's.

Social Security Bulletin Annual Statistical Supplement. Annually. U.S. Government Printing Office.

Soviet Military Power. Reprint of 1959 edition. U.S. Defense Department. Greenwood.

Statesman's Year-Book. Annually. St. Martin's.

The Statistical Abstract of the United States. Annually. Department of Commerce.

Strategic Survey. Annually. International Institute for Strategic Studies, London.

Time-Life Book of the Family Car. 1973.

Times Atlas of World History. 1984. Times Books.

U.S. Geological Survey Yearbook. Annually. U.S. Government Printing Office.

U.S. Industrial Outlook. Annually. U.S. Department of Commerce.

Webster's New Geographical Dictionary. 1980. G & C Merriam.

White Book of Ski Areas. 1984. Inter-Ski.

World Almanac and Book of Facts. Annually. Newspaper Enterprise Association.

World Book Encyclopedia. 1985. World Book.

World Fact Book. Annually. Central Intelligence Agency.

7

Packaging sections and stories

I'D PROBABLY read the paper more often if I knew where to find what interests me. Some days sports are mixed up with classified, sometimes they are in the B section. I want to reach in and find it right away.

An occasional reader

THIS IS MY IDEA OF A GOOD NEWSPAPER," the reader said. "I could go right to sports and business and get rid of everything else except the front news section" (Clark 1979, p. 30).

That bittersweet assessment by an out-of-towner seeing the *Chicago Tribune* for the first time strikes at the heart of traditional newspaper philosophy. Newspapers give readers the information they *need* and the information they *want*. If the newspaper is properly departmentalized, it is easier for readers to find what they want regardless of whether it is important, trivial, or both. Departmentalization also helps many readers tune out the unpleasant. Former Chief Justice Earl Warren once remarked that he turned to the sports pages, which chronicled man's achievements, before turning to the news, which chronicled man's defeats.

At least he knew where to turn. When you pick up some newspapers, you never know where the daily sections, if they even exist, will be. As a typical occasional reader told a researcher, "I'd probably read the paper more often if I knew where to find what interests me. Some days sports are mixed up with classified, sometimes they are in the B section. I want to reach in and find it right away." And a typical regular reader said, "I find it frustrating to look through stem to stern to find all the international or all the local news" (Clark 1979, p. 31). More readers said they liked the improved organization more than anything else in a redesign (Pipps 1985).

Readers are also frustrated when they are confused by the arrangement of elements on the page. When related stories are separated by unrelated stories or unrelated stories and pictures are positioned so that they appear to be related, confusion often results. One critic commented about a front page: "Once I'd worked out that the fine rule over the picture was probably meant to set it off from the headline, I then had to decide which story—the one to the left or to the right of the picture—actually went with the headline" (Pitnof 1980).

Readers are often jerked through the publication by jumps and reference lines. Readership surveys, such as those by Clark (1979) for the American Society of Newspaper Editors and the News Research Reports for the American Newspaper Publishers Association, remind editors that readers want their papers properly organized and easy to read.

Departmentalization

In study after study, readers tell us they want their papers organized. Editors have listened. Beginning in the late 1970s, they started arranging the content, not just by the larger divisions such as news and sports, but also by such subsections as local, state, national, and international news. But there is still work to be done. A table of contents in newspapers is a good place to start.

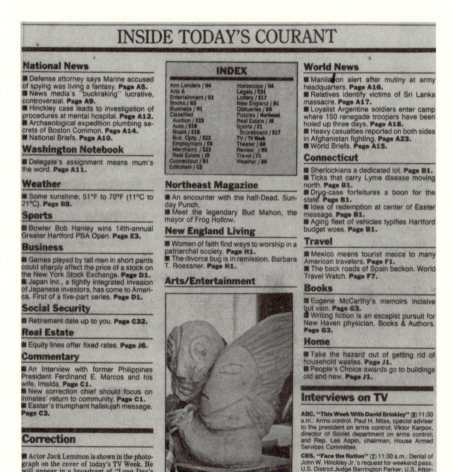

7.1. The *Hartford Courant* publishes a table of contents on Page 2 that goes far beyond a typical newspaper index in helping readers find what they want.

7.2. Features such as celebrity briefs and weather should appear in the same place in every issue.

7.3. This type of packaging makes the newspaper more useful to readers.

Few newspapers have contents pages such as that run by the *Hartford Courant* on Sundays (Fig. 7.1). Magazines such as *Time* have developed tables of contents to help readers through the publication and to increase readership of the stories cited. Despite the success of the magazines, most newspapers still rely on a brief index that tells but does not sell. Nor are the indexes complete. Newspapers have many more stories than magazines, and the stories are harder to find. Yet newspapers have been slow to help readers through the publication. The *Courant* and *New York Times* are among the exceptions.

Two reader characteristics must be foremost in the designer's mind: daily readership is a habit, and readers want the newspaper to be useful and enjoyable (Tipton 1978). A newspaper designer should organize the product before dealing with its aesthetic aspects.

Readers want to be as comfortable with their newspaper as they are with their slippers. Editors who pay no attention to the organization of their newspapers are likely to find that their readers soon will pay no attention to them. Editors should not irritate readers by making them search every day for the sports, features, or national news. We all are more comfortable with the familiar; the more familiar we can make our publications, the more secure our readers will feel with them. Robert Haiman, former executive editor of the *St. Petersburg Times,* wanted his readers to feel comfortable. He said, "I believe in the notion that there is a place for everything and everything in its place and in the same place *every* day."

If a newspaper is properly departmentalized and clearly labeled, readers are likely to find it useful and gratifying. They also will recognize and appreciate what the newspaper carries every day. Readers of the *Ledger* in Lakeland, Fla., know that celebrity briefs and the weather will always be waiting for them on Page 2 (Fig. 7.2). When the editors of Gannett's Reno, Nev., newspaper learned that readers thought they did not have as much national and international news as the competing San Francisco paper, they started measuring. They found that the Reno paper had as much coverage or more, but it was scattered throughout. The solution was to group the news by categories and label them clearly.

The size and production facilities of the newspaper dictate how easily departmentalization can be achieved and how many sections there will be. Some newspapers do not have the press capacity to divide their product into all the sections they would like. For those who do have the capacity, typical departments are General News, Business, Sports, Features, Food, Travel, and Religion. Each department may be broken down into subsections. General news often is divided into city, region, state, national, and international. The sports section is often split into spectator and participant events. The newsmagazines are strictly sectionalized, and even though the sections expand and contract, they do not move. By contrast, some readers often find their favorite subject matter rotating from section A to section B to section C. "Dear Abby" may appear in the news section one day and the feature section the next. Readers of such papers as the Fort Lauderdale *Sun-Sentinel,* however, not only know where Abby will appear, but her column is also packaged with other advice columns and labeled for easy access (Fig. 7.3).

While many newspapers have been quick to embrace departmentalization by content, they have done little to correlate the advertisements. A few sections, such as fashion and food, have compatible advertising and editorial content and are popular with readers. Unfortunately, they are the exceptions. A consumer who wants to buy a lawn mower has to search all the sections from news to sports to find the department store and hardware advertisements. Similarly, advertisements for such products and services as snow tires and tune-ups are likely to be scattered throughout the newspaper.

Although it is possible to group one-subject ads such as food, fashion, movies, and automobiles, it is more difficult to group all the ads for lawnmowers because they often are just one part of an advertisement containing many other items. However, if those ads were grouped by the type of store (discount or department, for instance), both the consumer and the advertiser would benefit. As computers take over the job of dummying advertisements, the ability to improve their organization increases. Locating advertising indexes in the same place in the front of the section would also help the consumer. Such organization is where design starts.

Improving the handling of jumped stories is another way to help readers through our publications. Most newspapers do not pay enough attention to the details of jumped stories.

One way to increase recognition of jumped stories is to put a symbol with the "see line" or jump line, the line of type that tells the reader where the rest of the story is located. By repeating that symbol with the line at the top of the continued story, editors are telling readers that they are in the right place. The symbol serves the same function as a road sign. Many newspapers use "See STORY, P. 12" as their see line. By adding "please," they can make friends among readers.

Both placement of the jumped stories and wording of the jump head are important. Consistency is the key to placement. Jumped stories should appear on the same page of the section every issue and should not leave a section. The *New York Times* sometimes continues a story into another section, a practice that is inconvenient for the reader. Ideally, jumps from the cover would be located on the back page of the section. However, that is a highly coveted advertising page and is often not available to editorial. Page 2 should not be used for jumps because it is impossible to clip stories that appear on both sides of a page. Wherever jumped stories are located, they should be located there consistently so subscribers learn where to look.

What they see when they arrive is often a one-word label over the jumped story. That is not enough. The advantage of a label jump head is that it is easily recognized by the reader who is following the story from the cover. However, few readers go directly to a jumped story. Most of them continue scanning the cover and may even read through the section before picking up on the jumped story. Others will not have seen the original story when they encounter the jump. A headline will attract more readers than a label. However, a headline that reflects the new material in the jump, rather than being a dull repetition of the cover headline, may not be immediately recognized as the same story. A combination of headline styles emphasizes the strengths of the two approaches.

The jumped headline should be a combination of the label and a headline that reflects the information in the portion of the story that is continued. There are several typographical ways of handling this combination. One is to use a hammer headline:

Tax impact

Governor's office:
Average family
faces $103 increase

Others are shown in Figures 7.4 and 7.5. The Fort Lauderdale *Sun-Sentinel* uses a bold rule above a one-word label. The rule acts as an identifying symbol for jumps. In addition to the label, however, each jumped story has a new headline. So do the jumped stories in the *Alexandria* (La.) *Daily Town Talk*. There the headlines incorporate the label into the headline and follow the colon with the new information. The continued line repeats the symbol that appears on the see line.

7.4. The Fort Lauderdale newspaper uses an identifying rule above continued stories and writes a new headline for them.

7.5. The *Alexandria Daily Town Talk* uses a boldface slug that repeats the key word in the original headline then uses a lightweight type for the new headline. The square bullet is the identifying symbol for jumps.

Secondary packaging

Packaging should not be confined to sections. Readers want organization by subject matter, but they also want organization and labeling of the content within a section. The editor's skill in packaging the material and communicating relationships visually determines how useful the publication is to the reader.

We communicate with our readers both explicitly (through the headlines, text, and pictures) and implicitly (through arrangement of material on the pages). Because the arrangement can say as much as the content, it is mandatory that we be careful not only about page balance but also about the relationships among the elements on the page. Being careful means never having to apologize for unwittingly saying something visually that was not intended. Such situations can be embarrassing. For instance, it was not the intent of the editor to imply that the well-known poet Nikki Giovanni was a gay soldier but, typographically, that was the message (Fig. 7.6).

7.6.   Editors can inadvertently send incorrect messages by the arrangement of elements. The photo is of the poet.

If you give readers an opportunity to make a mistake, many of them will. It is important to convey the correct relationships of elements on the page to help the reader avoid this possibility. For the same reason, typographical devices should be used to show when units on the page are not related. Editors have not always been careful in this regard. Until recently, many newspapers used 1-pt. cutoff rules whenever two unrelated elements came in contact. It was thought this thin rule would show the reader that the elements were not related. However, this technique is not always successful.

When newspapers adopted a more open look, most editors eliminated both column and cutoff rules. Many editors were puzzled about how to disassociate unrelated elements. Some have started using 2-, 4-, or 6-pt. cutoff rules. The heavier rules are more effective cutoffs than the 1-pt. rule and are also an integral part of the format because they add color and weight to a page.

Sometimes boxes are necessary. In Figure 7.7, the photo of the basketball player is in two modules; it could go with the story to the right or the left. Rules or boxes are needed to clear up the confusion. Never place a picture between two stories in the same module without taking extra steps to show the relationship.

7.7. This layout does not show which story and picture are related.

7.8. The layout says that the baseball story picture goes with the track story.

Rules, or the lack of them, are not the only problems on pages. Failure to put the photograph and story in the same module creates the same type of ambiguity. In Figure 7.8, the picture is of the Brewers celebrating; unfortunately, the picture is located in the track story module. In Figure 7.9, the photograph is located in the Social Security story module. However, it goes with the story to the left. Editors must do a better job of establishing relationships on the page.

Showing relationships

Through habit, readers have learned that the normal pattern for a related picture and story is a vertical package that starts with a photograph and continues down through the cutline, headline, and text. That flow pattern is based on the sound principle that the reader's eye is attracted by the photograph first and then travels out of the bottom of the picture. The cutline explains what is not evident in the picture, and the related headline and story are right there waiting for the reader. Editors who start the story at the lower left corner of the picture are taking advantage of the reader's propensity to go to a fixed left focal point. Type lined up evenly on the left provides a standard starting place for each line and can be read faster. Headline and copy lined up at the lower left of the related illustration (as in Fig. 7.10 under the picture of the man enjoying the Cinco de Mayo celebration) take advantage of a natural eye movements. The headline and copy block end at the right corner to complete the module.

Sometimes, however, it is not always possible or even desirable to arrange all related elements in a vertical package. If a different pattern is

7.9. The layout indicates, incorrectly, that the picture is related to the Social Security story. In fact, it goes with the story to the left.

7.10. One good way to establish the relationship between a picture and story is to start the story at the lower left-hand corner of the photo.

7.11. The placement of the headlines signals that they are not related to the photo.

used, it must indicate clearly where the reader should go. There are a number of ways to do this. One technique is to use the headline as a visual cutoff rule. If the reader expects the related story to start at the lower left corner of the picture, stories that are not related should start somewhere other than that position. In Figure 7.11 the headline, "A painful return to a tornado-torn city," starts one column to the left of the photograph. This arrangement signals the reader that the tornado story and the gardening picture are not related.

Headlines also can be used to connect related elements that are not in the normal vertical package. In Figure 7.12 the headline extends over the story and the related photograph about Brewer baseball fans. That ties the two together. So does the L-shaped copy wrap and the box around the package. Relationships on this page work well. The 1-column picture at the upper right goes with the story underneath it; the 1-column picture in the upper left is tied to the story to its left by the copy that runs alongside and under the picture. All the packages are in modules.

As noted above, boxes communicate relationships. Usually, the elements within a box are not related to those outside the box. Many editors err when they box a sidebar or related story but do not place the main story in the same box. The box sets the sidebar apart and competes with the content by telling the reader the sidebar is not related. Boxes are visual fences.

However, when the sidebar is a short related story surrounded by the larger story, it can be boxed without creating ambiguous relationships. In Figure 7.13, the story about the rifle that was aimed at Reagan is part of the Pope story; the rifle incident occurred while the two were visiting in Rome. The story about the rifle is clearly related to the visit with the Pope because it is tucked into the larger story. The tuck overrides the box.

By using modules properly, editors usually do not need additional typographic devices to show relationships. In Figure 7.14, the *Sun-Sentinel* packages a story, picture, and graphic in the same module. Each element

7.12. The relationship between the photo and the story about the Brewers' fans is established through the box, by running the headline over the story and picture, and by wrapping the copy underneath the picture.

7.13. Although a box normally separates, in this layout it is clear that the boxed story goes with the lead story because the copy wraps around it.

7.14. By working in the same module, the editors show the relationships among the Secord story, the picture, and the graphic.

has its own message, but together they carry a greater impact. The visual package communicates the relationship as well as the content.

Color also shows relationships. Asked to arrange circles, triangles, and rectangles, most people will group them by their shapes. But if the elements are presented in three different colors, most of the same people will arrange them by their colors. Color overrides shape. Editors must be wary of the way they use color on the page. If color is used in the title of a story or as a frame around a picture, the same color should not be used on an unrelated package unless the tint is changed dramatically. Readers will connect stories that have elements such as copy tints, headlines, or rules in the same color. However, the same color can be used on such nonstory items as teaser or promotional items and indexes without problems.

As we have seen, there are several ways to show relationships among elements on the page. Among them are the following:

1. Use a vertical package consisting of picture, cutline, headline, and story. The story should start at the lower left-hand corner of the picture and extend the width of the picture.
2. Extend a headline over a story and related picture.
3. Place related elements within the same box.
4. Surround a small element with a related story.
5. Wrap the copy in an L alongside and under a related element.
6. Wrap the copy in a U around a related element.
7. Run related stories in decks off a common headline.
8. Place all related elements in the same module.
9. Use a unifying device such as a logo, common inset, or rising cap letter or logo on all related stories.
10. Use color to show relationships.

Multiple-element packages

Sometimes the editors divide a story into many parts, or the story is so important or interesting that they use several elements to tell the story. That is when good packaging becomes even more important. Editors must clearly show relationships in an orderly way.

When a heat wave hit Missouri, editors at the *Columbia Daily Tribune* chose to tell of the event with two pictures and three stories (Fig. 7.15). Each element is in a module; the entire package is in a module. The package is boxed. Even though one of the sidebars is boxed, it is surrounded by other elements in the package to remove any ambiguity about relationships.

Labels, symbols, or any unifying device clearly identify a group of related elements and remind readers of what they have just read. The editor of a paper that had consistently published a good news story on Page 1 every day for almost a year was stunned when a subscriber complained there was never any good news on the front page. After the initial shock, the editor concluded that readers did not recognize the effort because the stories were not labeled "Good news." Labeling can identify small groupings of news as readily as departments. Readers want complicated events explained and relationships shown. Sometimes, however, it is impossible to put all the related elements in one place.

7.15. Two pictures and three stories are packaged in one module.

The *Washington Post* produced several stories a day out of the hearings on Iran and Contra aid in the spring of 1987. In an unusual but effective move, the editors pulled a quote, which was displayed centered at the top of the page, to tie together the three pages of coverage (Figs. 7.16, 7.17, 7.18).

7.16. The *Washington Post* created the pulled quote at the top of the page as the unifying device for its package of stories.

7.17. When the story moved inside, the pulled quote format appeared again.

7.18. The device was used on every page of this coverage throughout the hearings, not just on one day.

Labels can be designed in several ways. The reverse label (white type against a black background) is one method. The reverse can also be screened to produce white type against a gray border. This technique permits the use of a lighter weight on the page when desired. Many newspapers also use spot color (see Chapter 16) in place of the reverse or screen.

Logos, small graphic representations of the subject matter in which art and type are usually combined, also can be used to show relationships among either a group of stories or a series, stories that appear over a period of time.

Labels and logos give editors the opportunity to communicate with readers explicitly. These aids should be used more often. One reader suggested that newspapers could learn from supermarkets, "They label every aisle, and it makes it easy to find things. Newspapers don't" (Clark 1979, p. 31). Defining relationships for readers, whether between two stories or within a whole category of news, is important. Newspapers have been slow to capitalize on reader habits and desires, but progress is being made. As a result of such monumental efforts as the Newspaper Readership Project, a combined research effort of several newspaper-related organizations, and studies commissioned by individual newspapers, editors are learning and publications are changing.

8

Tabloids and Sunday magazines

PERHAPS one of the reasons that tabloids gained the reputation of being sensationalistic is because a tabloid page can carry three, maybe four news stories. If one of them happens to be about a rape, it gains more prominence than in a broadsheet. . . . It is therefore important for a serious tabloid to be careful in its type size and face design if it is to present all the news tastefully.

Paul Back
DIRECTOR OF DESIGN
Newsday

THE IDEA for an American tabloid newspaper came out of a visit between a son of a publisher of the *Chicago Tribune* and an English press baron. Joseph Medill Patterson told his cousin, Robert McCormick, of his meeting with Lord Northbrook, and in 1919 they started publishing the *Illustrated Daily News* in New York. They hoped to emulate Lord Northbrook's success with the tabloid *Daily Mirror,* which had a circulation of one million in England. Before achieving that kind of success, however, they had to slog through the yellow journalism sensationalism of the 1920s and 1930s and battle upstart competitors. The excesses committed in the name of circulation peaked in 1928 when the *News* brought in a *Chicago Tribune* staff member, Tom Howard, to surreptitiously take a picture of the execution of Ruth Synder, who had been convicted of murder. Public reaction to such sensationalism finally forced this type of newspaper to change or shutdown. The *News* changed and went on to become the largest general circulation newspaper in the United States. Unfortunately, the stigma associated with yellow journalism lingered long after the practices had been corrected, and it slowed the acceptance of the tabloid-sized paper. In 1940, Alicia Patterson, Joseph Patterson's daughter, started a tabloid on Long Island. *Newsday* has since become one of the most successful newspapers in America. Now owned by the Times Mirror Company, *Newsday* grew up with Long Island and, in content and looks, redefined the image of the tabloid. *Newsday* made the tabloid so respectable, in fact, that by 1979 even the conservative *Our Sunday Visitor,* the largest Catholic weekly in the country, had changed from broadsheet to tabloid and reported that reader reaction to the restyled paper was "overwhelmingly positive." On the other hand, the *Tempe* (Ariz.) *News* switched to tabloid but returned to broadsheet two years later because of reader complaints. The *Middletown* (N.Y.) *Daily Record* went from tabloid to broadsheet and then back to tabloid.

These days, the fear that a smaller paper will bring less advertising revenue, not the negative image of tabloids, keeps publishers from switching to the smaller size, which is widely acknowledged to be more convenient for readers. In tabloids, advertisers can buy smaller ads, usually at higher rates, and still dominate the page. Even a full page in a tabloid is only a half page in a broadsheet. Most national advertising is designed for broadsheet newspapers; tabloids often must reduce the ads to make them fit. Even if the reduction is proportionate, the reduced ads often look misshaped. The *Rocky Mountain News* in Denver shrinks its pages 2 percent to conform to standard advertising unit sizes.

As a consequence, tabloids are seen most often where they have existed successfully for years. There are 32 daily tabloids in the United States, but 6 of the largest circulation papers published are tabloids. They are also used by newspapers without much advertising (*Christian Science Monitor, Our Sunday Visitor*), by the minority press (*New York Amsterdam News, Chicago Defender*) (Figs. 8.1, 8.2), by high school and college publications, and by many weeklies. Some special-interest papers (*Village Voice, Rolling Stone*) are tabloids. The grocery-store papers (*National Enquirer, National Star*) are also tabs. Many broadsheet newspapers use tabloids for special theme sections, which usually revolve around an advertising promotion. Sometimes tabs are used to report the results of an in-depth investigation. The fastest growing segment of the tabloid market is city business journals.

8.1. The *New York Amsterdam News,* a black-owned newspaper, uses the tabloid format.

8.2. The *Chicago Defender,* which is 81 years old, uses the tabloid front as a mininewspaper.

They are also among the most innovative. Most newspapers also have Sunday magazines that are usually tabloid size or close to it. The growing number of Sunday newspapers and their corresponding Sunday magazines makes this type of tabloid an increasingly important product with a need for its own design philosophy. We will discuss the Sunday magazine later in this chapter.

Making the decision

Every successful business organization tries to maximize the strengths and minimize the weaknesses of its product. Publishers who are trying to decide whether to publish a broadsheet or tabloid must first know the advantages and disadvantages of each.

ADVANTAGES

1. Tabloids are more convenient for the reader to handle. At the breakfast table, the open broadsheet is big enough to cover three cereal bowls and the coffee; the tabloid is less intrusive. On the bus or subway, the tab does not have to be folded to be read.

2. Editors usually have more open pages. At *Newsday,* the first four pages are considered to be equivalent to the front page of a broadsheet. It is more economical for small papers with less advertising to set aside a full page for departments. An open page in a broadsheet represents twice the investment in the editorial product that the tabloid does.

3. Content, even within a section, is easier to divide in a tabloid than in a broadsheet where many stories on various subjects appear on a single page.

4. The tabloid size permits smaller papers to look and feel hefty with only half the content of the broadsheet. Falling advertising revenue and increasing newsprint costs forced the *Christian Science Monitor* to switch to tabloid. Where it only had 12 pages as a broadsheet, it has 24 pages as a tabloid.

5. Tabloids offer publishers more flexibility in the number of pages that can be added or subtracted. Depending on the press, broadsheet newspapers must go up or down in increments of two, four, or eight pages. The number of pages in a tabloid can be changed in increments of four at most plants.

6. Because of the preponderance of broadsheet newspapers, the tabloid offers publishers an opportunity to differentiate their product from others in the market. This is particularly advantageous to new publications in competitive markets.

7. The advertiser benefits by spending less money to dominate a page.

DISADVANTAGES

1. What advertisers gain, publishers lose. Although large advertisers may buy multiple pages of advertising, smaller merchants often settle for less than they would in a broadsheet. Rates can be increased to make up some of the difference, but only if the tab is operating in a noncompetitive market.

8.3. The *Chicago Sun-Times* uses large type to signal that readers are entering a new section.

2. Advertising and circulation success breeds problems. *Newsday* and the *New York Daily News* are too bulky. Successful broadsheet newspapers usually have problems with heft on Sunday, but tabs often face this problem several days of the week.

3. A smaller front page limits the number of elements tabloid editors can use to attract the same variety of readers obtained by the broadsheet. And when the "big event" occurs, such as a hijacking or the explosion of the Challenger, the broadsheet can use multiple pictures and stories on the front page. The tabloid cannot do this without sacrificing impact.

4. The tabloid cannot be sectionalized as easily as a broadsheet. The tab has only one section even though it may have pullouts (Fig. 8.3). The broadsheet, however, can be divided into numerous sections, depending on press facilities. A family of readers can easily distribute the broadsheet newspaper according to interest; this is much more difficult with a tab.

5. Tabloids still suffer from a lingering image problem. Present generations are not influenced by memories of yellow journalism, but some of them associate tabloids with sensational papers such as the *National Enquirer* and *National Star*. Even people who buy those tabloids do not necessarily want their news presented in the same format. The four most successful daily tabloid newspapers, the *Daily News, Newsday, Chicago Sun-Times,* and *Rocky Mountain News* try to maximize the advantages of their size. All are published in communities where mass transportation is available, yet all sell thousands of copies to homes also. If mass transportation was better developed in other large cities, the tabloid might be more popular because of ease of reading while riding. San Francisco and, to a lesser degree, Washington, D.C., have decent mass transportation systems. In those two cities, the second newspapers, the *Examiner* and the *Times,* might be candidates for tabloids, but both are established as broadsheets, and the disadvantages of a change in size probably outweigh the advantages.

Differentiating the tabloid

Beyond recognizing the advantages and disadvantages, editors must also identify the unique problems and possibilities that a tabloid presents, or it will be treated merely as a small-sized newspaper. The tabloid is different from a broadsheet newspaper in the following six areas: Page 1 philosophy, sectionalizing, spreads, sizing, typography, and jumps.

DEVELOPING A PAGE 1 PHILOSOPHY. Editors of broadsheets must decide whether they want a high or low story count, but tabloid editors must decide whether they want a low story count or no stories at all. On Page 1, tabloids have more in common with newsmagazines than with broadsheets. Both must concentrate on one or two elements because of size restrictions. Like the news weeklies, newspaper tabloids must retain immediacy while providing focus. That means stripping away the clutter. *Newsday* uses its front page as a poster; except for unusual circumstances, no stories start on Page 1 (Fig. 8.4). Instead, two to five stories are promoted with display type. Usually, though not always, there is an illustration with a reference line to an inside story. The *Daily News,* like the *Sun-Times,* uses

8.4. The perfect Page 1—explicitly telling the readers what the story means to them.

8.5. The *Sun-Times* uses large type on the small page.

8.6. The *Christian Science Monitor,* echoing a magazine look, uses small type but a newspaper format.

the front to sell its best story with display type and text and to promote other inside elements of interest. The *Sun-Times* (Fig 8.5) and the *Christian Science Monitor* (Fig. 8.6) treat Page 1 as a small-sized broadsheet. There are as many as four stories, all jumped, and a photograph.

There are five alternative ways to present the tabloid cover:

1. Use it as a poster to sell several stories insides. Both display type and illustrations can be used, but even one decently sized illustration will substantially restrict the number or items that can be teased (Fig. 8.7).

2. Use it as a mininewspaper page. That does not mean the pages will look alike. The *Christian Science Monitor* is a mininewspaper page; so are the *San Francisco Business Times* (Fig. 8.8) and *New Orleans City Business* (Fig. 8.9). What makes all of them different even though they have the same basic philosophy are the element counts, typography, and color. *City Business* is multicolored, *Business Times* has one spot color, and the *Christian Science Monitor* is black and white.

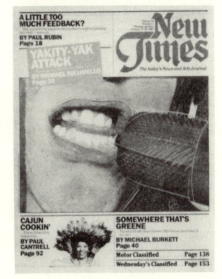

8.7. The *New Times* of Phoenix, Ariz., uses Page 1 as a billboard.

8.8. The *San Francisco Business Times* is deliberately understated in typography and layout.

8.9. *New Orleans City Business* uses lots of color and larger type to create an active page.

8.10. The *Baton Rouge Business Report* treats Page 1 as a cover instead of as Page 1. That means a large illustration and plenty of sell lines.

3. Emphasize illustrations. Instead of display type, use one, two, or even three photographs to sell the paper. The image would be more visual than that of a traditional newspaper.

4. Use a single cover illustration in the tradition of the newsmagazines. Overprinting permits giving the illustration a title and promoting other stories inside (Fig. 8.10).

5. All of the above. An editor may feel that the flexibility to choose any of the approaches on consecutive days is more important than being consistent. Any publication will discard a standard format to handle the big event; extraordinary news requires extraordinary handling.

It does not matter whether the cover contains news, display type, or illustrations because readers do not spend much time on Page 1 of a tabloid. That is why it is even more important for tabloid editors to lure the reader inside and provide a wealth of material there. Most of the major news tabloids open up the first four or more pages, but this varies with the size of the publication. The metros need several. Smaller publications, which may have only 24 to 28 pages, may need to open only the first three. The second and third pages are excellent places to sell the rest of the product. Most readers will go from Page 1 to Page 3 to Page 2. An editor may want to use the third page for an interesting story, news summary, or index. Page 2 is also a good location for items that appear every day, such as news summaries, indexes, tables of content, and in-depth weather reports (Figs. 8.11, 8.12, 8.13). Wherever these items are located up front, the first few pages are essential for creating reader traffic throughout the publication. Separate sections relieve broadsheet editors of some of that burden.

8.11. The *Business Report* runs both a table of contents and an index.

8.12. The *Monitor*'s index is one step more active than most. It includes teaser lines.

8.13. Inside, the *New Times* is in magazine format.

SECTIONALIZING. None of the successful tabs can adequately overcome the problem of size. *Newsday* publishes nearly 200 pages an issue. Some issues are as large as 250 pages.

To create internal departments, most tabs start sectionalized interest areas on the right-hand page so that readers can pull out the entire section. Unfortunately, unless readers work from the middle out, they will probably pull out several other sections too. *Newsday* developed a thumb index punch on the side of the paper to help readers find sections but dropped the idea. Many tabloids start the sports section on the back page. Some run a broadsheet food section tucked sideways into the tab. That section, which takes advantage of the full-page grocery advertisements, can easily be pulled out. The *Boston Herald* prints business and sports in a section that can be pulled from the middle.

Design is an important element in identifying sections. *Newsday* starts each section except sports with a magazine-type cover. The department is led with a large section identifier and a major illustration. Because it is not easy to separate sections physically, it is important that tabloid sections have different typographical personalities. This can be achieved by using a different, though compatible, headline face; using different column widths on open pages; running unjustified type in one section and justified type in another; and altering the horizontal-vertical emphasis to fit the content.

Examples of the varieties of ways of achieving this break can be seen in Figures 8.14 through 8.17. The *Rocky Mountain News* relies on the large Lifestyles header and the 3-column format to signal a change of content. The *San Francisco Business Times* uses a more effective device, white space, to set off its departments. It has a magazine flavor to it. The *Jackson Hole* (Wyo.) *News* has a distinctive script type to signal its arts section. *Crain's Chicago Business* maintains its high pacing even in Options (Fig. 8.17) but divides the grid into thirds. White space, a different grid, different typography, and different element count are ways of varying the pacing in the product.

8.14. When readers of the *Rocky Mountain News* reach Lifestyles, they immediately see a different grid.

8.15. Although appearing inside, this page, which introduces a section, appears to be a cover.

8.16. The distinctive script type introduces The Arts in the *Jackson Hole News.*

8.17. *Crain's Chicago Business* looks unbusinesslike in its feature section.

8.18. In its news section, *Crain's Chicago Business* looks like a newspaper.

8.19. Inside *Business Times,* the environment is like a three-piece suit.

For instance, in the softer feature or Lifestyle sections, ragged right type can be used to signify the less formal approach. In Business, the layout can be a more conservative vertical structure in the image of the *Wall Street Journal*. In Entertainment, it might be appropriate to use heavy rules freely, but in a Fashion section, thin rules (hairlines) would give a more dignified aura. Headline formats, if not the typeface, can also be changed according to section. The news can be presented in traditional style, while features rely on titles, labels, and readouts. The editorial section can emphasize summary decks to tell the reader the points made in the editorial column.

It is important to create different typographical personalities for each section, but the publication must be unified. This is done by providing standardized sectional identifiers (type and sometimes art) that convey the name of the section. Standardized identifiers can be designed by using the same headline face throughout, even if the format is different, using the same basic format for teasers on the section fronts throughout, or stipulating that all section fronts have summaries or standard indexes. The effort to unify the sections becomes more important as the differentiation between the sections increases. The points are not contradictory. Publications that do not choose to create separate personalities for sections have less need for standardized promotional approaches and indexes. On the other hand, publications that do create different personalities must show the reader that the sections are part of the same family even though they are different in content and approach.

Inside, the tabloid has an opportunity to adopt a newspaper or magazine format. A newspaper format would have headlines running over all the legs of the story, and the heads usually would be larger. A magazine format would be more vertical, have smaller heads, and permit type to wrap out from beneath heads. *Crain's Chicago Business* maintains a traditional newspaper approach (Fig. 8.18). The *Business Times* illustrates a magazine approach. Its briefs are run vertically, with 1-column heads, and the copy wraps (Fig. 8.19). Its news pages feature wraps and small heads.

SPREADS. The manageable size of an open tabloid permits the design editor to treat facing pages as a single unit. Even when stories or pictures do not use the gutter between facing pages, the designer should treat the pages or spread as one unit for purposes of balance and flow (Fig. 8.20). In the tabloid, it is often possible to continue stories and pictures from the left-hand to the right-hand page, and even the gutter can be used on the spread in the middle of a section. Using the gutter elsewhere is always risky because a continuous sheet of paper is not always available, and headlines and photographs may not line up properly.

When a double truck is done properly (Fig. 8.21), it takes advantage of the extra inch or so in the gutter and brings two vertical pages together into a horizontal spread. Notice that the copy and illustration flow across the gutter, and the space is not divided in halves or thirds. A different type of spread is illustrated in Figure 8.22. *Hamptons Newspaper/Magazine,* a resort-area publication, uses a consistent format of stacking ads on the left-hand page and using the two-thirds remaining for its spreads. The story starts on the left-hand side, but the headline always appears on the right-

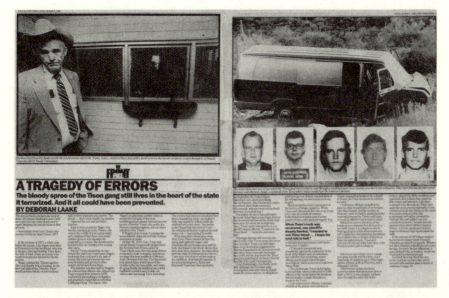

8.20. *New Times* designers treat facing pages as a single unit.

8.21. By using the double truck, facing center pages, the designer picks up another half-inch horizontally.

8.22. The photo and headline are on the right; the story starts at the left. If the approach is used consistently, readers may get used to it.

hand page. The advantage of this layout is that the weight of the ads and titles can be separated. While it usually is not advisable to separate the title or headline from the beginning of the story, readers of *Hamptons* would get used to it because of the consistency with which it is used. However, the spread could be improved by running a blurb or readout over columns 1 and 2 of the story.

RELATIVE SIZING. The most important design principle for tabloid editors to remember is that sizing is relative to the dimension of the publication. A 1-column picture in a broadsheet newspaper would look large in *Reader's Digest* or *TV Guide.* A 3-column picture in a broadsheet would look large in a tabloid. The fact that *National Geographic,* with its 33 by 52½ pica page size, has been able to establish itself as a quality photographic magazine is a testament to the principle of relativity.

Certainly a tabloid can never match the broadsheet newspaper's ability to run a picture 78 picas wide on Page 1. A photograph run as wide as the tabloid page will look large in relation to the size of the newspaper. Consequently, it is important for editors to use photographs properly in tandem to emphasize large and small shapes.

TYPOGRAPHY. Display type selection is also different for tabloids because there are fewer headlines and choices of size. Consequently, weight becomes the most effective way to show contrast. A headline schedule built around a bold or extrabold face would permit the editors to downsize heads, an appropriate measure for a tabloid. Smaller heads save space and preserve the proportions on a tab page. A lighter face should be available for decks and blurbs. However, as the *San Francisco Business Times* illustrates, lighter head schedules, when run small, create an entirely different tone. Contrast the *Times* (Fig. 8.8) with the *Monitor* (Fig. 8.6).

Tabloids are a more suitable format for mixing typefaces than a broadsheet (Fig. 8.23). A broadsheet usually has several headlines on a page, but most tab pages have only two to four. As a result, a headline schedule that used a serif for the main face and a sans serif for decks, or vice versa, does not have the potential for clutter that it would have on a broadsheet.

JUMPS. Jumps are a problem in any publication but, properly handled, are less so for tabloids than broadsheets. In a tabloid, however, the writing must be tighter to avoid the necessity of jumping a large number of stories. A medium-sized story in a broadsheet might jump past several pages and, in the process, make it difficult for the reader to follow. The tabloid can capitalize on its magazinelike format and jump to the next page, which is less annoying to the reader and is a pattern familiar to magazine readers. Continuing a story to the next page poses problems for editors, however. If the story starts on one of the first three or four open pages, the jump might occupy valuable space normally used to attract readers with a variety of interests. If the story is important enough that it has to be jumped, it ought to be able to carry its own weight in competition with the other stories fighting for space. When tabs jump stories several pages away, they lose

8.23. Tabloids should use different headline faces than most broadsheets to develop their own personalities. This one mixes two different races in a pleasing combination.

their advantage over the broadsheets. Readership surveys have indicated time and again that readers do not like jumped stories.

Tabloids can also jump from one page to a facing page without using continued lines if ads do not intervene. However, it is advisable to use a type takeout at the top of each page. A blurb or pullout quote, for instance, would be a good device to replace the jump head.

Tabloid philosophy

The Page 1 philosophy that tabloid editors adopt as well as the manner in which they handle sectionalizing and the special problems of dimension and proportion will determine whether the publication is treated as a mininewspaper or a genre with its own strengths and weaknesses. Too many editors of both broadsheet and tabloid newspapers never make the difficult decisions. The result is a publication that is unfocused in content and form. Although the basics of good design are the same for broadsheets, tabloids, and magazines, they each have their own special characteristics. Because the news tabloid serves the same audience as the more traditional broadsheet newspaper, editors often fail to distinguish it from the larger version.

With a clearly thought out philosophy, tabloid design editors can place their publications somewhere between the broadsheet newspaper and the weekly newsmagazine. The newsprint gives the tab a sense of immediacy. With 1 to 5 columns to a page, the tabloid designer can use many magazine techniques.

What is surprising is that college editors have not shown much inclination to break out of the traditional mininewspaper mold. Given the age and interests of the audience, the college paper would seem to have more in common with the *New Times* of Phoenix or *Rolling Stone* than the *Rocky Mountain News* or *Chicago Sun-Times*.

Sunday magazines

Newspaper Sunday magazines often are similar in size to the tabloid format. Sometimes they are even printed on newsprint. Often, though, they are printed on better quality paper stock and have a personality distinct from the daily sections of the newspaper.

The principles of design are constant from format to format, but some general practices are common among Sunday magazines. Most of these practices are based on the belief that the magazine audience is more selective and will take time to read that section. The following principles should be kept in mind:

1. A good advertising arrangement and proper editorial space is essential to success. Ad sizes should be restricted to full, half, and quarter pages (except perhaps in a special section for small advertisers) to create modular spaces for editorial copy. There should be at least one open spread (two facing pages) for the cover story.

2. The beginning of the editorial content must be established clearly. Some Sunday magazines are so full of advertising that the reader must turn several pages before finding editorial copy. Some surefire reader interest material should be up front. *Time* magazine runs letters. The *Kansas City*

Star Magazine runs a series of short items and a column.

3.   Begin each story with a strong focus. The reader should recognize immediately where each story starts. Use large type and photographs or illustrations for openers. The *Kansas City Star Magazine* used both to open a story on racist groups (Fig. 8.24).

8.24.   The striking spread signals the start of a major feature.

8.25.   In typical magazine fashion, the Orlando *Sentinel*'s *Florida Magazine* uses white space at the top of pages.

4.   Use plenty of white space in the magazine, especially around the type that starts the story. The magazine page should not be like the newspaper page, which is usually full from margin to margin. It is often more attractive to open a story about 30 percent of the way down the opening page (Fig. 8.25). White space in the margins is also important. The outer margin usually is larger than the interior, or interpage, margin. There should be more white space between the editorial copy and the advertising than there is between elements within the editorial spread.

5.   Although the white space in the margins enhances the text that it surrounds, that margin area can also be used effectively for bleeds—running a picture to the edge of the page. Bleeds permit larger picture display and provide page contrast.

6.   Design facing pages as one unit whenever possible. Create a strong horizontal left-to-right flow rather than a vertical flow. Refer back to Figure 8.24 to see how the *Star Magazine* treated two pages as one unit.

7.   Display typefaces appropriate to the content can be used without producing clutter because there will be only one typeface to a page. Newspapers with several different stories on each page usually cannot use different typefaces without producing a circus atmosphere. In a tabloid magazine, once a typeface has been selected, it should be used throughout that particular story to provide a unity of design and ensure reader recognition.

8.   Use titles and labels rather than news heads. Within reason, the designer and staff should write the headlines and then determine the format rather than specifying a format into which the content must be squeezed. There is always room for compromise, but the magazine staff should take advantage of the use of fewer stories to tell and sell the way they want.

9.   Avoid ending a story with a graphic explosion. In fact, it is usually

better not to place art or photographs on the last page of a story because they may compete with the opening of the next spread.

10. Have a strong reader feature at the back of the magazine. A significant number of readers move from the back to the front. Do not let them sneak up on you. The Orlando (Fla.) *Sentinel*'s *Florida Magazine* has a restaurant review column at the back; the *Washington Post Magazine* has a photo feature. The *Denver Post Magazine* has letters and a column.

11. Try to build a rhythm into your magazine. Do not bunch all the long or short stories together; alternate. Work closely with the advertising department to be sure you get enough space to hook the reader before the story disappears into the columns of advertising.

12. Do not use jump lines when stories continue on consecutive pages. However, try to place a sales pitch on each page, even if it is nothing more than a blurb. One metropolitan newspaper ran a single story for nine consecutive magazine pages without so much as a standing title, let alone a blurb. Each page represents an opportunity to get readers interested in the story.

13. Anchor your standing elements. Readers need to know where things are located.

14. Use the cover to advertise the magazine. It is just one of several sections available to Sunday newspaper customers and something must attract their attention to make them pick it up. *Esquire* says "read me" from the newsstand; the magazine says it from the coffee table.

The *Los Angeles Times Magazine* debuted in 1984 in a 50- by 65-pica format, much smaller than the normal newspaper magazine and much closer in size and execution to the popular magazines on news racks. In fact, with the glossy paper stock, high quality and quantity color, and basic 2-column grid, the magazine does not even hint of a newspaper (Figs. 8.26, 8.27).

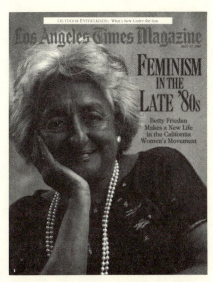

8.26. The *Los Angeles Times Magazine*, in size and feel, has a slick-magazine touch.

8.27. The designers used the two-thirds, one-third principle to divide the space horizontally. This provides a contrast in shapes and focus.

III

Newspaper Design

9

Management by design

HERE a designer has a firm hand in the initial process of selecting material. He makes news judgments. Beginning on the front page, he helps shape the consensus of what to give the reader. He has real power! That's design.

Edward Miller
FORMER PUBLISHER
ALLENTOWN *Morning Call*

WHEN HENRY FORD INTRODUCED the assembly line to produce his automobiles quickly and cheaply, he started a revolution in mass production. Ford proved he could manufacture a car in 93 minutes; others who followed his lead adapted the technique to include everything from the manufacture of cans to toothpaste.

As Ford was tinkering in Detroit with his new concept, newsrooms were already operating on the assembly line principle; reporters reported, writers rewrote, copy editors edited and wrote headlines, and layout editors placed it all in the paper. As the copy moved mechanically down the belt from reporter to layout editor, additional interpretations were added to the meaning and importance of the story.

Even after photography became an integral part of the publication, the assembly line process remained unchanged. At some point, usually after a story was already written, an editor would order a photograph, often specifying what should be photographed and how. The photographer would comply, the picture would be placed on the belt, and the layout editor would add it to the text and headline. It did not seem to matter that the layout editor probably had no more knowledge of how to handle photographs than the average reader.

Newspapers today carry more pictures and artwork and many have color, but their format is not unlike that in Ford's day. That is not surprising because newsroom organization has not changed substantially since that time.

Readers, however, and the ways they spend their working and leisure time have changed. Radio, television, and special-interest magazines (and soon home information delivery systems) have captured some of the readers' time and interest. Although technological developments permit

117

newspapers to publish a better, more legible product with increased speed, the organization of most newsrooms tends to fragment the work of highly trained, highly specialized journalists and put it in precast formats.

Traditional newsroom organization is a barrier to successful communication with the reader. Ever since photography became a part of the newspaper, the disadvantages of the assembly-line process have outweighed the advantages, but few editors recognize the problem. The result is a product that is often disorganized, seldom thought out, and usually difficult to read. The system fails to take advantage of the combined skills of the reporters, editors, photographers, artists, and designers.

Traditional approach

The traditional newsroom is organized vertically to move the raw materials horizontally. As Figure 9.1 illustrates, the decision-making authority flows downward from the editor to the departments. Meanwhile, each department produces its own end product—stories from the city desk, photographs from the photography department, headlines from the copy desk, and layouts from the layout desk. All the elements come together at the layout desk where one, two, or three persons will make decisions about the proper mix. This structure creates unnecessary barriers. Reporters usually are not consulted about editing changes, and photographers are seldom asked about selection, cropping, or display. Artists, if there are any, are often told to produce illustrations, graphs, and maps on short notice and with incomplete information. Furthermore, the editor who puts all these efforts together often does not know what is coming until it arrives.

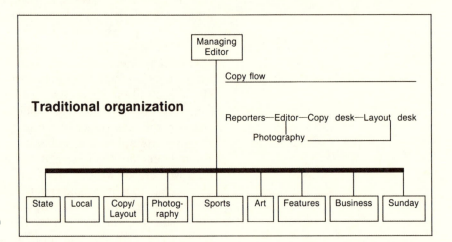

9.1. The traditional organization fails to assign responsibility for graphics to anyone.

Newsroom specialization is like the classic good-news, bad-news joke. It is good news when reporters know more about a particular field, such as medicine or the environment, or photographers know how to operate a camera, gather facts on film, crop for maximum impact, and display to attract attention. It is bad news when the division of labor inside the newsroom becomes so severe that journalists do not talk to each other any more than the employee who puts the engine onto the car frame talks to the employee who later screws in the headlights.

In the 1970s, some farsighted publishers, such as those in St. Petersburg, Fla., and Allentown, Pa., began to tinker with newsroom organization because of their growing awareness of the newspaper as a visual medium. Oddly enough, at most newspapers it was not the management experts who started this newsroom evolution but first the photographers then the designers.

Photographers argued loudly and often eloquently that the photo department needed to be more than a service agency that took orders but had no say about either the assignment or the display. These photographers saw themselves as photojournalists who were able to report with a camera, often more dramatically than reporters. They needed a chance to get into the newsroom flow and a voice in the planning and execution of the product as well.

It was only natural that journalists trained to deal with words were reluctant to invite photographers, much less designers, into the councils where news judgments were being made. There was, and still is, little appreciation for the total product in those councils. The efforts of professors Cliff Edom and Angus MacDougall, through the University of Missouri Pictures-of-the-Year competition, had a profound effect on the industry. Their students argued forcefully for the merits of photojournalism. Although many photojournalists went to magazines or free-lanced, many stayed in newspapers and fought the battle. Some won. Rich Shulman dramatically changed a small paper in Kansas before taking his talents to the *Everett* (Wash.) *Herald.* Brian Lanker, who worked with Rich Clarkson at the Topeka *Capital Journal,* helped transform the Eugene (Oreg.) *Register-Guard* into a visual medium. Bob Lynn brought the photographer's voice to the *Charleston* (W. Va.) *Gazette* and then the Norfolk (Va.) *Pilot and Ledger-Star* as graphics editor. For years, artist Frank Peters has reported for the *St. Petersburg Times* with maps, graphs, and charts. They and others like them convinced word-oriented editors of the importance of photographs and graphic presentation. Many editors resisted, and some still do, because they believed that a story, not a photograph, is the best use of space. Eugene Roberts, editor of the *Philadelphia Inquirer,* disagrees. His newspaper has won several Pulitzer Prizes, most for investigative reporting, and is considered one of the great newspapers in the country. Often overlooked is the fact that the editors at the *Inquirer* know they are working with a visual medium. When the National Press Photographers Association named Roberts Editor of the Year, he responded, "If I have any virtue as an editor in dealing with photography, it's that I don't know much about it, and I am quite willing to admit it." At the *Inquirer,* the photo director has the title of assistant managing editor and answers only to the managing editor.

At many newspapers, photographers still have little voice in planning. A University of Georgia Journalism School survey in 1983 found that only 17 percent of photographers are usually involved in the planning early, 24 percent were involved midway in the project, 39 percent after planning is complete, and 20 percent after the story is done.

Photojournalism produced at papers such as the *Inquirer, Pittsburgh Press, Sacramento Bee,* and *San Jose News,* combined with the growing body of readership research that showed that graphics do make a difference, began to change the face of U.S. journalism in the late 1970s.

Thomas Curley, director of research for Gannett, reminded his editors that "[the] causes of reduced readership and dissatisfaction with the newspaper are an unattractive appearance, poor packaging and the number of typos. Physical form often becomes an issue when something goes wrong . . . a small group, typically infrequent readers, finds reading a newspaper a chore. Good graphics attract them and help them understand a story" (Curley 1980).

It was not enough, however, to invite only the photojournalists into the mainstream of the newsroom. Artists, who were expected to work quietly in a corner of the room, and designers, who put the package together, started expressing their needs and showing editors how their involvement could attract attention and explain the content. As early as 1960, the *St. Petersburg Times* recognized that the presentation of information was as important as the content. At the Allentown *Morning Call,* art director Robert Lockwood and executive editor Edward Miller revolutionized the newsroom process. The design director became an equal to the assistant managing editor in making news judgments and coordinating the paper's content. Miller and Lockwood also experimented with "villages," teams that worked together and included everyone from reporters and photographers to pasteup employees.

In each case, the newsroom organization was changed to make the newspaper more understandable and easier to read.

Reorganizing the newsrooms

Any reorganization of the newsroom must be based on the goal of the organization. If, as it should be, the goal of the publication is to communicate, it follows that whatever the publication can do to make sense of the message will increase reader satisfaction.

The most successful communicators are those who recognize they are selling, not newspapers or magazines, but information. Information consists of both content and form. Publishers and editors who use all the tools of their medium will be successful. Those who do not are like the fighter who goes into the ring with one hand tied behind his back; neither the publisher nor the fighter is using all available resources.

Newsrooms are not organized to produce stories, type, artwork, and photographs that work together. Many stories have no pictures or graphs, and the traditional system facilitates the need to meet daily deadlines. If stories do or should have pictures, maps, or graphs, the system depends on the whim of the individuals doing the work. There are plenty of disaster stories.

At one newspaper, a five-member reporting and photography team worked for three weeks on a special fashion section. The two employees responsible for laying out the section found only the pictures and cutlines when they came to work They put together the entire section without any of the stories. The layout editors were not involved in the planning, and the section was a disaster.

At another newspaper, a reporter worked for days on an exclusive story about a local judge who was a client of the prostitutes who were being brought before him in court. The story contained a vivid description of the judge meeting the pimp in a seedy bar, walking across the dark street to a three-story house, and going up the carpeted stairs to the third floor to visit a prostitute. Although nearly two pages were devoted to the story, it did not have a single picture or piece of art. Why not? The reporter and his city editor failed to tell other departments they were working on the story until it was too late to add photographs or artwork without delaying the publication date. The story was written, passed on for editing and a headline, and placed in the paper in classic assembly-line fashion.

This sort of thing is happening less frequently, fortunately. Many papers, such as the *Seattle Times,* involve the expertise scattered throughout the newsroom in the planning on every major story and project. The result of one such planning effort was a series of stories on Seattle's homeless. As is obvious from the pages (Figs. 9.2, 9.3), the result was a combination of text, photography, and information graphics. The *Times* presented a package broken into digestible segments rather than throwing an overwhelming banquet at readers.

9.2. The *Seattle Times* used the team approach on the homeless project. The result was the integration of words and visuals.

9.3. A team approach does not guarantee success, but it does make it possible.

The *Times* took a team approach to the investigation. Such an approach will produce better newspapers too, but it is impractical to think that each story and picture that appears in a publication can or should be produced by a team. It is not unrealistic, however, to involve the appropriate departments in the planning, gathering, and preparation of all significant packages. That requires better management and a revised newsroom structure. In Figure 9.4, a new position has appeared on the newsroom chart, assistant managing editor—Design (A.M.E—Design). This position is at the hub of the newspaper. The design editor or a designee must be involved in both the daily production cycle and special projects and also have the authority to make news judgments.

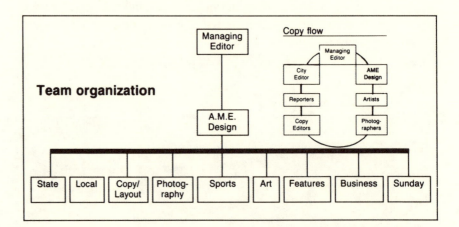

9.4. A more effective way to manage is to create a position for a design editor who has cross-departmental authority.

Design editors, whether they are called art directors, graphics editors, photo editors, or assistant managing editors, come from a variety of backgrounds. They may have been photographers, typographers, artists, or former copy editors who did layout. Because of the standards being established by these pioneers, those who follow will need to be even better qualified. For the design editors of the future, there are at least seven requisites:

1. They must be journalists. Design editors must understand news values, know how news and features are gathered, and be aware of readers' expectations.

2. They must be photo editors, though not necessarily photographers. They must be able to differentiate between potential picture situations and those that are not. In addition, they must know how to select, crop, group, and display pictures.

3. They must be artistic, though not necessarily artists, and must understand the principles of unity, contrast, balance, and proportion.

4. They must be typographers, know how to work with type, and use type legibly.

5. They must have a working knowledge of publication reproduction processes. The editor needs to know everything from programming the computer for proper type spacing to color production methods.

6. They must be able to work with others. Design editors must be able

to persuade others by earning their respect. In turn, they must respect others.

7. They must have the vision to think the unthinkable, the courage to experiment, and the wisdom to remember always that the reader must be served.

It is not necessary for the design editor to have firsthand knowledge of all the functions of the job. The designer needs to know the best spacing between letters in headlines and text, but a computer programmer can achieve the desired results. The designer needs to know how to use photographs, but a photo editor can make most of the day-to-day decisions. The designer needs to understand how color is reproduced, but the artist can make overlays.

Ironically, the smaller the publication, the more important it is for the design editor to have a broad base because it is less likely there will be computer programmers, photo editors, artists, or lab technicians to do the actual work.

Because of the nature of the job specifications, photojournalists who have backgrounds in typography are likely candidates for design editor positions. Regardless of whether the design editor is a former photographer, the photography and art departments must be elevated from service agencies (as diagrammed in Fig. 9.1) to departments on equal footing with other newsroom divisions (as show in Fig. 9.4). This will allow the photo editor to initiate assignments, make suggestions on photo orders from other departments, and even reject inappropriate requests. Such an action would be subject to an override only by the design editor or the managing editor.

It is essential that the authority of the design editor, photo editor, and chief artist be built into the newsroom structure.

If it is left to the preferences of the editor or managing editor, it can change overnight as editors move from one position to another. If authority rests on the shoulders of only one person, it also leaves with that one person. This is particularly true at small- and medium-sized newspapers that, like a campfire, glow brightly with the work of a single person but die as quickly as an ember when that editor leaves.

Once the structure exists, management must provide the means for the appropriate departments to work together. The assembly-line system requires cooperation but does not provide for the interchange of ideas or offer the benefits of collaborative efforts. The team system does.

The team system

Most newspapers still operate under a system in which reporters, working with the appropriate editor, gather the facts and write stories. When the stories are done, editors order photographs or artwork. As soon as those materials are available, they are given to a layout editor. Often, the preparation of the story takes days or even weeks, but the photography is expected to be completed in hours, and the layout must be finished by the deadline. The team approach, which involves more people earlier in the process, ensures adequate planning.

The composition of the teams is determined by the project. If it is a sports feature, the sports editor, reporter, and design editor (or designee) should be involved. At the initial conference, which may take only three minutes for some stories, the team determines the subject, focus, and deadline. The design editor might have suggestions about angles or tie-ins with other departments and may also assign a photographer to work with the reporter from the beginning. The reporter-photographer team might make decisions in the field that will change the focus. Even so, the words and visuals will still work together because of the team effort.

Planning sessions for other projects may need to include more people and be more formal. For instance, an investigative project should include the reporters and their project editor, the design editor, the copy editor, the photo editor, the chief artist, and the managing editor or assistant managing editor. The wide variety of perspectives strengthens the fact-gathering process. By involving all the persons who will be working on the package at some stage, management is making the most use of available talent, ego, and pride. Because everyone is involved and has a stake in the success of the project, they will work harder and understand what they are doing. Participating in idea and planning sessions is always stimulating to creative people. Ideas subjected to challenge and scrutiny become more clearly focused. The process is enriching for the participants and fruitful for the publication. The approach, however, requires more management ability than is needed to supervise the assembly line. It takes skill to select appropriate team members, conduct meetings, coordinate the efforts of various participants, and convince members to sacrifice some individual recognition or power to the group.

The advantages, however, far outweigh the disadvantages. The copy editor who is reading the daily memos along with the project editor is less likely to edit out essential information, edit in errors, or write a bad headline. Involving the design editor in the beginning of the project ensures that the photographers will have access to the reporters, people, places, and events as well as sufficient time to complete their work. Editors involved in a team effort at the *San Jose News* decided to devote a page to a national map. Type was to have been placed in each state to indicate the voting results and the map color-coded to the presidential election. Because the planning session was weeks before the election, the artist had time to prepare the map and discover that it would not work. The states would be too small to put type in them. Editors decided to print the map sideways (Fig. 9.5). They were able to switch because they planned and consulted rather than ordered.

Planning also permits artists to go into the field with the reporters, not two weeks later when conditions have changed. In addition, the design editor can have a series logo prepared ahead of time rather than one hour before deadline. Finally, the package can be designed for maximum impact in the appropriate space.

Scheduled events such as elections are naturals for the team approach because the date and participants are already known. It is the responsibility of the newsroom managers to assemble reporters, editors, designers, and photographers at the beginning of the election season to make plans for the entire campaign. Which reporters will be involved? Which photographers? How many out-of-town trips will be required? What kind of profiles should be done—issue-oriented, personality-oriented, or both? Should there be daily coverage or weekly wrap-ups? What will the campaign cov-

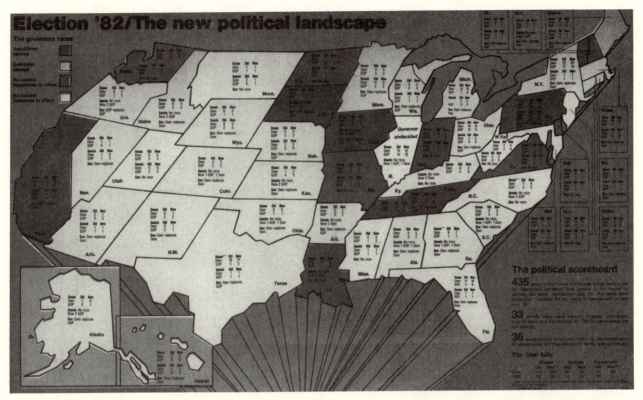

9.5. Because they planned ahead, editors at San Jose had time to change plans when they found out this map was too big for a horizontal broadsheet page. They rotated it.

erage be called? What would be an appropriate logo? What should the deadlines be for the major pieces? How much space will be available? What is the best method of reporting election results? Covering an election involves dozens of journalists. Those who work in newsrooms where all participants are involved from the beginning, goals are clearly defined, and ideas are sought from many persons instead of just a few will be more successful than those who work in an assembly-line plant.

At the *Star Tribune* in Minneapolis, the director of the special projects team creates what he calls the "backout schedule," which shows every deadline until publication. It indicates deadlines for reporters, photographers, and artists, and it also shows when the copy and management editors must complete their work. Such a schedule helps organize the team members and assigns responsibility to each.

Situations where teams work together reflect the awareness that newsrooms can be managed and that newspapers are a visual medium. Reporters are not the only fact gatherers in the newsroom; photographers and artists are too. Reporting for a visual medium includes gathering facts; writing the story; taking photographs; adding explanatory maps, charts, and graphs; writing headlines that tell and sell; and putting it all together so that it not only attracts and holds the reader's attention but is also legible and well written. Newsroom managers will be ready to compete in the twenty-first century if they recognize that photographers and designers are communicators, not decorators, and if they organize the newsroom to capitalize on their skills.

10
Principles of design

PAGE DESIGN should begin with the main illustration, and its size and shape should be regarded as a fixed element to which the other display elements have to adjust.

Harold Evans
EDITOR AND AUTHOR

WE ARE ALL ENGULFED by the work of designers. We encounter it in the clothes we wear, the cars we drive, the buildings we live and work in, the art we buy, and the publications we read. The principles of that design spring from our natural environment. The geometric proportions of our universe are reproduced in great architecture and paintings. The forms of leaves and the rings of trees have influenced designers for centuries.

Though the principles of design are fixed, the results are fluid. Engineering, architecture, art, and fashion change as needs and desires change. In the 1920s, the Model T was the right car; in the 1990s, we look for sleeker lines. The coliseums built in ancient Greece still influence architects, but today we build Astrodomes. Milton Glaser may owe something to Van Gogh, but even though we continue to appreciate Van Gogh's paintings, Glaser's colorful symbolic rendering of Bob Dylan in the 1960s did not look like Van Gogh's work. Aldus Manutius published a book in 1499 that has influenced publication designers for centuries, but book publishers today use materials from this decade. The texture and the type are different even if the proportions are not.

Graphic design, the planning and arrangement of elements on a page, appeared in magazines in the 1920s, about the same time Henry Ford brought the Model T off the first assembly line. In 1930, *Fortune* became the first U.S. magazine to combine words and visual concepts (Hurlburt 1976). Six years later, *Life* was born. The developing concept of photojournalism was nurtured to adolescence before *Life* died in 1972. Newspapers, a much older medium of communication, have been slower to wed words and visuals in a carefully designed product. Beset by a cumbersome advertisement arrangement on inside pages, a printing surface that still smudges and allows the print to show through, and unyielding deadlines, newspapers have always been the kid on the block with a dirty face and tattered clothes. Perhaps editors have been unwilling or unable to clean him up because generations of readers have been charmed by this messy kid. The pressures of competition finally succeeded in achieving what many visually oriented persons had been urging for years.

Struggling to maintain its share of the marketplace, the *New York Herald Tribune* turned to Peter Palazzo in 1963 for a redesign. Until then, redesign meant primarily a new typeface and occasionally a new nameplate. Palazzo, however, demonstrated that it could be much more. A graphics designer, not a journalist, Palazzo lowered the story count per page and introduced wider columns, more white space, better proportion, better use of photographs, better packaging and organization, and a different typeface (Fig. 10.1, 10.2). For the first time, a U.S. newspaper had truly been redesigned.

The *Herald Tribune* folded three years later, but the fallout from that redesign settled over the country. Suddenly, the design work at the *National Observer* and the *Christian Science Monitor,* both of which had been largely dismissed because they were not traditional newspapers, was emulated. Slowly, the momentum built. In the late 1960s, only a handful of newspapers had graphics directors or their equivalent. Ten years later, the pace had accelerated geometrically. Many newspapers began to look as contemporary and timely as their subject matter. Design had come to U.S. newspapers.

The look was changing because the process was changing. For nearly two centuries, layout editors served the unrelenting masters of deadline and story count in a repetitive process that was more concerned about production needs than readers (see Chapter 9). Layout editors react; designers plan. Layout is a manufacturing process; design is a creative process that traces its roots back thousands of years.

Design history

Most contemporary designers are products of one of two schools of thought: the Bauhaus/Swiss-Mondrian philosophy or the Push Pin Studio.

The Bauhaus school was established in Weimar, Germany, in 1919. The founders brought a Germanic precision and order to their teaching. When the Nazis closed the school in 1933, many of the faculty and students came to the United States. Some of them taught; others went to advertising agencies. Some, such as Paul Rand, worked for magazines. Their work was disciplined, functional, and imaginative because they had been influenced by the cubist revolution in painting. Piet Mondrian, a Dutch painter, developed many of the principles we still apply to the modular division of space and contrast in size and weight. They had also been influenced by the Swiss, whose application of functional Bauhaus thinking to typography produced the uncluttered approach to letter design. The popular sans serif typeface, Helvetica (Fig. 10.3), is a product of this school of thought. Its austere, functional lines give it a quiet dignity.

In physics there is a principle that every action has an equal and opposite reaction. The Push Pin Studio proved that this principle is as true in design as it is in physics. In 1957, a small group of illustrators, designers,

10.1.   Before the historic redesign, the *Herald Tribune* looked like all the other American newspapers.

10.2.   After the redesign, the *Herald Tribune* stood alone.

HELVETICA
The functional type

10.3.   Helvetica is used internationally on signs because of its high legibility.

and photographers formed a studio named a bit flippantly after a simple pin with a rounded head (Hays 1977). That name was the only simple thing connected with this studio. In the intervening years, the work of its designers has appeared in national advertisements as well as editorially in such magazines as *New York, Esquire,* and *Playboy.* Push Pin Studio is a genre of design that is as dissimilar to Bauhaus/Swiss-Mondrian as round is to square. While Bauhaus/Swiss is functional, formal, and rational, Push Pin is decorative, expressive, and intentionally irrational. For example, Bauhaus/Swiss eliminated curlicues because they were not essential to the reading process, but when Milton Glaser redesigned *New York* magazine, he reinstated them with gusto. His wild, colorful, abstract designs contrasted vividly with the austere look that was popular at the time. When Emilio Pucci, the fashion designer, was invited to a newspaper design seminar in Louisville, Ky., in 1974, he took decorative, hand-inked nameplates along and changed them each day (Fig. 10.4). The nameplates, he said, brought a "message of beauty, joy and serenity." They were impractical, fun, and straight from the Push Pin school of thought.

What had started as a backlash to functionalism became an established genre. By the late 1960s, art museum curators were cataloguing modern graphics in two groups: post Bauhaus/Swiss and Push Pin Studio.

Regardless of the philosophy to which designers subscribe, they all use the basic principles of design. Some follow them religiously; others know when to break them.

10.4. Emilio Pucci, best known for his fashion and interior designs, once proposed that the newspaper nameplate be changed each day for a new visual or esthetic message. (*Louisville Times* photo)

Principles of design

To know the principles of design is to know why you are doing what you are doing. No designer carries the list around consciously. Beginners, however, use the principles as guides until they are comfortable with the concepts. Although the names may be forgotten, the lessons never are.

There are five principles: balance, contrast, focus, proportion, and unity.

BALANCE. A square is perfectly balanced, but it is also monotonous. Similarly, formal balance in newspapers is dull and predictable, as were the people described as "square" in the 1960s. Formal balance is also the ultimate victory of form over content.

Formal balance had its heyday when the *New York Times* was its most visible proponent. It required balancing a 2-column picture at the top against a 2-column picture at the bottom and a 3-column headline at the top against a 3-column headline at the bottom. In short, balance was achieved by matching identical units. No matter what the news of the day, form took precedence over content.

While a formal balance format does not suit a newspaper's daily needs, any given design package can use formal balance successfully. The fashion spread on hats in Figure 10.5 is attractive, easy to read, and perfectly balanced. So is the interesting typographical treatment in the *Los Angeles Times* (Fig. 10.6).

Formal or symmetrical balance may be useful when building arches, but asymmetrical balance is more flexible and useful to newspaper designers. Balance is not achieved by merely using identical elements. Optical weights result from tones ranging from black to white. Tones, in turn, are provided by type in its various weights from light to bold, photographs and art, reverses and screens, rules, borders, and white space.

When two people are on a teeter-totter, they find the right balance by moving closer to or farther from the fulcrum. The weight is defined in measurable terms. Optical weight is not measured; it is observed. A small, dark shape balances a larger, lighter shape; white space in the margin balances the grayness of text type. A longer, narrow horizontal rectangle is balanced by a wider vertical one. The *Boston Globe*'s Home page (Fig. 10.7) illustrates balance through the sizing and placement of pictures and the use of white space. The dominant picture, combined with the subordinate one above it, creates the focus in the upper right-hand corner of the page. The narrow horizontal picture at the lower left illustrates the teeter-totter principle of balance. The white space helps to provide some relief, both in color and weight. It provides a buffer that sets the main package off from the rest of the page. The *Hartford Courant*'s Commentary page (Fig. 10.8) is also balanced from the left to right and top to bottom, but in a different way from the *Globe*'s. Instead of a symmetrical pairing of the dominant and subordinate photos, the *Courant* offsets the smaller photo to the right to start spreading the weight of the package away from the top left. The cartoon at the bottom provides a visual anchor.

Designers balance the right against the left and the top against the bottom. To achieve this, the designer places the major display element close to the optical center, which is slightly above and to the left or right of the mathematical center.

10.5. The designer used the formal balance on this layout.

10.6. The *Los Angeles Times* used type in an unusual way to move readers around the page and to give it balance.

10.7. The *Boston Globe* used white space and pictures to achieve balance. The bottom has a strong anchor.

10.8. Instead of symmetry, the *Hartford Courant* plays the graphic weights, including white space, against one another.

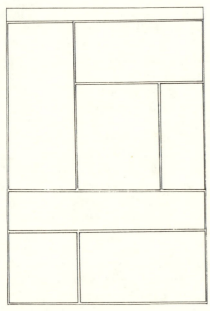

10.9. Weight and shapes should extend beyond the quadrants.

Dividing the page into quadrants is useful only if the design does not divide itself into four equal parts. Each of the four divisions should have some graphic weight to balance the page, but the weight should not be confined to the quadrant. It should extend vertically, horizontally, or both into other quadrants (Fig. 10.9), just as the heavier of the two persons of the teeter-totter moves closer to the fulcrum.

Designers working in modules have more control over weights on a page because their boundaries are defined. Meandering, irregular copy wraps make it more difficult to weight the elements visually.

CONTRAST. Writers contrast unlike things by using similes. For instance, "My newspaper is like my slippers—comfortable to sit down with at night." Writers contrast form by varying sentence length. Some sentences are long, rambling structures that, when used correctly, slow the reader and complement the subject matter. Some are short.

Designers contrast weights to balance a page. A 3-column photograph at the upper right can be balanced with a 3-column photograph at the lower left. The photograph can also be balanced with a large, multicolumn headline, white space, or a combination of all three. An 8-pt. rule can balance a block of text type.

Designers use type to provide contrast. For instance, bold type in the main head contrasts with light type in a deck or readout, sans serif type in the cutlines contrasts with roman type in the stories, ragged right contrasts with justified, all caps contrast with lowercase, 90-pt. type contrasts with 24-pt. type, and sans serif type contrasts with serif type. The *Kansas City Star* uses Goudy Bold as its basic display face (Fig. 10.10). By using Franklin Gothic as the accent head, designer Randy Miller was able to provide contrast. When a newspaper does not contrast serif with sans serif or vary weights within a face, the page will usually be monotonous.

Designers also contrast forms. Strong verticals give the impression of taller space and longer stories; horizontals appear to make space wider and stories shorter. A page divided into quadrants has no contrast of form, but a page divided into modules of varying rectangular shapes is full of contrast.

Dimension is an aspect of contrast too. The closer the object, the darker it appears. A small photograph placed adjacent to a larger one provides a contrast in size and adds dimension. To teach this principle to children, Johannes Itten of the Bauhaus told them to draw an outline of their hand on a sheet of paper. They then were told to draw, in their natural size, an apple, a plum, cherries, a gnat, and finally an elephant. The children said it could not be done because the sheet was too small. "Draw an old, big elephant—a young elephant next to it—the keeper . . . stretches his hand out to the elephant—in the hand lies an apple—on it sits a gnat" (Itten 1964). From that exercise, the children learned to contrast size by using light and dark colors and large and small shapes. Publication designers use the same devices.

FOCUS. Pages with focus clearly define the starting points and also show that an editor is not afraid to make decisions. To achieve focus, an editor

10.10. The *Kansas City Star* typography provides contrast from two type races.

has to decide what element or elements are most important or visually interesting and have the courage to let the design reflect that decision. Indecision confuses the reader and results in a meek or, worse, cluttered page.

Focus usually is provided by a dominant photograph. The impact that photography has in creating focus is illustrated by the pages from the *York (Pa.) Dispatch,* the *Los Angeles Times,* and the *Seattle Times* (Figs. 10.11, 10.12, 10.13). The *Dispatch,* the larger of two papers in a competitive city, carries no photographs on the front. There is no focus from photography or type. The *Los Angeles Times* is also vertical, but its type is bolder, and though its pictures usually are modestly sized, they start to provide a focus. The *Seattle Times* runs photographs large. The photograph of the woman clearly defines the dominant element. True dominance on a broadsheet page requires either a photograph wider than half the page or a vertical photograph of corresponding size. Three-column pictures on a 6-column page are just average and have little impact, but pictures wider than 3 columns provide both focus and impact.

10.11. It is difficult to achieve focus without a strong visual element.

10.12. The photo does not exceed half the width, but it comes close to achieving dominance.

10.13. The readers' eyes will go to the photo on this page first because it unquestionably is the dominant element.

Type can also be used effectively to provide focus. Newspapers traditionally have used large type on big-news events. The editors of the *Des Moines Register,* who seldom use large photographs on Page 1, provide focus with a banner headline that contrasts sharply with the vertical makeup (Fig. 10.14). More often, type is used to provide focus on feature pages or on packages within a page. Every design should have a focus, a major area of emphasis that identifies both the editorial decision and the reader's starting point.

From a broader perspective, the editor focuses on what is significant through the selection of elements for Page 1. Less important stories are found inside the paper. Similarly, department editors use their cover pages to provide focus for a section. There should be a progression from the focal point to the other elements on the page. It is not necessary for the designer to predict the readership path accurately. That is impossible. Readers will respond differently to printed stimuli. External stimuli such as noise or lack of time will also influence reading patterns. However, it is the duty of the designer to expose as many readers as possible to all the modules and remove anything that impairs legibility. Readers of poorly designed pages will skip some areas of the page altogether, not because they were not interested in the content, but because they did not notice the story. Readers move from large to small, (large photograph to small photograph), black to white, color to black and white, and top to bottom; but it all begins at the dominant element.

10.14. For the big event, even a vertical paper such as the *Des Moines Register* achieves focus with large horizontal type.

PROPORTION. Proportion, or ratio, has fascinated mathematicians, architects, and artists for centuries. Fibonacci, an Italian mathematician of the late twelfth and early thirteenth centuries, observed that starting with 1 and adding the last two numbers to arrive at the next created a ratio of 1:1.6 between any two adjacent numbers after three (1, 1, 2, 3, 5, 8, 13 . . .). Fifteenth-century architect Leon Battista Alberti believed that there was a relationship between mathematics and art because certain ratios recurred in the universe.

Leonardo da Vinci, who was not only an artist but also a mathematician, collaborated with a friend on a book titled *On Divine Proportion*. To Leonardo, proportions were of basic importance "not only . . . in numbers and measurement but also in sounds, weights, positions and whatsoever power there may be."

Finally, the classic definition of proportion was worked out by the architect-designer Le Corbusier in the early 1900s. He drew the human form with the left arm raised above the head. He then divided the anatomy into three uneven parts: from the toes to the solar plexus, then to the tip of the head, and finally to the tip of the raised hand. From this he developed what is known as the golden ratio. The ratio is 1:1.6, the same as Fibonacci's ratio. In nature, we see the same proportion in a daisy, a pinecone, and a pineapple, among others. The double-spiraling daisy, for instance, has 21 spirals in a clockwise direction and 34 in a counterclockwise position—a 3:5 ratio. The ratio of the printed to unprinted surface of a newspaper page with a 30-inch web is approximately 1:1.51; for a 28-inch web, it is 1:1.63. The 28-inch web, which the American Newspaper Publisher's Association began promoting in 1981 to standardize newspaper page sizes, is not only easier for the reader to handle but also closer to the proportions of the golden rectangle, which has the same proportions as the golden ratio.

Consciously or unconsciously, designers use that ratio when working with copy shapes on a page. The wider the story runs horizontally, the deeper it can go vertically and still maintain aesthetic proportions. On a 6-column page, a 4-column story 56 picas wide could be 30 to 35 picas deep from the top of the headline to the bottom of the story. As it goes deeper, it approaches the shape of the less pleasing square. Stories of 1 and 2 columns should be proportioned vertically in the same manner.

No designer actually measures the depth of the stories to determine if the ratio is correct. The eye recognizes what the calculator confirms. A sense of proportion is necessary for every designer.

Proportion is the vehicle for conveying the messages in both Figures 10.15 and 10.16. The first is a visual editorial from the opponents of nuclear weapons. The lonely dot in the middle represents the total explosive power we dropped on our enemies during World War II. All the other dots represent the explosive power in U.S. and Soviet arsenals. The shaded area in the upper left represents how much of the stockpiled weapons could cause a nuclear winter. Using the same principle of proportion, the people advertising breast screening show, not tell, the effectiveness of the technology they use to make the point that self-examination is not enough.

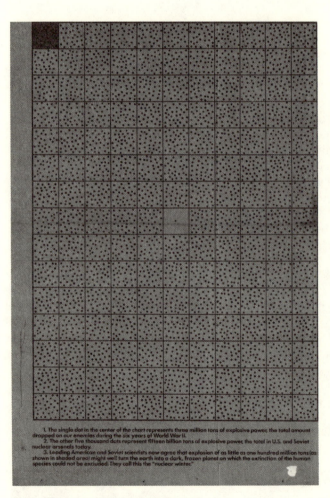

10.15. The point of this visual editorial is the proportion of all the explosive power in World War II compared to what exists in U.S. and Soviet arsenals.

10.16. Like the tumors, nothing has size or depth of color until it is compared to something. Type is not big or bold until there is smaller and lighter type by it.

In graphic design, proper use of proportion means avoiding squares unless they are required by the content. It also means being consistent about placing proportionally greater amounts of white space between unlike elements than between related elements. For instance, the designer might specify 24 points between the end of one story and the top of the next headline but only 14 points between the headline and the related story. The larger amount of space between the copy and the headline below disassociates the two when they are viewed against the lesser amount of white space between the headline and its related copy.

A good grasp of the concept of proportion is essential to anyone dealing with photographs. First, there is the proportion of the photo to the page. As we have already discussed, to dominate a page, a photograph must occupy more than half the width of the page or be proportionally sized vertically. The key is the size of the page. A broadsheet page requires one minimum size, a tabloid page another, and a magazine page such as *National Geographic* still another. Smaller pages require smaller visuals, a truism that many editors have not grasped. A 40-pica picture that runs margin to margin on a tabloid would not dominate a broadsheet page. In fact, 40 picas is a modest width on a broadsheet page, but impact is still possible with smaller sizes. A 40-pica picture in *National Geographic* bleeds the full width of a page.

Pictures should also be sized in proportion to each other. The 40-pica picture that looks so modest on a broadsheet page looks large when paired with one or more significantly smaller pictures. The smaller the subordinate picture, the larger the dominant picture appears.

Type also looks larger as the horizontal space it occupies grows smaller. A 48-pt. headline appears larger in a 2-column setting than in a 6-column format because it is larger in proportion to the space occupied. Type size is selected in part on the basis of the length of the story. Putting 3 lines of 24-pt. type over a 3-inch story would look odd because the headline would be one-third the depth of the story. Proportionally, there would be too much headline type. Conversely, a 3-line, 24-pt. headline over a story 18 inches long would also look odd.

Designers who have cultivated a sense of proportion work, within the limits of the content, in rectangles having dimensions that approximate 2:3 or 3:5. The resulting pages are aesthetically more pleasing.

UNITY. The designer must unify the work on two levels: the content and form of the individual packages within the publication and the various parts of the publication itself.

On the broadest level, unity is the art of making all the departments and all the sections of the publication appear to come from the same family but still allowing individuality within the various parts. Typographical unity does not mean homogeneity but does require a familial resemblance among the sections. This requirement can be fulfilled by using one family of headline type and varying other elements such as text width or setting. An alternative might be the use of two basic compatible faces, one for the main head and the other as an accent head.

Unity of publication means that sectional identifiers and column logos are the same throughout the paper. If the paper is large enough, logos may change from department to department but not within the department. Publication unity flows from a set of rules that everyone follows with few exceptions. The labels, for instance, on the Fort Lauderdale *Sun-Sentinel*'s editorial page are all centered and all have a 6-pt rule over them (Fig. 10.17). Spacing should be consistent between the lines of text type, headlines and bylines, and bylines and stories. In most newspaper plants, such control is possible because the specifications can be programmed into the computer. Most newspapers have design stylebooks for the same purpose as copy stylebooks—to provide consistency. The *St. Petersburg Times*'s book is 112 pages; the *Cincinnati Enquirer*'s is 94.

10.17. The labels on the interior of the page echo the label on the top of the page. That repetition creates unity.

Publication unity is even more important as newspapers develop a series of special-interest sections. It is important for these sections to have an identity of their own, but readers must recognize them as part of the parent organization. Before the *Los Angeles Times* was redesigned in 1980, John Foley, assistant managing editor for special projects, said the standard in-house gag was that the *Times* was six or seven papers under one banner. The *Dallas Morning News* runs a 24-pt. version of its nameplate underneath its sectional headings for such departments as Today, Metropolitan, Sports, and Business. The repetition of the flag also helps to unify the paper.

Unifying devices are necessary when a series or special package is prepared. Designers should make certain that readers recognize the package whether it jumps to the inside or appears again the next day. The Memphis *Commercial Appeal* solved this problem in its long takeout on a woman in rural Tennessee who teaches the Bible. The "Special Report" label and distinctive treatment of the title are repeated on each page where the story appears (Figs. 10.18, 10.19, 10.20).

10.18. The reader first sees the reverse slug and the title.

10.19. When the story moves inside, the reverse label and title appear in a smaller size.

10.20. As the story continues, the familiar label signals the way to the reader.

When form follows function, unity often results. Some stories, such as the Environmental Protection Agency's mileage rating for new cars, are basically lists, and the design requires more table than copy. Elections are stories of statistics and human emotions, and their design requires text, photographs, and charts. A fashion package has a different flow than one dealing with the eruption of Mount St. Helens. All these stories can be told more effectively when the message and design are unified.

On one level, the principles of design are esoteric; they cannot be subjected to quantitative analysis. On another level, they all have specific applications to the day-to-day operations of a newspaper. The better you understand the principles, the more confidence you will develop in your own judgments about design.

11

Understanding type

LETTERS are to be read, not to be used as practice models for designers or to be moulded by caprice or ignorance into fantastic forms of uncertain meaning. They are not shapes made to display the skill of their designers; they are forms fashioned solely to help the reader.

Frederic Goudy
TYPE DESIGNER

TYPE IS TO THE GRAPHIC DESIGNER what the bat is to the baseball player. When a batter hits a home run, the fans appreciate the feat; they do not ask what kind of bat was used. When a graphic designer successfully completes a publication, readers appreciate the pleasing presentation and the ease of reading; they do not ask the name of the typeface or the mechanics of reproducing it.

Because approximately 80 percent of the printing area in a newspaper consists of type, its selection and use is critical to successful communication. Yet, perhaps because it is so pervasive, type is often overlooked for the flashier tools of the designer—illustration, white space, and color. The headline face, the text type, and the design of the advertisements, which are primarily type, give each publication a personality. Many publications emit conflicting signals. The type says one thing, but the content says another. This Jekyll-and-Hyde effect is confusing and injurious to the communication process. Despite the importance of type, there are few typographers in newspapers or magazines. Consultants and designers may perform this function on a hit-or-miss basis, but often the day-to-day use of type is left to untrained personnel. Even so, given the proper type and instructions on how to use it, local staff members should be able to produce a daily or weekly product that is fundamentally sound typographically. Professionals who handle type every day should understand the basics of its use. This chapter discusses the design, language, grouping, and identification of type, Chapter 12 is concerned with legibility considerations, and Chapter 13 deals with the use of type.

Type design

Although the Chinese and Koreans first invented movable type, Johann Gutenberg was the first Western printer to use it. Furthermore, Gutenberg solved the problem created by the different widths of letters. Understandably, his first face was a modified reproduction of the handwriting used to produce sacred works such as bibles. From that point, further modifications were made to reflect the tastes and nationalities of the type designers.

Although type was the first mass-produced item in history, nearly four centuries passed after Gutenberg produced his type before a typecasting machine was invented, and it was not until the end of the nineteenth century that the entire process became automated. By then, many of the great typefaces still commonly used today had already been designed.

William Caslon, for instance, was an English typographer who lived from 1692–1766. The rugged but dignified Caslon face has staying power. It was used in the American Declaration of Independence and the Constitution. Over 100 years after it was cut, it became popular again following its use in the first issue of *Vogue* magazine. In 1978, designer Peter Palazzo brought it back once more in modified form when he redesigned the *Chicago Daily News*. In 1750, another Englishman, John Baskerville, designed a face that is known by his name and still commonly used today. Giambattista Bodoni, an Italian printer, developed a face in 1760 that was the standard headline in American newspapers from the post-World War II era through the 1970s. In 1896, another Englishman, William Morris, reacting to the conformity brought about by the Industrial Revolution, produced *The Works of Geoffrey Chaucer*. The Chaucer type he designed, combined with specialized initial letters and craftsmanship in design and printing, reawakened an interest in printing as an art form. Because his typefaces are highly stylized and personal, they are not used today for mass circulation publications, but his work influenced more than a generation of designers.

One of the people Morris influenced was Frederic Goudy, the first great American type designer. Goudy, founder of the Village Press, cut 125 faces, many of which are still used today. Goudy lived until 1946. At one time, the types he had designed, including the one carrying his name, dominated the American press. They fell out of favor after World War II, but when the 1980s brought a revival of the classic faces, Goudy was dusted off. When the *Kansas City Star* was redesigned in 1980 and the *Dallas Morning News* was redesigned in 1981, Goudy was chosen for the basic headline face.

The 1900s brought a host of typefaces—some were new; some were modifications of classic faces. Century Expanded was cut in 1900, Cheltenham in 1902, Cloister Old Style in 1913, Baskerville Roman in 1915, and Garamond in 1918. The interval between the wars produced two startling new faces. Paul Renner designed Futura in 1927; in 1932, Stanley Morrison produced Times New Roman for the *Times* of London. Futura, a geometric sans serif that is monotone in cut, ushered in an era of sans serif faces that brought us the popular Univers and Helvetica in the mid-1950s. Univers is used at the *St. Petersburg Times;* Helvetica, the most popular sans serif face among American newspapers, is used, among others, by the *Star Tribune* in Minneapolis and the *San Francisco Examiner.* Hermann

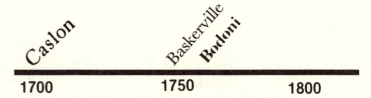

11.1. Even the oldest typefaces, when redrawn, are used today.

Zapf is the most successful contemporary designer. In the 1950s, he designed both Optima and Palatino, the face used in the redesign of the *New York Herald Tribune.*

The majority of typefaces commonly used by newspapers and magazines today were designed before World War II (Fig. 11.1). Tastes in type run in cycles, and some faces that are more than 200 years old are brought back periodically and modified to take advantage of technological innovations and modern tastes. The "modern faces," such as Helvetica, Univers, and Optima, already are 40 years old, but they are mere infants in the life of a type. The newspapers that rushed to embrace the modern look of Helvetica in the 1970s found themselves slightly out of step with fashion in the 1980s when the country began to turn back to traditional values. If Helvetica is put on the back shelf, it will be dusted off again later—maybe in 20 years, maybe in 50—just as the Caslons, Goudys, and Bodonis keep reappearing.

The introduction of photocomposition essentially stopped the design of new typefaces for use in general circulation publications. Foundries were busy converting their libraries to negatives for the new photocomposition machines. Most of the work involved modifying existing faces to take advantage of the new technology but still adhere to copyright laws. Bodoni, for instance, is now produced by six companies. Some of the alterations distorted the type and lowered the quality. By the late 1970s, great numbers of new faces were being designed for photocomposition, digital, and laser typesetters.

Technological developments

The proportion of primary strokes and serifs in metal type changes as the type size increases. When the font is produced in one size on a negative and enlarged through a magnifying glass, these proportions are not preserved. Most people would not notice (the difference is something like that between a designer's dress and its look-alike sold at chain department stores), but up close there is a difference. Digital and laser typesetters have overcome this problem by eliminating the need to enlarge or reduce the type; each letter is made a dot or stroke at a time. An excellent resolution laser typesetter, for instance, would print at 1,000 lines per inch. The higher the lines per inch, the smoother the edges and the cleaner the curves.

Because photocomposition permitted better control over letterspacing, kerning (letters set close together or even touching) and ligatures (two or more letters joined in a single unit) became common. When type was on individual metal slugs, the kern extended off the edge of the metal body and was vulnerable to breakage. That problem was eliminated in the phototypesetting process where the letters are on film rather than metal slugs. When Palazzo modified the Caslon face for the *Chicago Daily News,* he seized on

Century Expanded Cheltenham Goudy Garamond Futura English Times Univers Helios BAUHAUS AVANT GARDE GOTHIC

| 1850 | 1900 | 1950 | 2000 |

the phototypesetter's ability to kern and create ligatures. He shortened the cross stroke on the capital *T* and lowered the dot on the *i* to align with the top of the capital letters. Many newspapers have been able to take advantage of photocomposition, digital, and laser technology to make type more legible.

Now that designers are becoming comfortable with computer typesetting, a new generation of type designs is emerging to reflect contemporary tastes and demands. Type design has a history of fits and starts because it has been affected by such events as the Industrial Revolution, the world wars, and recent technological developments.

Now there are computer programs that will take a pencil outline of a typeface and convert it to the finished product. They can also produce the italics and condensed versions from one master design. That is a far cry from having to draw the specifications for every letter and every numeral in every size.

Language of type

The basic unit of all type designs is the individual letter. Just as we classify trees by the bark, leaves or needles, and shape, we classify type by its individual parts. Figure 11.2 provides a detailed examination of a piece of type. You need to acquire a working knowledge of most of these terms. The three main parts of the letter include:

1. *X*-line—literally, the top of the lowercase *x*. The *x*-height is measured from the top of the lowercase *x,* or any other lowercase letter without extenders, to the bottom. Because type within the same size can have different *x*-heights, it is critical to know that measurement as well as the size; *x*-height is a more exact method of measuring type size than points.

2. Ascender—that portion of the lowercase letter extending above the *x*-line. Capital letters are all the same and do not have ascenders or descenders.

3. Descender—that portion of the lowercase letter extending below the base line, or bottom, of the letter *x*. Together, the ascenders and descenders are called extenders.

The three basic parts are further divided as follows:

1. Bar—a horizontal or oblique (slanted) line connected at both ends. It is found in the letters *e* and *H*.

2. Bowl—the line enclosing a space. The letters *o, e, R,* and *B,* among others, have bowls. How the bowl is formed is one way of identifying a typeface.

3. Ear—on most faces, the *g* and *r* have a small distinctive stroke at the top right.

4. Serif—the unique cross-stroke at the ends of the basic letter form. A serif is ornamental, but when properly done it enhances legibility (see Chapter 12). Serifs are the principal means of giving a typeface a distinct personality.

5. Stroke—the primary part of the letter.

6. Stress—the thickness of a curved stroke, the shading of the letter.

7. Loop—a mark of distinction. The letters *o, c,* and *e,* particularly, may slant off center. Sometimes the bottom of the *g* is left open.

8. Terminal—the distinctive finish to the stroke on sans serif (without serifs) type. It may be straight, concave, or convex.

11.2.   Designers should know at least this much terminology of type.

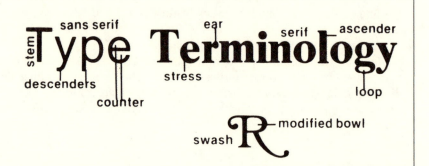

With these terms in mind, let us look at Bodoni Bold (Fig. 11.3). Bodoni is most easily recognized by the distinctive tail of the *Q,* which drops from the center and slopes to the right. The serifs join on the diagonal stroke of the *W,* and the *T* has drooping serifs. The *O, Q,* and *C* are symmetrical; there is no distinctive loop. The strokes are composed of consistent thick and thin lines to give each letter a precise, balanced quality. The stress of such letters as *O, G,* and *P* is vertical rather than rounded.

11.3.   Bodoni's weakness as a headline face is its hairlines.

Bodoni type: QWTOCGP

Type grouping

To enable typographers to communicate about type and ensure harmonious use, type has been organized into races, families, fonts, and series.

RACES. The race is the broadest system of categorization. Unfortunately, typographers cannot agree precisely on the number of categories. Too many leave typographers splitting hairlines, but having too few forces them to lump dissimilar type into the same race. The discussion in this book follows the guidelines of the authoritative *Composition Manual,* published by the Printing Industry of America. The categories are roman, square serif, sans serif, text letter, cursive, and ornamental.

ROMAN. The term roman has been used to refer to the straight up-and-down design of the type as opposed to the italic or slanted-right version. Originally, that was an incorrect use of the term, but it has became so common that it is now widely accepted. For the purpose of identifying races, roman is a classification of type that has serifs and thick and thin curved strokes. Some typographers believe roman is too general a designation and refer instead to three races: old style, modern, and transitional. These terms have no relevence to the time when the faces were designed. Instead, the terms refer to the style of type. Each of the three will be considered under the broad umbrella of roman.

Old style looks more informal because the letters are asymmetrical. The horizontal and upward strokes are light, and the downward strokes are heavy, but the differences between the strokes are minimal. The serifs appear to be molded or bracketed onto the stems. Garamond, for instance, is an old style typeface that bespeaks tradition and dignity (Fig. 11.4). Other well-known old style faces include Times Roman, Caslon, and Janson.

11.4.   Garamond, an old style face, is often used in advertising.

Garamond is an old style

Modern typefaces were introduced by Bodoni in 1760. His type was symmetrical and therefore had a more formal look. It also showed the influence of geometric forms. It is more precise than old style and has greater degrees of difference between the thick and thin strokes. The serifs were thin straight lines extending from the stems of the letters. As other faces were designed, the bowls became rounded, and the serif brackets were sharpened. Century Schoolbook, with its symmetrical, almost blocklike quality, is another example of a modern face (Fig. 11.5).

11.5.   Century, a modern roman, mixes well with Helios and Univers.

Century is a modern

As a category, *transitional* was created when succeeding generations of designers produced type that took characteristics from both old style and

11.6. Baskerville, a transitional roman, is a popular face in advertisements.

Baskerville is a transitional

modern. Baskerville and Caledonia, along with some members of the Century family, are generally classified as transitional (Fig. 11.6). They all have attributes of both old style and modern. Typographers do not all agree on which type merits the designation of old style, transitional, or modern, but a good reference book will help graphics editors avoid serious mistakes.

SQUARE SERIF. In square serif type, the strokes are nearly monotone in weight, and as the name suggests, the serifs are squared off in rectangles. Clarendon and Karnak are from the square serif race (Fig. 11.7). Square serifs were first designed about 1815 to be used in advertising. They preceded sans serif by about 30 years.

11.7. Many square serif types have Egyptian names.

Clarendon is square-serif

SANS SERIF. Befitting the mood of the day, the 1850s brought sans serif type. Sans is the French word for "without," and the type is without serifs. The type is easily identified not only by the lack of serifs but also by the uniformity in the strokes (Fig. 11.8). Sans serif type became popular in the 1920s as the Bauhaus school of thought (see Chapter 10) extended its influence. The purpose of the design was to eliminate all flourishes, including serifs, and produce a type that served the function of communicating without any of the aesthetic benefits that serifs offer. In the United States, the sans serif race was also referred to as gothic.

11.8. Helios is known by over 100 names, including Triumvirate.

Triumvirate is a sans serif

TEXT LETTER. This race, also called black letter, has type that is medieval in appearance. It is the style that Gutenberg used to print the Bible. Its designers were influenced by Gothic architecture, which was popular at that time. Cloister Black, Old English, and Goudy Text are examples of this race (Fig. 11.9).

11.9. Many newspapers use text letter in their flags.

Old English is a text letter face

CURSIVE OR SCRIPT. This race is also self-descriptive. The type is a stylized reproduction of formal handwriting (Fig. 11.10) and is most often found in formal announcements of events such as weddings and anniversaries.

11.10. Cursive is also used in graduation announcements.

Nuptual is cursive

ORNAMENTAL OR NOVELTY. This race is a catchall for those types that have been designed to portray a particular mood or emotion (Fig. 11.11) and is so unusual it cannot be used for other messages. The type is most frequently used in posters, movie advertising, cartoons, and display advertising. Newspapers occasionally use a novelty type on a feature page to reflect the content. For example, a computer type could be used over a story on the computer age.

11.11. Be careful using novelty faces in newspapers. Many are difficult to read.

JIM CROW IS NOVELTY

FAMILIES. Like all families, type families are basically similar but have variations. The differences are based on width, weight, and form. Some families have several members (Fig. 11.12); Caslon has at least 15, Cheltenham at least 18, and Univers nearly 30. The widths range from

Helvetica
Helvetica
Helvetica
Helvetica
Helvetica
Helvetica
Helvetica
Helvetica
Helvetica
Helvetica
Helvetica
Helvetica
Helvetica
Helvetica
Helvetica
Helvetica
Helvetica
Helvetica
Helvetica
Helvetica
Helvetica
Helvetica
Helvetica
Helvetica
Helvetica

11.12. Helvetica has a variety of weights and forms. These are just a few.

condensed to expanded; the weights from light to bold. Most types have two different forms, roman and italic. When the type is available in a special form, such as an outline or shadowed version, it is generally classified under the novelty race.

The width of a type is important when considering legibility and the amount of type that will fit on a line. It is figured on a character per pica (CPP) basis and is computed by counting the average number of letters that will fit in a given horizontal space and dividing by the number of picas. Thus, if the average number of characters that will fit on a 10-pica line is 32, the character per pica count is 3.2. If the average is 32.45, retain the fraction. The length of an entire lowercase alphabet of a single type size is called the lowercase alphabet length.

Unfortunately, even though the method of computing the alphabet lengths and characters per pica is standard, the results are not because of the way type producers have altered the face and spacing between letters. The CPP for Baskerville with italic when manufactured by Linotype in 10 point is 2.68; manufactured by Interytpe, 2.35; and manufactured by Monotype, 2.48. When comparing the CPP counts of typefaces, it is critical for the designer to know the type manufacturer.

FONTS. A font is a complete set of type. Nearly all families have fonts that include uppercase and lowercase type, punctuation, and symbols; some include an alphabet of small caps. Some also have ligatures, such as ff, ffi, fi, ffl, fl. Others have special symbols. A font of Century follows:

ABCDEFGHIJKLMNOPQRSTUVWXYZ

ABCDEFGHIJKLMNOPQRSTUVWXYZ

abcdefghijklmnopqrstuvwxyz

ff ffi fi ffl fl

1234567890 $ – % ¢

1234567890 $

1234567890

¡ ! □ ✔ ● ● ® © ° † * @ / £ & ( ) • / ¿ ? » «

+ = ÷

é ı ñ Ñ Ç ç

β

ª º

★ # [ ]

½ ¼ ⅓ ⅔

SERIES. The range of sizes available for each member of the family is called a series. When only metal type was available, size was an important consideration for the designer. Standard sizes of display type included 14, 18, 24, 30, 36, 42, 48, 54, 60, 72, and on up. Now that most newspapers have computer typesetting systems, publications no longer buy a series; they buy a font. Most computer typesetters can be programmed to set the type in any size desired, even in tenths up to 999 points. As a result, the term "series" is already a thing of the past.

Application

How this knowledge of type classifications, vocabulary, and history are applied is illustrated in the International Typeface Corporation (ITC) discussion of Weidemann, one of its new faces (Fig. 11.13). Noting that the typeface was commissioned in Germany by the German Bible Society, ITC reported in its publication (U & lc 1983) that one of the primary goals was to make a space-efficient type without sacrificing legibility. Thus "Weidemann was created with relatively narrow character proportions, a larger than average *x*-height, distinct character design traits, and optically even stroke thickness." ITC reported that compared to Times Roman, Weidemann can be read more rapidly. The designer, Kurt Weidemann, echoed old style roman design characteristics. His reasons, according to ITC, were:

1. The bracketed serifs of old style faces help to retain baseline definition.

2. The relatively even strokes in old style roman letter forms ensure a uniform typographic color, which results in less show-through on lightweight stock.

3. An old style face permits more distinctive shapes of individual letters than many other serif types.

Identifying type

The Printing Industry of America has compiled the following list of ten ways to identify typefaces:

1. Serifs. All type immediately breaks down into serif or sans serif, but the differences between types with serifs can be startling.

2. Terminations on top of the strokes of *E, F,* or *T.*

3. Weight of strokes. Are they thick or thin, and how much contrast is there?

4. Shape of the rounded characters *BCGOPQbcgopq.* Are the bowls symmetrical or balanced diagonally? How is the weight distributed?

5. Length of descenders.

6. Formation of terminals on *J* and *F.* The curves or angles are good clues to the identity of the letter.

7. Formation of the ears of the letters. Look particularly at the *r.*

8. The shapes of key letters of the font. Look at *a, e, g, r, m,* and *H.*

9. General proportions of the letter. Is the bar of the *H* located above, below, or at center? Are the letters equally proportioned or do they tend to be condensed or extended?

10. Overall appearance on the page when the type is massed. What is its personality?

Most graphics editors and designers have a working knowledge of 6 to 12 typefaces. For additional faces, they consult a type book. It is not necessary to memorize large numbers of typefaces, but you should become

ITC Weidemann Medium

abcdefghijklmnopqrstuvwxyz
ABCDEFGHIJKLMNOPQRSTUVWXYZ1234567890
ABCDEFGHIJKLMNOPQRSTUVWXYZ1234567890

Excellence in typography is the result of nothing more than an attitude. Its appeal comes from the understanding used in its plannin g; the designer must care. In contemporary advertising the perfect integration of design elements often demands unorthodox typog raphy. It may require the use of compact spacing, minus leading, unusual sizes and weights; whatever is needed to improve appeara nce and impact. Stating specific principles or guides on the subject of typography is difficult because the principle applying to one jo b may not fit the next. No two jobs are identical even though the same point sizes and typefaces are used. It is worthwhile to empha

6   Alphabet Length 68

abcdefghijklmnopqrstuvwxyz
ABCDEFGHIJKLMNOPQRSTUVWXYZ1234567890
ABCDEFGHIJKLMNOPQRSTUVWXYZ1234567890

Excellence in typography is the result of nothing more than an attitude. Its appeal comes from the understanding used in its planning; the designer must care. In contemporary advertising the perfect integration of design eleme nts often demands unorthodox typography. It may require the use of compact spacing, minus leading, unusual si zes and weights; whatever is needed to improve appearance and impact. Stating specific principles or guides on the subject of typography is difficult because the principle applying to one job may not fit the next. No two jobs a

7   79

abcdefghijklmnopqrstuvwxyz
ABCDEFGHIJKLMNOPQRSTUVWXYZ1234567890
ABCDEFGHIJKLMNOPQRSTUVWXYZ1234567890

Excellence in typography is the result of nothing more than an attitude. Its appeal comes from the understanding used in its planning; the designer must care. In contemporary advertising the perfe ct integration of design elements often demands unorthodox typography. It may require the use of compact spacing, minus leading, unusual sizes and weights; whatever is needed to improve appear ance and impact. Stating specific principles or guides on the subject of typography is difficult becau

8   90

abcdefghijklmnopqrstuvwxyz
ABCDEFGHIJKLMNOPQRSTUVWXYZ1234567890
ABCDEFGHIJKLMNOPQRSTUVWXYZ1234567890

Excellence in typography is the result of nothing more than an attitude. Its appeal come s from the understanding used in its planning; the designer must care. In contemporary advertising the perfect integration of design elements often demands unorthodox typo graphy. It may require the use of compact spacing, minus leading, unusual sizes and wei ghts; whatever is needed to improve appearance and impact. Stating specific principles

9   102

abcdefghijklmnopqrstuvwxyz
ABCDEFGHIJKLMNOPQRSTUVWXYZ1234567890
ABCDEFGHIJKLMNOPQRSTUVWXYZ1234567890

Excellence in typography is the result of nothing more than an attitude. Its app eal comes from the understanding used in its planning; the designer must care In contemporary advertising the perfect integration of design elements often d emands unorthodox typography. It may require the use of compact spacing, mi nus leading, unusual sizes and weights; whatever is needed to improve appear

10   114

abcdefghijklmnopqrstuvwxyz
ABCDEFGHIJKLMNOPQRSTUVWXYZ1234567890
ABCDEFGHIJKLMNOPQRSTUVWXYZ1234567890

Excellence in typography is the result of nothing more than an attitude I ts appeal comes from the understanding used in its planning; the desig ner must care. In contemporary advertising the perfect integration of d esign elements often demands unorthodox typography. It may require t he use of compact spacing, minus leading, unusual sizes and weights; w

11   124

abcdefghijklmnopqrstuvwxyz
ABCDEFGHIJKLMNOPQRSTUVWXYZ1234567890
ABCDEFGHIJKLMNOPQRSTUVWXYZ1234567890

Excellence in typography is the result of nothing more than an att itude. Its appeal comes from the understanding used in its planni ng; the designer must care. In contemporary advertising the perfe ct integration of design elements often demands unorthodox typ ography. It may require the use of compact spacing, minus leadin

12   136

11.13. ITC's Weidemann was designed with a large x-height but also a high count of characters per line.

acquainted with those most commonly used in newspapers and, especially, the publications you read regularly. The popular sans serif Helios, for instance, is identifiable by its uniform but dignified cut. It has short extenders, a square dot on the lowercase *i* and *j,* a distinctive capital *G,* and a straight tail on the capital *Q,* which is slanted and starts on the inside of the bowl. The stem of the *a* curves at the baseline.

Compare Triumvirate, another name for Helios, with another popular sans serif face, Univers (see Fig. 11.14). Univers also has a uniform cut, square dots over the *i* and *j,* and short extenders. However, Univers has a sloped bracket at the cross-stroke of the *t,* does not have the finial or line extending downward from the *G,* and the tail of the *Q* does not start within

ABCDEFGHIJKLMNOPQRSTUVWXYZ
abcdefghijklmnopqrstuvwxyz — Univers

ABCDEFGHIJKLMNOPQRSTUVWXYZ
abcdefghijklmnopqrstuvwxyz — Triumvirate

11.14. These two look alike, but compare *t, G,* and *Q.*

the bowl and is lower on the letter. The stem of the *a* finishes at the baseline.

Unfortunately, type identification is becoming increasingly difficult because of the barely distinguishable alterations performed for computer fonts. There is no effective protection for new typeface designs in the United States. The popular Helios, for instance, is produced with little or no variation under the names of Vega, Boston, Claro, Corvus, Galaxy, Geneva, Triumvirate, Helvetica, American Gothic, Ag Book, Newton, and Megaron. Optima is marketed by different manufacturers under the name of Chelmsford, Oracle, Orleans, Musica, Orsa, and Zenith. Palatino also has several imitators including Palateno, Elegante, Patina, Andover, Palladium, Pontiac, Michelangelo, and Sistina. By whatever name they are known, however, they are still Helios, Optima, and Palatino.

12

Legibility of type

READING is the most important part of the whole design. If you limit this—if you slow down the speed of reading—I think it is wrong.

Hermann Zapf
TYPE DESIGNER

F OR MORE THAN 60 YEARS, researchers have been studying the variables that affect legibility. The findings have been enlarged significantly since Miles Tinker's pioneering studies in the 1920s. His work in later years, notably with D. G. Paterson, added significantly to the body of knowledge about legibility. The Merganthaler Linotype Company published *The Legibility of Type* in 1936 and a similar volume in 1947 in an attempt to distribute the research findings from the ivory tower to the grass-roots level. B. W. Ovink published *Legibility, Atmosphere-Value and Forms of Printing Types* in 1938. Sir Cyril Burt published the landmark *Psychological Study of Typography* in 1959. Tinker's 1963 *Legibility of Print* pulled together hundreds of studies that he and others had conducted. Bror Zachrisson and his colleagues at the Graphic Institute in Stockholm spent ten years researching legibility variables, and the results were published in *Studies in the Legibility of Printed Text* in 1965. Rolfe Rehe compiled the results of hundreds of tests in his 1979 book, *Typography: How to Make It Most Legible.* The studies continue, but dissemination of the results to the people working with type daily in American newspapers still lags far behind the research. For example, in 1980 the assistant managing editor of design for the *New York Daily News* suggested in an industry newsletter that the American Society of Newspaper Editors should put together a presentation for editors on legibility of type.

For too long, knowledge of legibility has been buried in academic journals or limited to the province of professional consultants. It is necessary, however, for the men and women who work on newspapers every day to have the opportunity to learn and understand the factors that affect legibility. The daily examples of type that is overprinted; reversed; or set too small, too narrow, or too wide indicate that many editors have still not awakened to the need to remove typographical barriers between the reporter and reader.

Perhaps the reason that many editors are just beginning to inquire about the proper use of type is that, for the first time, they have control over the typesetting and have the flexibility to be creative. With video display terminals in the newsroom, the editor can program the type size, width, and leading for each story without slowing the production process. In addition, the letter and line spacing can be altered in both text and display type. A new era has begun, and editors are asking the right questions. The new graphics design editors will need to have the answers.

This chapter distills the results of hundreds of legibility research projects, but it is not a substitute for reading the original research. Several studies and books referred to in this chapter are listed in the References Cited and list of Additional Reading sections at the end of the book.

Legibility considerations

Legibility and readability are often confused. Legibility is measured by the speed and accuracy with which type can be read and understood. Readability is a measure of the difficulty of the content. Some typographers however, consider readability to be the result of how you use a typeface. Noted typographer Allan Haley says, "It is therefore possible to take a very legible typeface and render it unreadable through typographic arrangement." Legibility research has been conducted by typographers, educators, journalists, printers, and ophthalmologists, all of whom have a stake in the printed word.

Some research methods are more useful for testing legibility factors than others. The visibility measurement, for example, tests reading speed by controlling the amount of light. This is useful for measuring the effect of contrast. Another method resembles the familiar eye test and measures what can be read at various distances. This test is most useful for work with large advertisements such as posters and billboards. Many other testing methods have been used through the years, but the most effective has been to measure reading speed while controlling all but one variable, such as line length. Researchers have also been able to track eye movement by using still cameras, video cameras, and various electrical devices. The results show that we read in saccadic jumps, the movements from fixation point to fixation point. For a split second the reader pauses, and reading occurs. The reader scans shapes, not individual letters, and fills in the context. The right half and upper portion of the letters are most helpful in character recognition. To illustrate how readers fill in the forms, one researcher gave this •xa•ple of • se•te•ce •it• mi•si•g l•tt•rs.

The results of all these tests are not uniform. Some of the discrepancies are attributable to incomplete control of the variables, others to the different measuring methods that are used. The measurement of legibility is an inexact science, but there are some general principles that can be extracted from the great body of research.

Legibility factors

Legibility is determined by at least nine factors:

1. The reader's interest in the text

2. Type design
3. Type size
4. Line width
5. Word and letter spacing
6. Leading, or line spacing
7. Form
8. Contrast
9. Reproduction quality

In the testing process, reader interest is controlled by comparing results against a control group. However, the editor who is publishing a daily or weekly product is interested in the level of reader interest because it is critical not only to legibility but also to sales and customer satisfaction. By the same token, the quality of reproduction, which depends on the paper and the printing process, is very important. In tests, researchers can control reproduction quality carefully. Editors, unfortunately, cannot. The newspaper is printed on an off-white, flimsy paper called newsprint. The texture is disagreeable, and the resulting contrast between the black type and the background is not as good as that found in magazines using coated paper. Other variables, however, can be manipulated with little or no expense to the newspaper. The most important factor to remember is that no one variable can be taken by itself. For instance, leading requirements change as the type and line width change; if the type size is changed, several other variables must be altered also.

TYPE DESIGN. For textual material, the basic choice is serif or sans serif type. A study conducted in 1974 for the American Newspaper Publishers Association by Hvistendahl and Kahl (1975) found that roman type was read seven to ten words a minute faster than sans serif type. The roman (serif) body type faces that were used included Imperial, Royal, and variations of Corona; the sans serif faces were Helvetica, Futura, Sans Heavy, and News Sans. The researchers found that the subjects in the study read the roman text faster and two-thirds said they preferred it. This study confirmed the earlier work by Tinker and Paterson (1929), who found that a sans serif face was read 2.2 percent more slowly than a roman face (Dowding 1957). Robinson et al. (1971) found it took 7.5 percent more time to read sans serif than roman. Serifs are important in preserving the image of small letters.

This limited research does not mean that newspapers should never use sans serif in text. It does mean, however, that editors should seriously question the advisability of using it in quantity and perhaps might want to consider restricting its use to special sections or features. For instance, some newspapers that use a roman text type use sans serif in the personality, people, or newsmaker features. It is also often used successfully in cutlines.

Only a handful of the roman text faces are commonly used by mass circulation publications. Corona, Ionic No. 5, Imperial, Times Roman, and Excelsior have proven themselves on newsprint. The *Los Angeles Times* chose an extended version of Paragon when it redesigned in 1980. Bookman is a distinguished text type, but some typographers shy from it because it takes more space than most of the other commonly used faces. Other text possibilities include Cheltenham, Plantin, and Century.

Like all type, these text faces have been marketed by different companies under different names. To guide your search, here (according to Monotype) are some of the common synonyms (key to typeface manufacturer: Autologic, AI; Compugraphic, CG; Harris, HI; Itek, IT; Monotype, MO; Linotype, LI):

1. Ionic No. 5, LI: News No. 9 and News No. 10, CG; Regal, HI; and IC, IT.

2. Times New Roman, MO; Times 2 New Roman, AI; English Times, CG; Times Roman, HI and LI; and TR, IT.

3. Excelsior, Paragon, and Opticon, LI; News No. 14, CG; Regal, HI; and EX, IT.

4. Corona and Aurora, LI; Crown and Nimbus, AI; News No. 2, No. 3, No. 5, and No. 6, CG; Royal, HI; CR, IT.

5. Imperial, HI; Bedford and New Bedford, AI; News No. 4, CG; Gazette, LI.

TYPE SIZE. The proper size of type is closely related to the line width and subject matter. Tinker (1963) found that moderate type sizes (9- to 12-pt. range) are the easiest to read. A discussion of type sizes in points, however, can be misleading. The *x*-height is a more accurate measurement of the actual size of the type (Fig. 12.1). When testing legibility, Poulton (1955) had to use 9.5-pt. Univers and 12-pt. Bembo to equalize the *x*-heights. Another researcher found that 60-pt. Univers Bold, 72-pt. Caslon Bold, and 85-pt. Bodoni Bold were needed to get an *x*-height of 12.6 mm. The *x*-height of Linotron's 9-pt. Helvetica is 4.8 points, but its Caledonia is 3.8. The difference is in the length of the extenders. If there are long extenders, the size of the bowl is smaller; if there are short extenders, the size of the bowl is larger and the type appears larger. *X*-height, then is the critical determiner of type size.

12.1. *X*-heights are more accurate than point sizes.

9 pt.: Futura Univers   Helios   Clarendon Book

A smaller type size can be used for reference material such as sports scores, box summaries, or classifieds because readers do not read large amounts of it. When the columns are wider, as for editorials, a larger type size is needed. Depending on the *x*-height, 11- or 12-pt. type is appropriate for material set wider than 18 picas.

Most editors acknowledge that newspapers should use a larger type size; the *Fresno Bee,* the San Diego *Evening Tribune,* and the *Arizona Republic* are among the few who use 10-pt. type. The *Charlotte* (N.C.) *Observer* uses 10.4-pt. type with 9.7-pt. leading, and the Providence (R.I.) *Journal* uses 10.5-pt. type with 9.8-pt. leading. Both use Bedford. The Bend (Oreg.) *Bulletin* uses 10.5-pt. Century type with 10.5 leading. Of the 314 American and Canadian newspapers that responded to a National Readership Council request for text type samples in 1980, 103 indicated their body type was less than 9 points. Most of those, however, were using Corona which has a large *x*-height, or a modification manufactured under another name. Even though there have been improvements, more needs to be done. Editors reluctant to lose space to larger type are ignoring a significant portion of the potential audience. Poindexter (1978) found that 8.5 percent of the nonreaders did not read newspapers because of poor eyesight. A Gannett researcher found that 16 percent of the subscribers wanted larger type and that the percentage was even higher among people over 50, who are among the most loyal newspaper readers. Another newspaper found that one-third of its readers wanted larger type (Curley 1979). No newspaper should be using type smaller than 9 point with a good *x*-height.

LINE WIDTH. In newspapers, column widths range all the way from slightly less than 9 picas to 18 picas. Some newspapers do not have a standard setting for pages with no ads. The *St. Petersburg Times* permits setting between 11 and 22.6 picas for its 9-pt. Century Schoolbook. Other newspapers specify the widths for type. The *Star Tribune* in Minneapolis, for example, permits only two widths.

Newspaper column widths have historically been shaped by advertising rather than by legibility considerations. Advertising is sold by the column inch, and 8 columns produce more column inches than 5 or 6 columns, even though the total space on the page does not change. Consequently, newspapers were loath to change to a 6-column format even when it became commonly known that it produced a more legible line length. Such a change also required a sizable increase in advertising rates on a column-inch basis to maintain the same income per page. As a result, some newspapers converted to a 9-column advertising format and a 6-column news format.

The 6-column format was an improvement over the 8-column format because the line widths are between 12 and 14 picas for most newspapers. Tinker and Paterson (1929) found that a line width of 18 to 24 picas provides the easiest reading when 10-pt. type is used. This width provides 10 to 12 words per line, which they found to be the optimum number. Because most newspapers use type at about 9 points, the 12- to 14-pica range produces nearly the same number of words per line. Hvistendahl and Kahl (1975) found that the highest reading speed was obtained when they set roman type in 14-pica columns.

In the 1980s, advertising again forced a change in column widths. In its first-ever attempt to standardize columns to attract national advertisers, the industry settled on a format that reduced column widths to about 12.2 picas in the 6-column format. That width is nearly the same as it was when newspapers had 8 columns but wider pages.

WORD AND LETTER SPACING. We read by perceiving shapes and groups of words. If words are   widely   spaced   like   this, it slows reading speed considerably. More stops are necessary, and words must be read as individual units rather than as parts of phrases. For newspaper purposes, type is read most comfortably when word spacing is between 3 to the em and 4 to the em. (An em, you will recall, is the square space of the letter *m* in the type size being used.) The term 3 to the em means one-third of an em spacing. Word spacing should not be greater than the leading.

The spacing between letters also affects the speed of reading. By tightening letterspacing, more words can be printed in the same amount of space. With proper handling, this can increase reading speed. Condensed type in particular, whether text or display, should not have a large amount of letterspacing.

Up to the point that the letters lose their shape, the closer the letters are, the faster we will read them because we will take in more of them during each eye pause. However, every letter needs some space around it, or it loses its recognizable form (Fig. 12.2).

12.2.   Too much space between letters wastes space and slows reading time; too little also slows reading time. The first line in each set represents spacing as programmed by the manufacturer of the typesetting equipment; the second has minus two units and the third, minus five units.

Letter spacing
Letter spacing
Letter spacing

Letter spacing
Letter spacing
Letter spacing

LEADING. The correct amount of leading depends on the width of the line and the size and design of the type. Unleaded material generally slows reading speed (Becker et al. 1970), but too much leading can have the same effect. For newspapers that have columns in the 12- to 15-pica range and use 9-pt. type, Tinker (1963) found that 1-pt. leading is desirable. He also found that 10-pt. type set solid (no leading) was read faster and was more pleasing to the readers than 8-pt. type with 2-pt. leading (Figs. 12.3 to 12.5). However, newspapers can easily use a half-point of leading. It saves space without reducing legibility.

12.3. The examples are set in Futura (left) and Corona.

9 pt. with no leading

The amount of leading required depends upon the width of the line, x-height and design of the type. For newspaper purposes, 9 pt. type set at 12 to 14 picas should have about 1 pt. of leading.

The amount of leading required depends upon the width of the line, x-height and design of the type. For newspaper purposes, 9 pt. type set at 12 to 14 picas should have about 1 pt. of leading.

12.4. Futura has a much smaller x-height than Corona.

9 pt. with 1 pt. leading

The amount of leading required depends upon the width of the line, x-height and design of the type. For newspaper purposes, 9 pt. type set at 12 to 14 picas should have about 1 pt. of leading.

The amount of leading required depends upon the width of the line, x-height and design of the type. For newspaper purposes, 9 pt. type set at 12 to 14 picas should have about 1 pt. of leading.

12.5. Type with small x-heights can be set with less leading than type with large x-heights.

9 pt. with 3 pts. leading

The amount of leading required depends upon the width of the line, x-height and design of the type. For newspaper purposes, 9 pt. type set at 12 to 14 picas should have about 1 pt. of leading.

The amount of leading required depends upon the width of the line, x-height and design of the type. For newspaper purposes, 9 pt. type set at 12 to 14 picas should have about 1 pt. of leading.

There are some situations where the designer will have to apply common sense because research does not answer all the questions; for instance:

1. Type with a large x-height generally needs more leading than type with a small x-height because the large x-height has shorter descenders and gives the impression of less space between lines.

2. Sans serif type generally needs more leading than roman type because sans serif has a strong vertical flow and leading will counteract this. Roman type with a strong vertical flow, such as Bodoni, also needs more leading.

3. Less leading is needed on certain copy such as editorials because the reader does not spend much time on it.

4. Leading for headlines can be much tighter than for body copy because the reader does not spend much time reading them. In fact, some newspapers have gone to minus leading in headlines. The *St. Petersburg Times* sets 24- and 30-pt. headlines at minus 2-pt. leading; type above 36 points is set at minus 4-pt. leading.

FORM. The design of the type and how it is used affects legibility. For newspapers and magazine purposes, editors are primarily concerned with the legibility of text type between 8 and 12 points. Readers prefer moderate designs, neither too condensed nor too extended, for textual material. The shape of the bowls and, for roman type, the design of the serifs are also factors. The space within the bowls determines legibility (Roethlein 1912), which is why boldface is less pleasant to read in large quantities. Boldface type has heavier lines and less white space within the letters. As a test, compare a typewritten page from a typewriter that has not been cleaned against one that has. It is far more difficult to read the page when the letters are filled in. If the serifs are too fine, they may not reproduce well on newsprint in small sizes. That is why some modern roman types such as Bodoni, with its hairline serifs, are not used as text type. Among the sans serif type, the differentiation among letters is even more important than it is for roman faces. News Gothic has been successful in this regard (Poulton 1955).

Once the typeface is selected, the editor must decide how emphasis will be added. Boldface in small amounts is a good method. Italic type, on the other hand, takes longer to read and readers do not like it. "In general," Tinker (1963) concluded, "the use of italics should be restricted to those rare occasions *when added emphasis is needed*" (italics added).

Text or headlines in all capital letters should be avoided, except as special treatment, because it slows reading speed and displeases readers. Because readers perceive shapes, IT IS MORE DIFFICULT TO READ ALL-CAP MATERIAL. THE SHAPES BECOME UNIFORM, AND THE READER IS FORCED TO LOOK AT INDIVIDUAL LETTERS RATHER THAN WORDS AND PHRASES. A headline style that requires capitalization of the first letter of the first word and proper nouns only is more legible than one that requires capitalization of all words. In addition, the more capitals used, the more space required. All-cap style in text or headlines is not economical. An occasional headline or title in all caps, however, has a negligible effect on legibility.

Another aspect of form that is increasingly coming into question is whether to justify the copy to produce an even right margin or run it unjustified (ragged right). The research to date suggests that there is no significant difference in reading speed between justified and ragged right copy (Fabrizio et al. 1967). Hartley and Barnhill (1971) found no significant differences in reading speed when the line length was determined by grammatical constraints and hyphenation was avoided whenever possible, when about 33 percent of the lines were hyphenated, or when type was set ragged right over double column formats of varying widths.

While there may not be a difference in reading speed between justified and unjustified lines, there certainly is a difference in appearance (Figs. 12.6, 12.7). Justified type in narrow newspaper columns requires a great deal of hyphenation and causes variation in the space between words. Unjustified type permits the editor to standardize the word spacing and avoid illogical breaks in words. When type was hand set, unjustified type was much faster to produce, but now that a computer justifies the lines, that advantage has been nullified.

12.6. Type set justified has a formality.

Type set justified

Type set justified looks more formal. It is appropriate to news content. Type set ragged right is more relaxed. It is appropriate for soft news and features. There is no significant difference between the two in reading speed.

Type set justified looks more formal. It is appropriate to news content. Type set ragged right is more relaxed. There is no significant difference between the two in reading speed.

12.7. Ragged left should be avoided; ragged right works well.

Type set ragged right

Type set justified looks more formal. It is appropriate to news content. Type set ragged right is more relaxed. It is appropriate for soft news and features. There is no significant difference between the two in reading speed.

Type set justified looks more formal. It is appropriate to news content. Type set ragged right is more relaxed. It is appropriate for soft news and features. There is no significant difference between the two in reading speed.

The choice of justified or ragged right type is reduced to a question of personality. The *Hartford Courant* claims it was the first American newspaper to use ragged right throughout the newspaper. When the Allentown *Morning Call,* which had used ragged right frequently, appeared set entirely in ragged right, the publisher did not notice for two weeks. Neither, apparently, did the readers. There were no objections.

Justified type is formal, and the orderliness of the margins gives a feeling of precision and control, factors that may enhance a news product. Ragged right type is informal, more relaxed, less precise. Consequently, it may be more appropriate for feature sections. If ragged right is chosen, it is preferable to use a modified ragged right type, which permits hyphenation whenever a line is less than an established minimum length, such as 50 percent of the potential line. This eliminates unusually short lines, which are noticed for their contrast rather than their message.

Ragged left type should be avoided except in small amounts such as a short cutline set to the left of a photograph. If the reader does not have a fixed left-hand margin, reading speed is seriously impaired. Ragged left should never be used in textual material of any significant length.

CONTRAST. The contrast in color between the type and its background is another important factor in legibility. Black and white offers the most contrast and therefore is the most legible. The reverse, however, is not true. White print on a black background slows reading speed significantly

12.8. Although the design is striking, especially in color, the copy is nearly unreadable. Type should be enlarged and run only in small amounts if reversed.

(Holmes 1931). The dramatic effect that can be achieved by reversing type must be balanced against the loss of legibility. Reversed type should only be used in small quantities, such as a paragraph or two, and in larger than normal type, such as 14 or 18 points. When it is not, the copy often becomes unreadable (Fig. 12.8).

When color is laid over type, it should be treated the same as reversed type—larger than normal and in small quantities. Only pastel colors should be considered, and they should be screened. Black print on yellow paper, and red print on white paper have scored well in legibility tests (Tinker 1963).

Newspapers are fighting an increasingly difficult battle to produce a legible product. As newsprint prices have increased, the quality of the paper has decreased. In the mid-1970s, in an attempt to restrain increasing costs, newsprint mills dropped the basis weight of newsprint from 32 to 30. The lighter paper is easier and cheaper to make but, according to an analysis by the Knight-Ridder group, has caused expensive web breaks and reduced printing quality. Now the newsprint industry is proposing to lower the basis weight to 29 or 28.5. Unless new inks are developed, the result for newspapers will be more show-through of ink from one side of the page to the other. This in turn will decrease legibility.

REPRODUCTION QUALITY. If the quality of newsprint continues to decrease, it will become even more difficult to control other variables, such as camera and press work, that affect the quality of reproduction. Offset presses need a good-quality paper. As the basis weight for newsprint decreases, the pressroom operators have to work even harder to control the amount of ink. Unfortunately, there is a limit to how much the operators can do to prevent show-through with lighter weight paper.

While the texture of the paper does not directly affect legibility, it does affect the reader's attitude toward the product. It is almost impossible to read a newspaper these days without getting ink all over your hands and perhaps even on your clothes. NBC television correspondent Irving R. Levine always wears gloves when he reads a newspaper, a practice that invites curious glances, not to mention comments.

Selecting text type

While x-height, set width, and color are important in selecting a display typeface, many editors put a premium on aesthetics and trends. Text type, however, is less susceptible to trends. It is the workhorse of the newspaper—not much appreciated, but if it does not work, the publication is in trouble.

Earlier in this chapter, we cited several potential text typefaces that will work well. All of them meet the basic criteria: uniform or nearly uniform stroke widths, good x-height and shorter than average set width. In addition, whichever typeface is selected, editors ought to use the medium weight or slightly bolder than medium weight.

Of the typefaces shown in Figure 12.9, Olympian and Corona have the best x-heights; Nimrod and Ionic are right behind them. The typefaces with the shortest lowercase alphabets are Times New Roman, Imperial, and Jubilee.

The problem for newspapers is that the faces with the best x-height usually have the widest set width or longest lowercase alphabet. To alleviate this problem, many newspapers are programming their typesetting machines to slightly condense their text type. That way the large x-height can

IONIC NO 5 – 1925 – C. H. Griffith – Mergenthaler Linotype

abcdefghijklmnopqrstuvwxyz
ABCDEFGHIJKLMNOPQRSTUVWXYZ

EXCELSIOR – 1931 – C. H. Griffith – Mergenthaler Linotype

abcdefghijklmnopqrstuvwxyz
ABCDEFGHIJKLMNOPQRSTUVWXYZ

TIMES NEW ROMAN – 1932 – Stanley Morison – Monotype

abcdefghijklmnopqrstuvwxyz
ABCDEFGHIJKLMNOPQRSTUVWXYZ

CORONA – 1940 – C. H. Griffith – Mergenthaler Linotype

abcdefghijklmnopqrstuvwxyz
ABCDEFGHIJKLMNOPQRSTUVWXYZ

JUBILEE – 1954 – Walter Tracy – British Linotype

abcdefghijklmnopqrstuvwxyz
ABCDEFGHIJKLMNOPQRSTUVWXYZ

IMPERIAL – 1957 – Edwin Shaar – Intertype

abcdefghijklmnopqrstuvwxyz
ABCDEFGHIJKLMNOPQRSTUVWXYZ

MODERN – 1969 – Walter Tracy – British Linotype

abcdefghijklmnopqrstuvwxyz
ABCDEFGHIJKLMNOPQRSTUVWXYZ

OLYMPIAN – 1970 – Matthew Carter – Mergenthaler Linotype

abcdefghijklmnopqrstuvwxyz
ABCDEFGHIJKLMNOPQRSTUVWXYZ

TIMES EUROPA – 1972 – Walter Tracy – Linotype Paul

abcdefghijklmnopqrstuvwxyz
ABCDEFGHIJKLMNOPQRSTUVWXYZ

NIMROD – 1980 – Robin Nicholas – Monotype

abcdefghijklmnopqrstuvwxyz
ABCDEFGHIJKLMNOPQRSTUVWXYZ

12.9. Of these faces commonly used as text type, Olympian, Corona, Nimrod, and Ionic have the largest *x*-heights; Times New Roman, Imperial, and Jubilee have the best lowercase alphabet lengths.

be preserved while increasing the number of characters per line. Newspapers must be careful, though, not to condense the type so much that legibility suffers.

Editors must avoid the temptation to change the size of type without considering the line width, leading, and type design. Editors must eschew the dramatic at times to produce the legible. Nevertheless, every factor discussed here can be violated to a minimal extent. Type can be reversed if it is done in small quantities and in larger type. Newspapers that publish editorials in 10-pt. type but run only one editorial a day can probably get by with little or no leading even though 10-pt. type is usually not set solid. Screening type decreases the contrast and thus the legibility, but as a labeling device it can be effective. A 5 or 10 percent screen over type should be used only on short stories, perhaps 10 to 12 inches at maximum. If the story is longer and a screen is used, increase the size of type. There is no doubt that all caps type is more difficult to read than lowercase, but a two- or three-word headline in all caps is not going to make a measurable amount of difference in reading speed. All these factors should be considered in relationship to one another.

13

Using type

A MESSAGE that we hear is soon forgotten, but the one that we see and read is more permanent because it penetrates memory on more than one level and can be referred to over and over again. This explains the growing significance of typography as a world-wide communication tool — a tool that we must improve steadily by studying it as we use it.

Will Burton
TYPOGRAPHER

J UST AS THE CLOTHES WE WEAR reveal our personality, the type that is used to dress our newspaper says a great deal about the publication. Type is an essential part of a newspaper's personality. Imagine reader reaction if the *New York Times* was set in Cartoon typeface, the *Wall Street Journal* in Egyptian, or the *Philadelphia Inquirer* in Futura Light. Those type choices would be as inappropriate as wearing a T-shirt to a formal dinner party. Researchers have shown that laypeople are able to attribute characteristics to type similar to those used by professionals (Tannenbaum et al. 1964) and that the selection of a correct typeface appears to make more difference with some types of content than others (Haskins 1958). Benton (1979) found that the sans serif face Helvetica was not perceived as differing significantly from serif faces Garamond, Bodoni, Palatino, and Times Roman, except that it was considered more modern. For years, many newspapers used a more feminine face in the women's section than elsewhere. Haskins and Flynne (1974) found that even though readers ascribed feminine characteristics to certain typefaces, the use of those faces in the section did not affect readership. Not enough research has been done to determine whether readership is enhanced by appropriate typefaces, but it is generally conceded that selection of type does have connotative impact. That is, type imparts an emotion, a feeling. The successful designer uses type with the understanding that the form is part of the message and not a decoration.

The selection of a proper headline face rests on legibility consideration, the image the editors wish to project, the tradition that needs to be preserved, and the mood and life-style of the community. After World War II, Americans were hungry to improve their lives. A home, two cars, and vacations became possible for millions. Americans trashed the old and devoured the new. During a period like that, a modern typeface such as Helvetica has a strong appeal. Moods change, however.

When the oil embargo overturned the world economy in the late 1970s, Americans first elected a president who preached self-denial and then one who advocated a return to traditional values. Throughout the country, there was a strong yearning for the "good old days," and political conservatism enjoyed a revival. For the first time in years, functionalism became more important than looks.

The theme of the administration that took office in 1981 was "A New Beginning," but it was based on a return to classic American values. At that time, many American newspapers going through redesigns selected classic typefaces instead of the more modern ones. The *Dallas Times Herald* and the *Los Angeles Times* adopted Times New Roman. The *Kansas City Star* chose Goudy Bold. The *Milwaukee Journal* adopted Baker Argentine. Other newspapers sensed the mood of their readers and followed suit. Times change; tastes change. There is no "right" display face. Type should be chosen on the basis of its legibility, its connotative image, its credibility, and the mood of the community in which the paper is published.

Type is a large part of the newspaper's personality. A sudden change is shocking. For example, if nameplates were exchanged between newspapers, the resulting combinations of type would immediately indicate that something was wrong. The personalities would have been changed.

To check the personality of your paper, draw up a list of opposite characteristics (traditional, modern; credible, not credible; old, young; aggressive, passive; cold, warm) and put them on a 1 to 10 scale. Compare the staff's perception with that of an audience sample. This kind of measurement is also a good way to field test a proposed type change.

Assuring contrast

Once editors have decided upon the image desired, they have four basic methods to provide contrast with the display face:

1. Choose one weight of one typeface and use size differentiation only.
2. Choose one typeface with two or more weights.
3. Choose one typeface and use italic or oblique of the same face.
4. Choose different but complementary typefaces.

A fifth option, which is not desirable, is the use of any typeface from condensed to extraextended. These styles should be avoided for the main display face because their legibility is not good; the readers do not like them; and with the extended faces, editors cannot get as many letters into a headline. Although a condensed version can be built into the basic headline chart, it should be used judiciously (Fig. 13.1). It is better to use these special faces for standing features such as departmental identifiers and column logos.

13.1. Although condensed type offers a better head count, it is unusual to use it as the primary display face.

13.2. Because it uses such bold display type, the *St. Petersburg Times* uses smaller sizes.

SIZE DIFFERENTIATION. Traditionally, newspapers have relied upon more than one size of type to relieve the dullness that is inherent in the use of a single weight of type. When the size differentiation is not present, the page lacks interest. It is possible to produce successful pages that rely only on size to provide contrast with type, but the task is formidable. In fact, it is impossible if the basic face is a bold weight. As type increases in weight, type size should decrease. Newspapers such as the *St. Petersburg Times,* which uses Univers Bold for its basic face, do not need as much size to carry a page. As a result, the range of type sizes used is much smaller. A typical *Times* front page (Fig. 13.2), for example, ranges between 30- and 60-pt. type. Most headlines are 36 and 42 points. However, newspapers that use a medium weight often range above 80 points, and 48-, 60-, and 72-pt. type is seen frequently. Futura, because it is gray, generally needs more size (Fig. 13.3). The Baltimore *Sun* uses Bookman in two weights (Fig. 13.4), both light compared with the bolder look of the *St. Paul Pioneer Press Dispatch* (Fig. 13.5).

13.3. Futura, because of its light color, needs more size. In the extra bold versions, it looks short and squat.

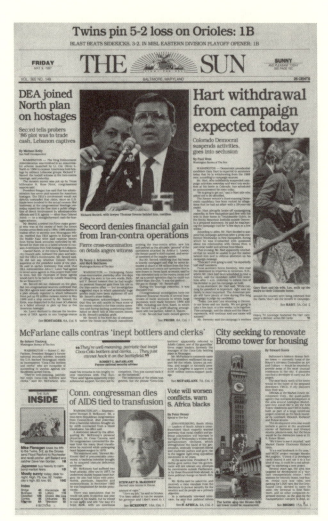

13.4. Bookman, used by the Baltimore *Sun,* is an attractive, dignified typeface that connotes tradition.

WEIGHT DIFFERENTIATION. If designers select a single display type-face for editorial content, contrast can be achieved from weight differentia-tion. One face helps to ensure the designer of concord, the blending of typographical elements to give a uniform impression. When all the type is the same weight, however, the uniformity produces dullness; bolder and lighter weights provide pleasing contrast. A designer should work with at least two or three weights. The basic headline face is usually in the medium to bold range. Different weights are used most effectively in readins, readouts, blurbs, and decks. Some newspapers, the *Arkansas Gazette* among them, obtain contrast by alternating bolder and lighter weight type in main heads throughout the page. This approach is more suited to a paper with a vertical format such as the *Gazette*. The interplay of typographic color (Fig. 13.6) is much more effective than the use of one color (Fig. 13.7), which was used at the *Gazette* previously. The two colors in the vertical format help to solve the problem of tombstoning. However, for most papers in a horizontal format, the interplay between the bold and the

13.5.   The *Pioneer Press Dispatch* uses two weights of English Times; the bold is much blacker than either Bookman or Futura in the two preceding examples.

13.6.   The *Arkansas Gazette* now uses two weights of Helios to lend the page a pleasing contrast of type weights.

light in the same headline shows off the contrast to better advantage (Fig. 13.8). Even with weight contrast, size differential is important. Editors need to downsize heads when using a bold or extrabold weight for hammers or labels. For instance, if the hammer is usually twice the size of the deck, the size differential may be only one step (from 36 to 30 points), particularly if the hammer is set in bold or extrabold type and the deck is medium or light. In each of the examples in Figure 13.9, two weights of type are used. In the first, there is one size difference; in the second there are two.

CONTRAST BY FORM.   Some designers prefer to achieve contrast by using the italic or oblique of the basic face. *Time* magazine, for instance, uses Century italic, a serif, as a contrasting deck head to the sans serif, Franklin Gothic, main head. Because of the small page size and subordinate position in the headline, italic type usually is only 12 to 14 points. Some italic faces lose their graceful lines in larger sizes and are not as suited

13.7.   Formerly, the *Gazette* used one weight of Futura, which is not as black as Helios. The new typography is crisper.

13.8. While the *Gazette* alternates bold and light as the primary head, the *Morning Call* uses bold as the primary head and light as the secondary head. The adjacent positions emphasize the contrast.

Bold weight
It can be used in smaller sizes
Medium weight
It requires more size to set it off

13.9. The interplay of type weights provides color contrast, but it also affects the sizing of type.

13.10. The redesigned *Fort Worth Star-Telegram* (see pre-redesign example Fig. 13.3) contrasts Times Roman bold with medium italic, a change of color and form.

for newspaper use where larger sizes are needed. The *Milwaukee Journal*'s Baker Argentine has an attractive italic, and the redesigned *Fort Worth Star-Telegram* (Fig. 13.10) uses the italic of its Times Roman successfully. The oblique, or slanted right, versions of the sans serif and square serif faces have none of the elegance of italic and are best used in small sizes, such as in blurbs. Some newspapers, however, do use oblique as a contrasting face.

CONTRAST BY RACE. A few newspapers are starting to use typefaces from different races in their basic formats. It is a noble but risky experiment. If the proper types are not matched, the effect will be the same kind of clash that results from mixing a striped shirt with plaid slacks. In addition, because of the high story count on most newspaper pages, clutter is always a danger when two typefaces are used.

A knowledge of the type continuum can help avoid mismatched types, and lower story counts can mitigate the clutter. The type continuum arranges type much the way a color wheel arranges colors. The continuum (Fig. 13.11) ranges from text lettering to square serifs. To be effective, the contrast must be sharp. Timidity in type choice produces conflict. That is why a designer would not mix two types from the same race, such as Helvetica and Futura. The *Kansas City Star* selected Goudy Bold (modern roman) for its basic face but uses Franklin Gothic (sans serif) for decks (Fig. 13.12). The mix works. The types are from adjacent races, a basic rule

Text

Old Style

Transitional

Modern

Sans serif

Square serif

13.11. For headline formats, some serifs and some sans serifs are a complementary match.

13.12. The *Kansas City Star* contrasts two type races, roman and sans serif.

13.13. *USA Today* uses two weights of Times Roman in addition to Helios. That much mixture leads to a high-activity page.

when mixing type. The weight contrast, however, is not as successful because both typefaces are bold. A sans serif in a lighter face would have been more effective, but the bold was chosen so smaller sizes could be used to save space. *USA Today* uses Times Bold and Times Medium for weight contrast. But it also uses Helios Extra Bold Condensed for its teaser lines and over a special cover story (Fig. 13.13). Richard Curtis, assistant managing editor, said their goal was to produce a high-energy paper without being circusy.

Not all serif faces complement all sans serif faces. Look for contrasting characteristics when seeking a match. For instance, Helvetica, Univers, and Franklin Gothic all have characteristics similar to sans serifs: the strokes are uniform and functional and the color is strong. Now look in the serif race for types with contrasting characteristics. In faces such as Century, Janson, and Caslon we find classic forms with enough contrast in stroke widths but not so much as to lose the hairlines in printing. If we were to look for a matching face for the sans serif Futura, which is less bold than Helvetica, Univers, and Franklin Gothic and has a smaller *x*-height and slightly longer extenders, we might see a match in a serif typeface such as Bookman, which has nearly uniform strokes and a solid color (Fig. 13.14).

This is Triumvirate Bold
Century italic is a good contrast

This is Caslon Bold
Univers is a good contrast

This is Futura Bold
Bookman is a good contrast

13.14. When carefully selected, types from different races offer a pleasing contrast.

When you are matching text letter, cursive, or ornamental, you are almost always forced to use sans serif as the contrasting face. A cursive type would clash with a serif face; they look similar enough to appear to be a mismatch. Most novelties are so stylized or so busy that a sans serif is needed as a calming match. Occasionally, square serif will also work. Some sans serifs can be used with some square serifs also.

In the days when most newspapers had as many as 20 stories on the front page, it would have been impossible to have two basic faces. Now that most newspapers have lowered their story count to 10 or less, it is possible to work with two typefaces without cluttering the page.

SPECIAL OCCASIONS. It is often difficult to decide when to deviate from the newspaper's basic face to choose a type that reflects the content of a specific story. A newspaper page has several elements on it; the use of a special typeface for one or more of them invites discord. Even the news weeklies (*Times, Newsweek,* and *U.S. News and World Report*) stick to their basic face or faces. Like newspapers, their element count is high. Other magazines, though, have fewer stories, and their openings are often separated by several pages. Consequently, the use of type appropriate to the content of each story does not cause disharmony because each spread is a separate unit of the magazine, and the type from one story is not adjacent to the type of another. In certain circumstances, however, newspaper designers can use type other than the basic display face with great success. For instance, type appropriate to the content might be used without risk to the unity of the publication on section fronts, particularly those with one subject; on picture pages, which often give designers an opportunity to meld mood and type; and in special sections such as investigatory projects or evaluations of new car models. Care must be taken, however, to tie the section to the main paper with identifying symbols such as a reduced version of the newspaper's nameplate or repetition of the department identifiers.

It is not advisable to change faces, even on one-subject pages, because it might disrupt the reader. If readers fail to recognize the page as part of their paper, the designer has failed. It is more appropriate to change faces on pages that do not appear regularly, such as picture pages or one- or two-page special reports.

Judicious use of a special type, often a novelty face, for a story heading (Figs. 13.15, 13.16) can be fun. This technique is best relegated to feature sections.

13.15. On special packages, designers should be free to use a typeface that matches the content of the story.

13.16. The playful message in the type design is reflected in the story. The type treatment, therefore, is successful.

Working with display type

Headlines inform and entertain. They make history, incite emotion, and cause people to laugh or cry. In most cases, however, they are dull.

Newspaper headline writers have been straitjacketed into some unusual formats. Once it was fashionable to write headlines that exactly filled each line. At another time, headlines had one to two counts less in each succeeding line—the stepped-down format. Narrow columns and capitalization requirements further restricted the ability of headline writers to tell and sell stories. Developments in newspaper design that accompanied the introduction of cold type eased some of the restrictions but also took away an essential element of the headline—the deck. Functionalism was incorrectly interpreted to mean that decks were superfluous. The fact that decks allow headline writers to tell the story more accurately and fully was overlooked. The elimination of decks for design purposes was a case of form over content. Both form and content are served by the increased use of well-designed display type.

For the most part, the decks that are reappearing are decks only in the sense that they are subordinate to the main head. Traditionally, decks were 1-column wide and 3 or more lines deep. Now type that is subordinate to the main head appears in a variety of forms—readins, readouts, one line, multicolumn, summary boxes, and blurbs. Main heads bring with them the tyranny of headline counts, but some of the subordinate head styles avoid the restrictions of count. Readins and readouts, for example, are not counted. The readin leads into the title or label of the story (Fig. 13.17). A readout is not tied to the main head in the same sentence (Fig. 13.18).

Writing headlines can be a
frustrating experience. But the
readin format is one way to avoid

HEADLINE TYRANNY

13.17. This readin format lends itself to feature pages.

The
aftermath
of a
VOLCANO

When the grief subsides,
the residents discover that
they have to get back to business.
But what do you do when your
business is buried under mud?

13.18. The readout works in both news and features.

One of the most effective headline formats was initiated by the *Tampa Tribune* and now is used regularly by the *Portland Oregonian* (Fig. 13.19). The newspaper uses what it calls "nut graphs" under many of its headlines. A derivation of the readout, the nut graph, according to the *Tribune* stylebook, "should say that extra something that the headline would have said had there been room. It tells readers why the story is important to them by giving additional information to people who scan headlines. Nut graphs never repeat the lead and never are lifted word for word from the copy."

Many editors will tell you that the number one source of complaints from readers is headlines that are misleading, incomplete, or unfair. That is understandable because most headlines are four to seven words. It is impossible to tell and sell a story and put it in context in so few words. Devices such as nut graphs permit editors not only to be more complete and fairer but also to set the hook deeper in the scanning reader, the person who is looking at the pictures and headlines on the page. Headline writers do not

13.19. The nut graph, seen on the *Portland Oregonian*'s stories, is a hybrid between a traditional deck and a blurb. It helps tell and sell the story.

13.20. Another version of the nut graph is used on the lead story. In this case, the graph is the first paragraph of the story.

have to count the characters in the nut graphs as they do the main head; they write them as they would a blurb complete with articles and periods. The *Tribune* research department reported that of the 69 percent who classify themselves as regular readers, 62 percent said they "almost always" read the nut graphs and 16 percent said they occasionally read them (Clarke 1986). Others newspapers would do well to emulate the format. Another version of it is a takeoff on a typical magazine layout; the deck is the lead of the story (Fig. 13.20).

Designers should take advantage of every opportunity to use display type to attract the reader's attention. Special stories should have special treatment, but run-of-the-mill stories such as city council and school board meetings need display treatment too. Summary boxes are especially useful when reporting on meetings where several votes are recorded. The lead of the story will probably be the issue judged by the reporter to affect the most readers. Even if the reporter is right, "the most readers" will probably be a minority. Because the headline reflects the lead, readers who are not affected by that particular issue will probably ignore the entire story. Readers are self-centered; they look for information that helps them. A summary box is one way to reach readers, many of whom are essentially newspaper scanners (Fig. 13.21). Without the summary box, scanners who travel or live on or near Broadway, ride the buses, or live on the north side may never have known the council took action that might affect their lives.

Council approves $20 million sewage project

xxxxxxxxxxxxxxxxxxxxxxxxxxxxxxxxx
xxxxxxxxxxxxxxxxxxxxxxxxxxxxxxxxx
xxxxxxxxxxxxxxxxxxxxxxxxxxxxxxxxx
xxxxxxxxxxxxxxxxxxxxxxxxxxxxxxxxx
xxxxxxxxxxxxxxxxxxxxxxxxxxxxxxxxx
xxxxxxxxxxxxxxxxxxxxxxxxxxxxxxxxx
xxxxxxxxxxxxxxxxxxxxxxxxxxxxxxxxx

In other action, the council:
• **voted to widen Broadway;**
• **cut the West and Tenth street buses;**
• **put the north side fire station on hold**

13.21. Almost every story reporting a meeting with multiple actions should have a summary box.

Another type of summary box is illustrated in the innovative and humorous pullout labeled "Leader board" (Fig. 13.22). The grouping of golfers by categories (High and dry; Next in line; Wet, willing; Soaking their egos) is not only worth a chuckle but it is informative. Most important, it is a quick read that can stand alone, but it teases the reader into the text.

The scanning reader can also be stopped by type used as blurbs, readouts, or quoteouts. These terms refer to the use of type (usually in the 14- to 18-pt. range) to highlight a quote, relate an anecdote, or set the stage for confrontation. The *Tampa Tribune* used type in this way when it quoted two of the people involved in the Brian Bosworth story (see Fig. 13.18). Editors designing pages must find ways to use display type and visuals to entice the reader into the stories. There are several devices: use pullout quotes and blurbs, combine quotes with photographs, run pullout statis-

13.22. The summary box on the golf story is informative and entertaining. Be careful to edit redundancies out of the story with summary boxes, though.

tics, create summary boxes, and many others. The *Charleston* (W.Va.) *Gazette* created one when it reversed type out of the title (Fig. 13.23). Ideally, the type would have lined up with the beginning of the story, but the editors correctly did not flop the photo to achieve it. The *Ledger-Star* of Norfolk, Va., attractively combined a quote and the dominant picture (Fig. 13.24). There are dozens of other ways to do it, some are yet to be invented. Figure 13.25 shows five more examples.

The average reader spends about 15 to 20 minutes with the daily newspaper. Even if scanners are not enticed to read the whole story—and some will be—they should be given as much usable information as possible. Readers who find their newspapers useful are likely to continue subscribing.

13.23. The *Charleston Gazette* combined type and the photo for a striking display.

13.24. The display of the quote draws attention to the story.

HIGHLIGHTS OF GERALDINE FERRARO'S NEWS CONFERENCE

❝I think what you have received is probably more financial disclosures than you have from any other candidate in the history of the United States and from any other spouse.❞

❝I probably brought it on myself by promising more than I was able to deliver. But I ended up delivering it, didn't I?❞

❝A look at my record over the past 5.4 years . . . would indicated that at no time did I violate any trust that was placed in me by my constituents.❞

The Dallas Morning News: Mark Smith

"I have really not felt discrimination, maybe because I knew what should be there. If I don't like what's going on, I do something about it. I was real lucky."
— Esther Buckley

MATT GRIFFIN

"There's a bunch of cash going out and someday you hope to get a bunch of cash coming back. But, you never know for sure."

'We have no superstar but we've got a good group of hustling players. Getting to the regional gave this team incentive. We lost twice in the district, but here we're starting over again.'
—*Carl Childress*

St. Petersburg Times — MAURICE RIVENBARK

'And then they gave out these 'crickets' which we had never seen before. They explained that they would be our principal means of identification during the invasion which would take place that night.'
— Rep. Sam Gibbons

13.25. The number of ways to use type to sell the story are limited only by the designer's imagination.

CONTENT CHANGES. Designers are using a greater variety of headline formats. Some newspapers are also reevaluating rules about content. The standard rules are sound: use the active voice; use a subject and verb. For years, the headline has done yeoman's work and permitted journalists to process hundreds of stories against a deadline. However, such admonitions as "never use titles or labels" need a rehearing. Combined with subordinate type, titles can help editors avoid the extreme statements that traditional headline rules often force. Flexible headline formats and content rules alleviate the problems of attribution in headlines over controversial stories that highlight only one of many charges and one of the denials, and use large bold type for only one of several findings of an investigation. Do not hesitate to deviate from the tried and proven headline approach if the message can be told better by using alternative formats or content.

Type can talk

Now that designers have the flexibility to use type more creatively, it can do more than just carry the letters; it can talk. When we speak, we add inflection to emphasize a point. We speak softly sometimes; other times, loudly. Similarly, inflection can be added to type by capitalization, changing the size or weight of type, or varying the form from regular to italics. Most of the time, type only carries words. For instance,

Let my people go

Printed in that manner, it directs the reader to give each word equal emphasis. If the story's theme has a different focus, inflection can be added to the last word as follows:

Let my people GO

Without changing the words, the meaning can be changed again:

Let MY people GO
or
LET MY PEOPLE GO

In the last line, the speaker is shouting. Additional variations include changing the shape of the headline and using size differentiation

Let my people GO

or changing the shape and form:

Let my people GO
or
Let my people **GO**

Used to its potential, type attracts attention, tells what the story is about, converts scanners to readers, creates a focal point, adds inflection, and entertains and pleases with its aesthetics. The pages in Figures 13.26 to 13.29 illustrate the range and power of type.

13.26. By manipulating the *f,* the designer was able to echo the cross, an effective integrating of type and topic.

13.27. The editors of the *Seattle Times* wanted to draw attention to the opening of an important series. They chose to use only type on the front page to signal that this was different.

13.28. By using uppercase and lowercase, bold and light type, the designer was able to add inflection to the type introduction.

13.29. Because the inflection is so effective and so well integrated with the photo, nothing more needs to be said.

Type can speak in other ways too. In Figure 13.30, internationally known designer Herb Lubalin made type speak with great simplicity and strength. The "Families" nameplate is the work of a genius.

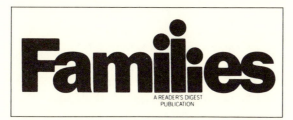

13.30. By manipulating the letters, the designer is sending a double message.

However, it does not take a genius to improve the use of type in newspapers, but it does take a knowledge of the alternatives and the willingness to try. It is time to unleash the power of type to reach our readers.

Integrating words and visuals

Advertising agencies form creative teams to work on a client's campaign. The team is composed of specialists who work in the context of the other team members. Their product is the best that the team can produce. Newsrooms operate, for the most part, on the Lone Ranger principle, which holds that each individual applies his or her expertise to the problem, then passes it on to the next person. The product is the best that a group of individuals working alone can produce.

But it is not as good as can be produced. In Chapter 9, we discussed the advantages of the team approach on projects ranging from sectional covers to election coverage to investigative reporting packages. When it comes to integrating the words and visuals in the display, newsrooms either have to adopt a team approach to the design, make certain someone coordinates the work, or provide for one person to cross the specialty lines. Fragmented work produces fragmented information.

Too many newsrooms separate the function of headline and title writing from design, cutline writing, and pullout writing. In fact, in some newsrooms, those four tasks are done by four different people. That approach does little to integrate the words and the visuals on the page into a coordinated package in which all the elements combine to offer readers an enticing, comprehensible message. Copy editors who are writing headlines without seeing the accompanying pictures are not going to be able to write a headline that ties the picture to the story. Editors who write cutlines without seeing the headline or pullouts are going to be redundant or misleading.

Even on pages where there is adequate time, journalists often fail to integrate the heads or titles and the key photograph. In Figure 13.31, the title "Form Follows Function" doesn't mean anything in the context of the dominant photo. In this case, the title may be better than the photo. We are missing a photo showing the Country Market clearly. In figure 13.32, "Braced for action" leads a reader back up to the dominant photo in a search for braces on the teeth. Only after we see the other photos of the child in leg braces do we realize the intent of the headline. The correct information is there, but the message is open to misinterpretation. Like writers, designers should be clear and unambiguous. In this case, the best picture is not the one that tells the story. The solution, assuming that a full-body picture of the child in leg braces walking toward the camera is not on the negatives, is to reshoot or to rewrite the title.

When one person is responsible for writing or coordinating the package, each of the elements supports the other. The reader sees several reasons to read the story. We see examples of this in Figures 13.33 to 13.35. The headline under the tuba player (Fig. 13.33) could not have been written unless the writer had read the story and was looking at the photo. Another nice touch: the deck plays off the secondary photo. The cutline avoids redundancy but does not tell us as much as it could. Besides identifying the two people, the cutline tells us that the woman is putting her head in her hands and laughing. Cutlines should not tell what the reader can see. What we cannot see is where or when or why this is happening.

13.31. The headline writer did not follow her own advice. The title and the dominant picture do not reinforce each other.

13.32. The headline, appearing under the head shot, could mean braces for the teeth. The title needs to work with the lead picture; in this case, the wrong picture leads the page.

13.33. When the headline writer has read the story and is looking at the picture, there is the opportunity to tie the words and visuals together.

13.34. The title appropriately echoes the illustration. Subordinate type is missing to define what slice of this issue we are to read.

The title "Religion & Politics" is echoed nicely in the illustration (Fig. 13.34). What is missing is subordinate type to identify what slice of the issue we are going to read.

Newsday integrated the hands into the title in its coverage of Hands Across America (Fig. 13.35), and the *Chicago Tribune Magazine* illustrates what happens when the artist knows the story (Fig. 13.36). It is no accident that the title with the drawing of the former mayor as Napoleon is "Jane Byrne in Exile."

Visuals, cutlines, headlines, and pullouts should exist in a symbiotic relationship.

13.35. The designer made the photo and type work hand in hand.

13.36. The photographer, or in this case the illustrator, can work from a title. The result is an integrated package free of ambiguity.

14

Designing sections

THE design of a daily newspaper is a difficult undertaking. Compromise on the niceties of typography is inevitable, control of layout minimal, and perfection unobtainable.

Alan Fletcher
GRAPHICS DESIGNER

SOMETIMES I FEEL THAT THEY [the local paper] are out to hassle me," a participant in a readership study said. "You can't find things, you're always turning pages, and the whole paper begins to fall apart."

Enter the designer with the tools to keep the paper from falling apart. The tools include organizational talents, labels, and unifying devices. Like a carpenter, the designer constructs the newspaper from the solid footings of sections. When the designer is finished and the occupants move in, they soon become familiar with every nook and cranny. It is hoped they will also feel comfortable with it.

The designer should approach the job with an understanding of how people go through a newspaper, why they read it, and what competes for the reader's time and attention. Most of all, the designer should have an appreciation for the function of a newspaper. As long as that function is primarily to inform, there can be only one guiding principle: Keep it simple.

Keeping it simple does not mean talking down to readers in writing or graphics. It does mean that designers should use writing and typographical devices to explain rather than decorate, to organize the paper, to favor the familiar over the dramatic, to be more concerned about reader reaction than peer reaction, and to allow form to follow function.

With these goals in mind, the discussion now turns to the specific parts of the newspaper. We will begin with two items of importance to all sections: segmenting and relieving grayness. Then we will turn to discussion of design.

Segmenting the package

Some stories roll in upon readers like ocean waves. There does not seem to be any end. None of us would try to drink the ocean, but we might be surprised how much we do drink little by little over the course of our lives. The same is true with stories. People who would not read a 40-inch story might read four 10-inch stories. People who would not read a 100-inch story might look at pictures and information graphics and read three 15-inch stories. Breaking banquet stories into digestible bites is called segmenting, a concept that designers are going to have to master in the 1990s.

Segmenting begins at the stage that the story is proposed. Reporters must recognize that they are not writing for a super reader; most people are not willing to consume reams of text in a single sitting. Readers unwilling to commit themselves to start reading a 25-inch story may be willing to start a 10-inch story. The reporter must understand that unless the story is especially compelling, it should be broken into shorter takes.

Segmenting also is the result of breaking out some information into photographs and information graphics. Segmenting is running a table or chart instead of grinding numbers up in text. Segmenting is using all the tools available to tell the story.

Segmenting is what the editors of the *St. Petersburg Times* did with a story on journalism ethics (Fig. 14.1). Three journalists and a journalism professor were asked what they would do in four cases; readers were also asked. The *Times* broke the story into several pieces over two pages: the introduction, the four case studies, how the readers would react, and how the editors would react. In addition, the *Times* conducted a reader poll, the results of which were presented in a table. The packaging diverts attention from the length (several thousand words) to the content.

The Rochester *Times-Union* used a similar approach in its package on local heroes (Fig. 14.2). Instead of one long story on the people nominated by readers, the editors used a nicely handled type introduction to the sidebar and picture on each nominee. Both the *Times* and *Times-Union* successfully separated the title and introduction from the stories that followed. Do not expect the package title to double as the title of your lead story. Make the separation clear.

The *Wichita Eagle-Beacon* used segmentation when it produced its innovative *Weather Book,* a tabloid combining text and information graphics. Editors organized the information by months. Although 28 pages long, the story is really 12 stories, each of which is broken into text and graphics (Figs. 14.3, 14.4).

14.1. The *St. Petersburg Times* segmented a long presentation on newspaper ethics. Because the package looks like several shorter stories, readership will probably be higher than if it were one long article.

14.2. What is one long story on local heroes is divided into several short stories.

14.3. The *Wichita Eagle-Beacon* special tabloid on weather was divided by the 12 months.

14.4. The segmentation permitted better integration of words and visuals and was more inviting to readers.

Segmentation should also extend to spot news stories. City council or school board stories should not automatically be 20 inches. Working from an agenda, reporters can anticipate natural subdivisions, and editors should plan two or more stories in addition to a box summarizing the action. Every state's legislature is worth several stories a few times during the session. Editors should design a format for segmenting and packaging the information. One such approach is shown in Figure 14.5. Such a package may run on the second front or inside. It does not preclude a major legislative story from running on Page 1 as long as there is a refer line to the package. On some days, there would be no package; on others it might be 3 columns wide and on yet others, 6 columns or perhaps even two rows. The format forces the reporters to break the information into segments.

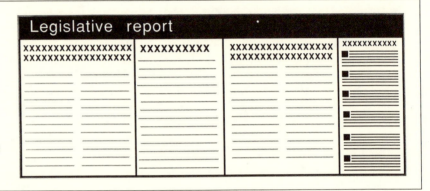

14.5. Packages such as this and derivations of it allow editors to break stories into parts and still show the relationship among them.

14.6. This type of drop-in allows the reader uninterrupted access to the story.

Relieving grayness

Even when stories are longer, and some must be, designers should attack them. Only a complacent designer would pour long stories into the column troughs without providing visual relief.

Even without pictures and graphics, editors' toolboxes are full of tones ranging from white to black and of contrasting shapes and techniques to make long stories look shorter. Let us examine the options.

1. Blurbs. Used primarily to tease the reader, blurbs also provide visual relief. Usually set in 14- or 18-pt. type, they are often set off by rules. The weight depends on the overall design of the paper. Blurbs, which can be interesting lines from the story or quotes, normally are placed at the top of the leg of type. That is because some readers will make a mistake if they encounter a pullout in copy and bounce from the top of the quote to the top of the next column. An even worse error, however, is running a pullout over more than one column of your setting. That almost ensures that the reader will make a mistake. The solution is shown in Figure 14.6. Readers can continue around the quote. Another way to drop the pullout into the copy is shown in Figure 14.7, but this device requires a wider column setting. In feature displays, an oversized pullout can attract readers and relieve the grayness (Fig. 14.8). The type pullout is effective, but type combined with a photo or graphic (Fig. 14.9) is more so. It combines the two elements that attract scanners.

18A ST. PETERSBURG TIMES ■ SUNDAY, MAY 1

Study finds women tending to stay in 'traditional fields'

By FRANCES CERRA
Ⓒ New York Times

NEW YORK — Although the number of women enrolled in law, medical and business schools has been increasing dramatically in recent years, most college women are still studying for traditionally female occupations where jobs are scarce and relatively low-paid, according to a recently published study.

The study, conducted by Pearl M. Kamer, the chief economist for the Long Island Regional Planning Board, and published in a recent edition of *The New York Statistician*, concludes that if women "continue to cling to traditional, female-intensive professions," the gap between their earnings and those of male college graduates will remain wide.

According to 1978 figures compiled by the U.S. Census Bureau, the average female college graduate working full-time earned 60 percent of the salary of a man with the same education.

The author of the study says there is a need for a 'major push to guide women into faster-growing "nontraditional" professions such as mathematics, economics, business and the physical sciences.'

Miss Kamer reported that this gap was likely to continue well into the 1980s. A. J. Jaffe, special senior research associate at the Columbia University Graduate School of Business, developed projections indicating that in 1987, 71 percent of all doctoral degrees earned by women would still be in such fields as education, library science, fine and applied arts, English and foreign languages.

Miss Kamer said in an interview that she had been surprised by her findings. "We tend to focus on the exceptional women as role models, but this obscures the fact that most women are not moving into traditionally male fields rapidly," she said.

As a result, Miss Kamer asserted in her article, there was a need for a "major push to guide women into faster-growing 'nontraditional' professions such as mathematics, economics, business and the physical sciences."

Miss Kamer's study documents the presence of more and more women on college campuses, both as undergraduates and graduates.

14.7. This drop-in only works with wider settings.

selves from the market and their accountability to it. It's absurd!

"[It's as if] you owned a house and somebody came along and offered you one-and-a-half times what you paid for it, double what you paid for it — geez, let's say double what *anybody else* would pay for it, that's more like what we're talking about, you know — and you said, 'Gosh, I can't sell it because my gardener's sitting there on the lawn shooting at the guy who's making the offer.' That's all these guys are, you know — the gardeners. 'And not only is the gardener shooting,' you say, 'but he won't even talk to me about whether I want to sell it.' Well, that's crazy! Get rid of the damn gardener, I say."

Of course, it's not quite as black-and-white as that, and Carl Icahn probably knows it, too. But the ultimate dissident pose serves him well. He's got a persuasive argument, and a shared interest, and he's got all the money he needs to mount and continue his fight. In fact, he can't afford to lose — if he did, his next opponent might perceive him as weak. "Hey, I'm not Robin Hood," he says — it's a favorite refrain. "Obviously, I'm in this to make money.

"This is a very tough game. It's not always so pleasant when I come. But, see, very often the price you pay for smiles and friendliness is that the deal never gets done.

"See, most guys want to be liked in this business. They buy stock but what they really want is to buy friends. They don't see that in this game, it's a chess game. It's a poker game. Collecting money is a game: you get a lot of money, you win.

"It's the best game there is."

Carl Icahn grew up an only child in Bayswater, a working-class section of Queens. His mother was a schoolteacher, his father a lawyer whom Icahn has described, characteristically, as a man "without very much capital." Icahn remembers having few friends, but excelling in school, and boasts that he was the first student his high school ever sent to Princeton.

"I wouldn't say that I was extremely happy there," he recalls. Much of the social life at the college revolved around its various fraternitylike and highly stratified eating clubs. Icahn's "wasn't the best, and it wasn't the worst," he says. He majored in philosophy, won a prize for his bachelor's thesis, "An Explication on the Empiricist Criterion of Meaning," and was invited to continue his studies on the graduate level. But he went to medical school instead.

"I was there because I didn't want to go into the army. I was a little unsure of what I wanted to do in the world — you know, if you're a doctor then you *must* be sure of yourself. And then there was financial security. But I hated it, and I couldn't do what I hated, so I quit."

After a six-month hitch in the army, he looked for work on Wall Street. He joined the Dreyfus Corporation as a trainee, becoming a broker just in time for the bull market of 1961. "I made a lot of money buying stocks. A lot of people were making a lot of money, because the market was rising and you could buy convertible bonds at 90-percent margin." But in 1962 the market went to hell and the margin calls came in. "I lost everything I had in one week. It was so bad that I sold my white convertible Galaxie for $2,500 to get enough money to eat and pay the rent. That's what hurt the most — I really loved that car."

He vowed never again to play the stock market. (He still refuses to, confiding, "A lot of people ask me, 'What's the market going to do?', and they're disappointed when I say, 'How do I know?' ") His crisis taught him that there's no strength in numbers when everyone falls; you just get buried. It also educated him to the value of developing an offbeat specialty and thus maintaining a measure of control. As a former colleague put it, Icahn has prospered "by being where the action isn't. . . . Carl doesn't like crowds. It's easier to find a new game with no other players."

Icahn took a job managing options for Tessel, Patrick & Company in 1963, long before the Chicago Board Options Exchange was established to standardize that market. He moved to Gruntal & Company the next year and stayed there for four.

"In those days the options business was unpopular. It was too complicated for most people and it didn't get much commission. No one really knew what they were worth. But I got myself a bunch of sellers all over the country. Maybe they wanted to sell options on 100 shares of International Widget for $4 apiece — I'd call them back and say I got them $5. 'Hell,' they'd say, 'there's this guy up in New York just gave me $100 I didn't ask for.' It was a good way to get ahead. So I learned options and these guys loved me. I was one of the few honest guys in the business."

Then in 1968, with $150,000 of his own money and $400,000 on loan, he secured a seat on the New York Stock Exchange. Icahn & Company went into arbitrage, specializing in the many new classes of securities produced in the aftermath of the paper-for-stock business consolidations of the late 1960s. Icahn earned a reputation as a workaholic even among his driven Wall Street colleagues, arriving at the office early and leaving late, and taking home with him the voluminous prospecti, proxy statements, and annual reports that were his new bedtime reading.

> ❝**I lost everything I had in one week. It was so bad I sold my white convertible Galaxie for $2,500 to get enough money to eat and pay the rent. That's what hurt the most — I really loved that car.**❞

14.8. The pullout quote replaces the headline on this page of a continued story in a magazine.

U.S., Soviets optimistic about arms agreement

WASHINGTON (AP) — American and Soviet officials expressed optimism yesterday that the two sides could reach an arms control agreement soon, but cautioned that snags could develop that would scuttle progress made last week during talks in Moscow.

"I think that there is a possibility now to reach an agreement, if there is a real willingness to do so without raising any artificial obstacles," Viktor Karpov, the chief Soviet arms control official, said on ABC-TV's "This Week With David Brinkley."

Karpov said that during his talks with Kremlin leaders in Moscow last week, Secretary of State George Shultz was given "an exact deal that would lead to the meeting of Mr. President (Reagan) with our general secretary (Mikhail Gorbachev), in the autumn or at the end of the year" to sign arms agreements.

On another program, Richard Perle, the assistant defense secretary who oversees Pentagon arms control matters, expressed similar guarded optimism.

"I would think the chances are quite good for a summit ... provided we settle the issue of verification, and provided we get a satisfactory solution to the short-range missile problem," Perle said on NBC-TV's "Meet the Press."

The United States is considering a proposal discussed last week by Shultz and Gorbachev under which each country would eliminate all of its medium-range missiles in Europe, while keeping up to 100 of the weapons on its own territory. Gorbachev also proposed eliminating short-range missiles in Europe, an idea that has raised concerns among some NATO allies and American lawmakers wary of the Soviet conventional force advantage in Europe.

Departing NATO Supreme Com-

"I think there is a possibility now to reach an agreement, if there is a real willingness to do so without raising any artificial obstacles."

Viktor Karpov, chief Soviet arms control official

mendously cautious."

"All the time ... it looks better and then somebody throws in a monkey wrench and then it goes worse, so I am cautious, but I would say there was never such a chance given to any president of the United States as now," he said.

Three American officials on the programs differed about the budgetary implications of a removal of some American and Soviet weapons from Europe.

House Speaker Jim Wright, D-Texas, said on "Meet the Press" that with an arms control agreement,

"separate areas" for blacks and Hispanics.

"No, no, no, he didn't say anything like that," said Wright, who was interviewed by "Meet the Press" in West Berlin on his way back from the Soviet Union. "He's got more sense than that. After all, he's not foolish. He was talking in terms of what they are trying to do to create more integrity for their ethnic minorities in their country."

14.9. Type and visuals together are stronger than either alone.

14.10. The more abundant use of white space signals that the content on this page is different from the news pages.

14.11. Anytime a story has steps or a list, emphasize the numbers, even if only in a subhead, to increase comprehension.

2. White space. White relieves gray just as much as black does. Newspapers traditionally have packed material onto the page; white space is thought to be wasted space, but it serves a purpose, especially in special displays and longer stories. White space gives the *Philadelphia Inquirer*'s daily magazine page a relaxed, comfortable feeling (Fig. 14.10). Pictures not run flush, layouts that leave a half column or even more of white space at either side of the package, and additional white space between elements are all techniques that relieve grayness.

3. Inset and rising capital letters. When the first line of copy comes off the top of the capital, it is called an inset cap; when the first line comes off the bottom of the capital, it is called a rising cap. Inset caps add black tone to an otherwise gray mass; rising caps add black tone and white space where the letter extends above the copy. The size of the caps depends upon the design of the package. A modest size for caps is 30 to 36 points. Some designs, usually poster sectional fronts, include caps at 60 to 80 points.

4. Subheads. Subheads can make long stories look like a series of shorter stories. Scanners often start reading a story at a subhead then, if interested, go back to the beginning. Subheads should be larger than the text (11 or 12 points with 9-pt. text) and placed at logical transitions in the copy. The old method of placing them every four paragraphs does not increase reader comprehension. Subheads, like headlines, should be written to attract attention. Use about a line of space above the subhead, but the subhead should be tight to the copy below. This spacing establishes relationship and airs out the text.

5. Varying settings. A page that is text-heavy benefits from the relief that different column widths provide.

6. Ragged right setting. Like slightly opened venetian blinds, a ragged right setting permits white space to invade the textual gray.

7. Rules. With the proper amount of white space above and below them, rules as heavy as 12 points bring black or a spot color to the page and can help organize the material.

8. Screens. A light gray screen over copy provides a different tonal quality. Be careful to preserve the legibility of the copy.

9. Invent your own. The possibilities are endless. One enterprising graphics editor who was working with a story that had five steps designed a series of copy breakers that not only relieved the grayness but also served as a map for the reader (Fig. 14.11). Chronology lends itself to use of dates or times as copy breakers.

Design by section

Many of the design challenges are common to all sections, but each section has its own personality.

NEWS. The front page *is* the paper. It is the first thing the reader sees, it sets the tone, it announces what is important. Through its structure, typography, visuals, and element count it has a personality.

The *Wall Street Journal* is defined by its vertical format. So is the *Des Moines Register* (Fig. 14.12) and, to a lesser extent, the *Star Tribune* of Minneapolis (Fig. 14.13). A vertical format offers the opportunity to run

14.12. The *Des Moines Register* is consistently vertical in its news section.

14.14. The *Pittsburgh Press* has a reasonably high element count . . .

14.15. . . . but compared to *USA Today,* the *Press* looks calm.

more stories than a horizontal format. It also creates a line of tombstones and often leaves the bottom of the page without a strong visual tug to create an anchor.

Most papers use a combination of horizontal and vertical elements. The combination approach is the most flexible, the most responsive to the news, and the most able to offer a surprise each day.

Whether the paper is vertical or horizontal, a key factor in the paper's personality is the element count. Some editors count stories, but a more important factor is the number of elements for the window-shopper. Readers scan visuals and display type. Each story is an element because it has a headline, but each visual, each promo, each brief is an element. *USA Today*'s front page is the ultimate in element count; the *Pittsburgh Press* has a reasonable element count but a much more relaxed pace than *USA Today* (Figs. 14.14, 14.15).

Readers of the 1980s have told researchers they want more activity on the pages. Teasers or promotional items and briefs increase the element count and thus the activity. Color also increases the activity on the page.

The trade-off for higher element counts is less space to display the day's big news. *USA Today*'s front page is essentially the same every day unless there is a catastrophe. The higher the element count, the more framing there is. The frame defines the built-in features; in Figure 14.16, we see the progression from teasers over the flag to teasers and briefs, run either vertically or horizontally. The X indicates the space available for the display

14.13. The *Star Tribune* is also vertical, but it has stronger bottoms than the *Register.*

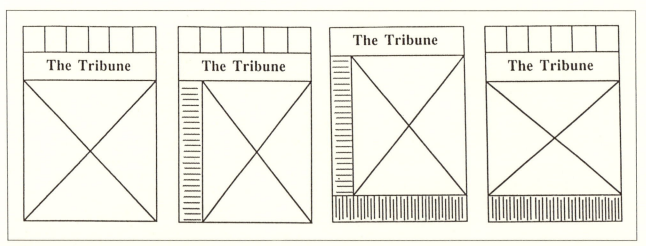

14.16. Framing defines the space for standing features, ranging from teasers to columns. The X is the space left for the day-to-day report.

news. As framing increases, flexibility decreases. Severe framing impinges on good photographic display. *USA Today*'s Page 1 photo is pigeonholed into a formatted space. The papers in Figures 14.17 to 14.19 illustrate some variations of framing.

14.17. The *Kansas City Times*'s frame consists only of a vertical down the right.

14.18. The *Los Angeles Herald* has an inverted L frame.

14.19. The *Marin Independent Journal*'s frame consists of a horizontal strip at the top and bottom and the index space at bottom left.

Once we have reached the news display space, whether it is the entire page or a poster, we go back to basics:

1. Create a dominant element.
2. Establish an anchor at the bottom if a frame does not provide one.
3. Establish relationships.

Many newspapers publish an offbeat or good news item on Page 1 daily. Special treatment is needed to differentiate it from the news. Consistency is the key. The story should be located in the same place and have the same nonnews headline format on it. The *Boston Globe* uses a hammer head over a boxed story that appears daily on the bottom of the page to help identify it (Fig. 14.20).

The question of whether to use teasers and briefs is one that has to be answered in each market. The newspaper industry, like most others, is trendy. With 1,700 daily newspapers, we should expect more variation than we see. Instead of shoehorning all the elements that fit on a page and calling it a quick read, someone should be publishing a front page that is truly a briefing on the major news. Why doesn't anyone devote a quarter of the front page to a well-designed table of contents? Why aren't broadsheets as innovative as the more restrictive tabloids? Tradition and economic forces are powerful buffers against innovation. Someone, however, is going to overcome them.

14.20. The one-time use of a hammer head signals to the reader that this is a different kind of story than the others on the page.

INSIDE NEWS. News should be organized by categories and labeled. Readers should know the logic of the packaging and become accustomed to the consistency. While section labels are usually large, inside news labels should be small (Fig. 14.21).

14.21. Not all page labels need to be large; pages within a labeled section should be appropriately small.

Editors should examine the newspaper carefully to identify material that should be pulled together. Records often are found on several pages; pulled together, they should be anchored in one position and run in the same format every day.

Once the news section is organized, there are these points to remember:

1. Work off the edge of ads to create modular spaces (see Chapter 4).

2. Try to keep photos and graphics as far away from the ads as you can. If the ads pyramid right, place a photo at left.

3. Do not box a story on top of an ad. It looks too much like the advertising.

4. Run briefs vertically if possible. On short stories, the fewer breaks to the next column, the better.

5. Vary the rhythm on a page containing two or more stories by using a wider setting on one.

6. Avoid using Page 2 as the jump page. Make your paper reader friendly. It is difficult to clip stories that appear on the front and back of the same page.

7. Pages 2 and 3 are important for establishing readership. Fight to keep these pages as open as possible.

8. Consider creating, not just an index, but a table of contents. Magazine editors have discovered that a table of contents attracts high readership and that people who read something there are more likely to read the full story than those who do not. Newspapers have many more articles each day than a magazine, yet few make an effort beyond an index to help the reader find anything, let alone encourage them to read it. The table of contents is both a map and a tease for the stories.

The *Arkansas Gazette* uses its table of contents as a combination map and briefs (Fig. 14.22). The *Washington Post* offers a similar approach (Fig. 14.23). A typical example of a story line is "Chilean gets up to 7 years in Letelier murder . . . A19." While magazines do not carry nearly as many items in their tables of contents, they do a better job of promoting the ones that are there (Fig. 14.24). The newspaper table of contents of the future could include the best of both these newspaper and magazine formats. In turn, that development might open the front page for more news display by taking some of the teasers off the page. Editors creating tables of contents should also include advertising alphabetically by store name. It would be a thoughtful reader service.

FEATURE SECTIONS. Lifestyle, Food, Entertainment, Arts, and Travel often have separate staffs and separate sections. The problems, however, are shared.

The poster or billboard (one-subject pages) was popular in lifestyle sections until the mid-1980s. Then the move to create more active pages reached many feature sections. The impact is illustrated in pages from the *Detroit News* (Fig. 14.25) and the Fort Myers (Fla.) *News-Press* (Fig. 14.26). Detroit uses an upside down L to frame the page. The format at the top offers quick-read items. That is one way to increase the element count

BRAVING BLIZZARD: A couple braves a blizzard Monday as they take a stroll along Atlantic City's Boardwalk. The bad weather was part of storm that hit much of the Northeast. (Article on Page 6A.)
—AP Wirephoto

14.22. This table of contents offers an extended headline and a page location. The table is a readership item in itself.

THE WASHINGTON POST INDEX

14.23. The *Washington Post* publishes an extensive table of contents, but it relies on headlines only and lacks any promotion.

14.24. *Adweek* magazine combines an index and promotion in its table of contents. Newspapers would do well to combine the high element count of the *Arkansas Gazette* and *Washington Post* with the display approach of **Adweek.**

14.25. Feature sections are looking more newsy. Most have gone to high-element pages with frames.

14.26. The Fort Myers *News-Press* is framed top, bottom and side; what is left is a miniposter page.

14.27. Even when newspapers present one-subject pages, most segment them. The *St. Paul Pioneer Press Dispatch* presented this subject in four segments.

and still set aside a decent area for display. The *News-Press* uses the same strategy at the bottom of the page with short takes on new and interesting products. Both pages have a dozen elements.

By contrast, the *St. Paul Pioneer Press Dispatch* devotes only a 2 by 5 space to a table of contents. The remainder is devoted to one story presented in four segments (Fig. 14.27). The *Detroit News* food page has 17 elements, but they are arranged in an orderly fashion. The use of numbers in the how-to feature is particularly effective (Fig. 14.28).

Here are some guidelines for section fronts:

1. There is still room for one-subject pages, but the package should be in segments.

2. For high-element-count newspapers, establish a frame and stick with it. Designers tire of the formats a long time before readers do. Use the frame to increase your element count and use the rest of the page for your major display.

3. You have more opportunity because of time and subject matter to use the range of storytelling devices available. Make the best of them. Your pages should use maps and charts, illustrations and photography.

4. Design with type. Manipulate the letters and stack the words (Figs. 14.28, 14.29). Use type appropriate to the content if your stylebook permits (Fig. 14.30).

5. Even if you do not design with type, make use of alternate headline formats. A banner headline on a feature page is out of place; save it for

14.28. Seventeen elements are shoehorned into this page, but they are organized to remove clutter and confusion.

14.29. Type design helps focus attention on the story by providing focus to the package and inflection to the title.

14.30. The type says the word and connotes the shaking of a quake.

14.31. The *Hartford Courant* uses white space to help differentiate between news and feature sections.

news. Titles, labels, readouts, and blurbs should be used regularly.

6. Use wide settings for your feature stories and narrow settings for your quick reads and listings.

7. Use white space in inventive ways (Fig. 14.31). The *Hartford Courant,* for instance, uses more white space between elements in its arts and entertainment section than in its news section. That helps establish a sectional personality.

8. Tease stories that are inside. Be aggressive. Sell.

INSIDE FEATURES. Many feature-section editors have to deal with calendars, columnists, weddings, and engagements. Each presents special challenges. Probably what they have most in common, however, is that journalists dislike dealing with these items and readers enjoy reading them. They are too important to be overlooked.

Just as creating a records page is important in the news section, creating a good calendar is important in many feature sections. The calendar should appear in the same place and at the same time. The typography should be legible and should differentiate between categories of information (calendar name is the major category, followed by the day of the week or a subject category followed by a specific listing). Any listing, calendar included, works better in a vertical format than horizontal because the vertical minimizes breaks in the copy (Fig. 14.32).

Space or lack of it is the arbiter of whether advice columns are pack-

14.32. Any compilation of short items works better in a vertical format than horizontal because it minimizes the breaks in the short items.

14.33. If space permits, package items such as advice columns on the same page.

aged or not. If possible, do it. The *San Antonio Light* expanded its daily advice package from a third of a page to a full page. It offers a potpourri of material to readers in an active, organized fashion (Fig. 14.33). If advice columnists cannot be packaged, they at least should be anchored. Like calendars, they should appear in the same place and at a regular time.

Numerous short stories cause one problem common to feature sections. Grouping them under common subject headings creates a larger graphic element, which is easier to handle, rather than running them as small, stand-alone stories. The Milestones page (Fig. 14.34) brings many small items together on a well-organized, easy-to-read page. Small newspapers that run club news should gather all items in a roundup. The lead report rates a larger headline; the others trail with 14- or 18-pt. heads.

Weddings and engagements present another challenge to designers. To make these items useful to the readers, keep the copy with the photograph. Readers can cut them out in one piece. One solution is to create clusters of photographs and run copy beneath the related photograph (Fig. 14.35). If the copy runs short, leave the white space.

14.34. Group short items and create a large graphic. Both readers and the designer benefit.

14.35. The challenge is to keep the copy with engagement, wedding, and anniversary pictures and still present an organized page. This is one successful solution.

SPORTS. A hybrid, sports offers the timeliness of news and the interest of features. The sections should reflect that integration of content.

Most do. Some choose to emphasize the feature; some, news; and some, both. The Fort Lauderdale *Sun-Sentinel* combines the two by creating a miniposter in the middle of the page to feature a magazinelike cover

---

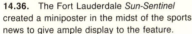

14.36. The Fort Lauderdale *Sun-Sentinel* created a miniposter in the midst of the sports news to give ample display to the feature.

14.37. The combination of element count, large photos, and bold type gives this page a high-energy look.

story (Fig. 14.36). The column and the index are standing features on the page. The *Los Angeles Daily News* has a higher pacing, in part because of the element count, in part because of the heavier, Helios extrabold type (Fig. 14.37). Where the *Sun-Sentinel* leaves the ears of its section header open, the *Daily News* fills them with two teasers and an index.

Regardless of the pacing, all sports sections have available to them action pictures, reams of statistics waiting for a chart to happen, and good quotes. The sections should reflect that content by sharp photo editing and generous sizing and frequent use of charts, tables, and pullout quotes.

Most sports editors rely on roundups to save them from being inundated with stories. With the overlapping seasons, they are often faced with basketball, football, soccer, and hockey at one time. Roundups permit them to reduce the hundreds of game stories to briefs. *USA Today* (Fig. 14.38), like most sports sections, runs a headline only on the lead game and lets the others trail behind. Most newspapers run box scores on the agate page, but it is easier for the reader if the box score is with the story.

Sports agate is the ultimate in record keeping. Designers must present a huge body of statistical data with the least amount of space and the highest amount of legibility the paper can afford. Most newspapers are running 7-pt. agate type. At that size, and considering the kind of information in the scoreboards, designers save space and increase legibility by going to a 7- or 8-column format with gutters of about 6 points. The narrow format holds the word count per line at a reasonable level and leaves fewer unfilled lines. In 12- or 13-pica columns, items such as standings are spread out just to fill space. The Fort Lauderdale *Sun-Sentinel* (Fig. 14.39) uses an 8-column grid but doubles up on it as necessary.

Designers of sports agate should also:

1. Build in a variety of medium and bold type. Readers need the visual relief.

14.38. *USA Today* runs a headline over the lead story in its roundups; the rest have only the score as a subhead.

197

2. Use sans serif type. It is more legible in agate than type with serifs, which often disappear. A slightly condensed face will save significant amounts of space. Little or no leading is necessary.

3. Use a combination of bold type and rules to break up the mass of agate gray. Some newspapers use drawings or symbols of the sports, but be careful; it is easy to get junky.

4. Use column rules. Narrow columns with narrow gutters need column rules to separate the type.

5. Use a window on the agate page for relief. A window is a space, usually carved into the top middle of the page, that contains anything from a cartoon to television listings (Fig. 14.39).

In its weekly tabloid sports format, the *Denver Post* integrates the agate listings with stories in a double-truck spread (14.40). The *Post,* which runs a 9-pica agate, picks up nearly a column by using the gutter.

BUSINESS. Unlike sports, business sections have to create most of their visuals because what they cover does not lend itself to action photography. In addition, because most people take money seriously, the tone of the business section is also less flippant than sports.

But that does not mean the sections need to be dull. Some people think information graphics were invented with business editors in mind. That is not true, but business editors certainly benefit from them. So do readers. The daily grist of the business section is numbers. Charts and tables are not only useful but also essential. Diagrams help explain how the economy

14.39. Narrower columns are more suited to sports agate than wide columns. Agate pages should be built on a 7- or 8-column grid.

14.40. The *Denver Post* makes excellent use of the gutter in the double truck for its sports agate.

works better than long blocks of text do. In fact, charts and tables are so useful that business editors must resist the temptation to fill the pages with boiler plate graphics—syndicated graphics with no local angle and often questionable connection to the story they accompany. By printing the syndicated graphic, the editors forgo their traditional editing role. Syndicated graphics are fine if they truly illustrate the accompanying story and if the newspaper has the ability to adapt them locally.

But just because information graphics are so obvious does not mean that other forms of storytelling are not available. Editors can use illustrators to draw the people they are writing about or they can do photographic portraiture. Good portraiture photography goes far beyond the usual newspaper head-and-shoulders shot. While editors should use all these forms of storytelling, one should come to dominate the pages, and that will establish the personality of the section.

Like all other section editors, the business editor starts with the framing. Will there be teasers, columns, and briefs on the cover? The *Los Angeles Daily News* uses the wide-column technique effectively to run briefs down the left (Fig. 14.41). The graphic in the lower left assures them of weight at the bottom of the page. That page has a distinctively different pace than the *Denver Post*'s business page. The *Post* starts with a blank slate; there is no framing (Fig. 14.42). The page has more of a feel of features than news. The *Dallas Morning News* is somewhere between the *Daily News* and the *Post* in activity (Fig. 14.43). The *Morning News* Digest is modest, but the element count remains relatively high because of the number of stories started on the front. All five of them jump.

14.41. The frame on the *Los Angeles Daily News* business page consists of an upside down L.

14.42. The *Denver Post*'s business page will vary more day to day than the *Daily News* because there is no framing.

14.43. The *Dallas Morning News* effectively uses pictures and information graphics in its business section.

200

14.44. Roundups should be formatted. The narrow columns reflect a quicker pacing.

14.45. The wider columns communicate a slower pacing, but the content indicates high pacing.

Regardless of where they appear, roundup packages require time and attention to create but should be formatted so that the wheel does not have to be invented each day. Figures 14.44 and 14.45 show both a narrow- and wide-column approach. The narrow column reflects a quicker pacing; the wider column is slower and may be inappropriate for briefs, which by their name, ought to be quick reads. The challenge is to use space efficiently yet provide good display for the copy. The designer favors vertical formats, uses rules and headers to separate and organize, and spins off tables if they are the most efficient way to tell the story (Fig. 14.46). Tables and lists use space efficiently, are easy to read, and can be formatted, which saves the editor time daily. The lists from the *San Francisco Business Times* are functional and typographically sound. Labels, rules, and the interplay of bold and medium type helps direct the reader through the copy (Fig. 14.47).

14.46. Tables can use space efficiently in presenting a lot of business data, but designers should be careful not to run them wider than necessary.

14.47. This page is functional because the design is appropriate to the content. The use of white space and typographic color helps relieve the gray and organize the material.

One problem business and sports sections have in common is dealing with agate. Business editors usually are responsible for the stock market report. The designer should consider building a window on the stock page (Fig. 14.48). The window is a collection of market statistics; its placement with the stocks airs out an otherwise dense-pack page. Windows can also go alongside (Fig. 14.49) or, on the tabloid where the pages are shorter, over the top (Fig. 14.50).

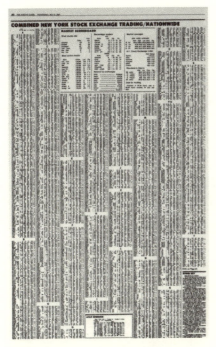

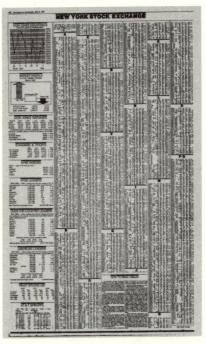

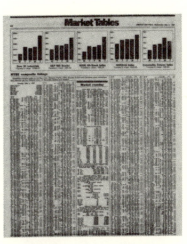

14.50. Even on the smaller tabloid pages, visual relief is welcomed on stock pages. This newspaper does not offer the reader any help in finding a particular stock.

14.48. By building a window into sports agate and business stock pages, the designer provides visual relief. The alphabetical letters relieve the gray and help direct the reader.

14.49. The vertical window combining tables and charts offsets the denser stock tables. The Fort Lauderdale *Sun-Sentinel* uses letters and rules to divide the page.

Column widths for agate depend on the amount of data your newspaper includes. Those that publish only the name of the stock and high and low points can use a 10-column grid. Those that run the stock name and six classes of data use a 9-column grid (14.48). The columns are about 9.6 picas wide with 6-pt. gutters. Vertical rules must be used to separate columns. As for the sports agate, the type should be a slightly condensed sans serif set tight.

Stock listing pages do not need to be pretty; they need to be functional. That means that stocks should be easy to find. The *Boston Globe* simply runs the letters of the alphabet; the Fort Lauderdale *Sun-Sentinel* uses a 4-pt. rule to help organize and segment the table. The *Chicago Sun-Times* does not offer the reader any help in finding stocks (Fig. 14.50).

EDITORIAL. The editorial or opinion pages traditionally are the most static of any page in the newspaper. The news, sports, features, and entertainment change daily, and the pages reflect that change. The editorial page content generally consists of opinions from the newspaper editors, columnists, cartoonists, and readers. A few newspapers use photographs to support an editorial point; some use photos or artists' drawings to illustrate the concerns in readers' letters. These are admirable improvements. Photographs, especially, are strong editorial devices that increase readership and add impact. Another area that tradition rather than logic dominates is the signatures on letters. Readers will look to see who the writer is before reading; why not put the signature at the beginning of the letter?

Nonetheless, the editorial page is properly static in format. Most newspapers prefer to create an environment in which issues are discussed rationally. Credibility could be damaged by flashy display, but that does not mean the pages have to be dull. The appropriate use of photographs aids and does not hinder the editorial viewpoint. Deviation from the traditional format should be saved for special occurrences.

The designer's first goal is creation of the proper editorial personality, which should be noticeably different than the news pages. Once the per-

14.51. The Memphis *Commercial Appeal* offers a summary of the editorial. It serves those too busy to read but also may attract some into the editorial.

14.52. The *Los Angeles Herald Examiner* draws attention to letters by running them in sans serif type.

sonality has been identified, there are two other major concerns: providing contrast to differentiate between the newspaper's opinion and the opinion of others on the page and anchoring the recurring elements.

Because form is part of the message, contrast must be built into the page to separate the newspaper's opinion from the rest of the page. This can be achieved by setting the editorial column significantly wider than the rest of the copy, using larger type or using a different text face. When the contrast is missing, the readers have to guess whose opinion they are reading. Labeling is important too.

The Memphis *Commercial-Appeal* labels its editorials and runs a summary of its editorial position before launching into the editorial, a helpful gesture for those too busy to read and a tease for readers who are window-shopping (Fig. 14.51). The *Los Angeles Herald Examiner* directs attention to the letters from readers by setting them in sans serif type in contrast to the rest of the page (Fig. 14.52). The *Des Moines Register,* in keeping with its overall design, is vertical on the opinion page too (Fig. 14.53). The editorials are set in the standard 6-column grid. They are set much wider in

14.53. The vertical *Des Moines Register* stays with the 6-column grid on its editorial page.

14.54. The *Reston Times* switches to a 5-column grid on its editorial page.

the *Reston Times,* a suburban Washington, D.C., paper (14.54). They also receive more of the spotlight on the page. Editorials are also set off from the rest of the page in the *Columbia Missourian,* which runs them horizontally (Fig. 14.55).

14.55. Newspapers are not required to run their editorials down the left. The *Columbia Missourian* runs its horizontally.

14.56. On Sundays, the Louisville *Courier-Journal* uses a double-truck format to give its editorial pages a distinctive look.

Editorial and op-ed (opposite the editorial) pages are logical places to use a 4- or 5-column format. With no advertising, the designer has an opportunity to create a grid that reflects the content. Wider columns are appropriate. Designers should also think about the visuals. In addition to the editorial cartoon, will there be photographs? Line art? Caricatures?

Designers should also think about how white space will be used. More white space between elements would air out the page, which is type-heavy.

Op-ed pages should be treated as part of the package. The Louisville Sunday *Courier-Journal* certainly treats the two pages as a single unit by running the title across the interpage gutter (Fig. 14.56). The *Courier-Journal* also has an unusual typography. The sans serif, all-caps hammer heads are all the same size, a reflection that on commentary pages journalists are not evaluating news with the placement of stories and sizing of

14.57. Letter writers get special treatment on the *St. Louis Post-Dispatch*'s op-ed page. Artists illustrate some of the letters.

headlines. The interplay between the bold head and light author's name creates a pleasant contrast. The readers get excellent display on the *St. Louis Post-Dispatch*'s op-ed page (14.57). The sketches relieve the page of its grayness and highlight readers' comments.

15

Designing accessories

READERS are getting a well-planned, guided tour through a potentially awesome wilderness of information, building great reader involvement, the one most important ingredient in product renewal.

Belden Associates
RESEARCH FIRM

ACCESSORIES are, by definition, secondary. In a newspaper, the design accessories include the nameplate, teasers, labels, bylines, and logos. Readers do not buy a newspaper to look at accessories, but these accessories help readers find their way through the publication. Like a king's aide, accessories should be seen and not heard. They do their job when they direct readers to the content, not to themselves. Accessories are the road map of a publication.

Nameplate

The nameplate, or flag, sets the tone for the newspaper. Its design is important because it is usually the first thing the reader sees. Seven factors should be considered:

1. Personality
2. Flexibility
3. Importance of each word in the name
4. Insignia
5. Letter and line spacing
6. Customizing
7. Subordinate elements

PERSONALITY. The nameplate can say to the reader, "This is an old-fashioned newspaper," or "This newspaper is up-to-date." The difference between traditional and old-fashioned is a thin line that often involves the elements included in the flag. When it is unnecessarily cluttered, it can communicate an amateurish quality. The type in the nameplate of the Baca County (Colo.) *Plainsman Herald* has a weak personality and is surrounded by clutter that detracts from the credibility of the newspaper. One solution would be a visual pun that makes the nameplate as simple and "plain" as the name (Fig. 15.1).

Plainsman Herald

Exclusively serving the people of Baca County, Colorado

15.1.   Flags should not be cluttered.

The type chosen to convey the name can be old without being old-fashioned. The *New York Times* uses a variation of Old English type. The nameplate of the *New York Times* speaks of tradition and credibility, and the news section, at least, is in tune with the tone set by the nameplate. The *Post-Dispatch* is a modern paper with a traditional flag (Fig. 15.2), which is the newspaper's way of saying that it has a long and proud tradition but also recognizes that the product and its form are continually changing. The *Seattle Times* uses a modernized version of the Old English face (Fig. 15.3) to preserve the image of tradition while updating the product. Other newspapers have completely severed ties with the past. Some, like the *Sun* at

15.2.   The *St. Louis Post-Dispatch* flag is without frills in type or design.

15.3.   The *Seattle Times* modernized a text letter face.

Biloxi, Miss., had little past. The *Sun* was started in 1973. The nameplate conveyed the message that this newspaper was a young, bright product. However, when it was merged with its sister paper, the *Sun Herald,* the symbol disappeared (Fig. 15.4).

15.4.   Since the *Biloxi Sun* and *Herald* merged,
the sun does not rise.

Personalities do not change overnight, and neither should nameplates. Proposed replacements should be allowed to simmer in the newsroom. Determining the connotation of a type is an inexact science at best, and editors should get as many reactions to the proposed replacement as possible before making a decision.

FLEXIBILITY. Some editors like nameplates that can run the entire width of the paper or can be used in a narrower format. Newspapers with short names may be able to run either a 5- or 6-column flag by adjusting the amount of white space at both ends. Editors should be reluctant to vary the flag width more than one column because it is the major identifier each day. Flexibility is less important than familiarity.

IMPORTANCE OF WORDS. Because all the words in a newspaper's name are not of equal importance, the designer can subordinate some words to others by changing size and boldness of type. This gives the designer a chance to use larger type for the main part of the name. For example, if "Stillwater" was of equal importance with *News Press* (Fig. 15.5), the type would have to be much smaller to accommodate all the letters. Instead, the designer subordinated "Stillwater," and as a result, *News Press* is big, bold, and brash. Some newspapers have dropped "the" from the name; others have subordinated it by running it in smaller type. When the *St. Paul Pioneer Press* and *Dispatch* merged, the new name was so long that management had little choice but to subordinate "St. Paul" (Fig. 15.6). The *Centralia* (Mo.) *Fireside Guard* emphasizes "Guard" to produce a modern nameplate (Fig. 15.7).

15.5. Not all words are treated equally in all nameplates.

15.6. "St. Paul" is subordinated to the rest of the name, which is long enough anyway.

15.7. The Centralia paper chooses to emphasize "Guard" and stack the words.

INSIGNIA. It is easy to clutter a nameplate, but a simple insignia can help establish the identity of the paper. The insignia can reflect the area or a major landmark, or it can be a trademark for the newspaper. Whatever the insignia, it should be simple and fit neatly into the nameplate. The eagle in the *Albion News* flag (Fig. 15.8) overpowers the type. South Carolina papers in Columbia and Kingstree both use trees in their flags. The spacing in the *State* flag (Fig. 15.9) is so generous it looks as if the tree forced itself in. The tree is integrated naturally in the *News* flag (Fig. 15.10).

15.8. Some symbols overpower the words.

15.9. The tree is not integrated into the flag; it simply sits between the two words.

15.10. By using tight spacing and allowing the branches to shade the *N*, the editors integrated the tree into the flag.

SPACING. As a rule, the spacing between letters should be tight. Kerning and even ligatures should be considered. Horizontal spacing should also be minimal. In Figure 15.5, "Stillwater, Oklahoma" lines up with the top of the *N* to produce a compact nameplate. In contrast, there is excessive space in the *York County Coast Star* because the symbol has not been integrated into the nameplate (Fig. 15.11).

YORK COUNTY COAST STAR

15.11. Because the eagle has not been integrated into the flag, much space is wasted.

CUSTOMIZING. Some nameplates can be easily duplicated by anyone with access to typesetting equipment, others are hand drawn, and some use standard type in an individualized manner. It is impossible and unnecessary to design a nameplate that cannot be duplicated, but it is desirable to customize it. The *Detroit News* has a simple nameplate, but notice how it was customized (Fig. 15.12). The Th is run together as a ligature; the ear of the *r* overlaps the *o*; the *e* and *s* sit under the serifs of the *w*. As already mentioned, an insignia, especially when neatly integrated, individualizes the nameplate.

The Detroit News

Today
MOSTLY CLOUDY
Tomorrow
CLOUDY,
SHOWERS
Details on Page 10D

— Tuesday —

June 9, 1981
108th YEAR NO. 291

15¢

MICHIGAN'S LARGEST NEWSPAPER

15.12. The *Detroit News* has both a ligature and kerning.

However, if you are going to attempt kerning, be consistent. The spacing from the typesetter is full of optical illusions, as the *Fairview Heights* (Ill.) *Journal* discovered (Fig. 15.13). The computer put normal spacing between the *Fa* combination, but it was fooled. The eye can see that the *a* should be tucked closer. The *He* and *Jo* combinations are also begging to snuggle together. The *rv* combination in "Fairview" is touching, but there is a sliver of space between the *rn* combination in "Journal." Be consistent in your spacing.

Fairview Heights Journal

Member: Suburban Newspapers of Greater St. Louis

| VOLUME 13, NUMBER 7 | 2007 HIGHWAY 50, FAIRVIEW HEIGHTS, ILLINOIS 62208 | WEDNESDAY, SEPTEMBER 14, 1983 | Circulation Audited And Certified By | 20 CENTS |

15.13. Spacing should be optical, not mechanical. Notice the discrepancy in spacing between the letters.

SUBORDINATE ELEMENTS. The design of the nameplate includes the name of the paper and all those elements that surround it—insignia, folio lines, cutoff rules, weather blurbs. Too many elements cause clutter; the fewer there are, the better. For example, in Figure 15.14 the Slidell (La.) *Daily Sentry-News* almost gets lost between the folio information to its left and the index at the right. The insignia even extends into the promotion boxes above. The Henderson (Ky.) *Gleaner,* which uses the same Helvetica type, is much cleaner (Fig. 15.15).

15.14. Be careful of clutter.

15.15.   Often, less is more.

The weight of cutoff rules should be selected carefully so there is a clear delineation to show where the nameplate ends and the news begins. When this is not clear, the lead headline often sits uncomfortably close to the type in the nameplate. If the flag is ever dropped to permit promotion boxes or a story to run above it, at least a 1-pt. rule should be placed between the flag and the material above. Generally, the weight of type in the flag dictates the weight of the cutoff rule—bold type, bold rule.

Information that goes with the nameplate should be handled as simply as possible. Folio information usually runs below the name in small type. Occasionally, when the name of the paper is short, it may be run vertically at the left or right of the nameplate.

Labeling

Sectional logos, or identifiers, are labels to tell readers where they are in the paper. They are read differently than headlines and text. They receive only a glance, like the sign on a restroom door. Large sectional logos, such as the ones used by the *Seattle Times* (Fig. 15.16), make a bold statement at the beginning of each section. The *Dallas Morning News* uses 72-pt. type for its logos, a 4-pt. cutoff rule, a 24-pt. reproduction of its nameplate, and a 2-pt. cutoff rule (Fig. 15.17).

With space at a premium, some newspapers have looked at sectional logos as one place to conserve. This can be done by using variations of a typeface. For instance, bold type can be run smaller without losing impact and condensed or extended variations might be appropriate, although extended would save more space than the more vertical condensed type. If the type in the nameplate is not customized, using a variation of it in the sectional logos provides unity and contrast at the same time. Screening the type produces the same effect.

Refers or teasers to inside stories can be built into the sectional logos, but if it is done in one, it should be done in all. The teasers should be handled carefully to avoid clutter.

Whatever typeface is selected, it should be compatible with the type used on the rest of the page and in harmony with the personality being created throughout the publication.

Labeling extends beyond the tops of the pages, however. A designer must create categories of information; each category has a different-sized label. For example, working from large to small, category 1 would be section fronts; category 2 would be inside page labels; category 3 would be the label for standing features such as Daily Records or Newsmakers; and category 4 would take us into labels within the category 3 feature. By establishing categories, the designer can achieve consistency throughout the paper. Editors who follow can identify the correct label by identifying the category.

PM TUESDAY

A day at the races
Laurel, a Longacres bettor since 1933, has some tips for the unwary
B 1

SCENE
Bob Marley, reggae king, dies of cancer
B 1

NORTHWEST
State begins scaling down tax breaks
A 12

WEATHER
Mostly cloudy
High, low 60s, low, upper 40s
Details, C 2.

The Seattle Times

Washington's largest newspaper

Copyright, 1981, Seattle Times Company

TUESDAY
May 12, 1981
★ ★ 52 pages
25¢

Syrians fire missiles at Israeli jets

CHTAURA, Lebanon — (AP) — Syrian antiaircraft missile batteries fired at high-flying Israeli jets over the Eastern Bekaa Valley

plans to knock them out to give President Reagan's Mideast troubleshooter more time to defuse the crisis.

The reports, if confirmed, would be Syria's first use of its Soviet-made surface-to-air missiles since they were moved into

The incident appeared to be a display of Syrian determination to keep their antiaircraft missiles in Lebanon and use them if chal-

dominate all of Lebanon if they controlled Lebanon's skies and its central mountain peaks.
"War would be inevitable, and

Department undersecretary, on a three-nation Mideast tour to try to avert a military showdown.
Habib was in Jerusalem today

Scene
The Seattle Times   Tuesday, May 12, 1981

INSIDE: Dear Abby **B 3**   June Almquist **B 3**
Erma Bombeck **B 3**   TV **B 4**   Visual arts **B 5**
Comics **B 6-7**   Troubleshooter **B 7**   Films **B 8**

B SECTION

Business Thursday
The Seattle Times   Thursday, May 14, 1981

INSIDE: Maritime **C 2**
Stock exchanges **C 4-5**
Aerospace **C 7**

C SECTION

Sports
The Seattle Times   Thursday, May 14, 1981

INSIDE: Outdoors plus **D 12, 13**
Celtics hope to clinch title tonight **D 8**
A look at women's collegiate sports **D 4**

D SECTION

News/Classified
The Seattle Times   Thursday, May 14, 1981

INSIDE: Classified advertising **E 4-19**
General news **E 20**
Deaths and funerals **E 19**

E SECTION

General News   The Seattle Times   Thursday, May 14, 1981

F

15.16. In labeling, consistency is not just a virtue; it is a must.

Metropolitan

Tuesday, June 9, 1981   ©The Dallas Morning News, 1981   The Dallas Morning News   15 A

15.17. The miniflag is an effective way to help label sections.

Promoting the content

Selling the content of the paper is becoming an increasingly popular as well as necessary function of the editorial department. Teasers are usually placed across the top of Page 1, down the side, or anchored at the bottom. The location depends on how the newspaper is trying to market itself.

Papers that have significant newsstand sales often run the teasers over the top; those located in smaller communities with insignificant newsstand sales can move the teasers to the bottom of the page. For papers that have limited access to news pictures, the bottom-of-the-page teaser box serves as a needed visual anchor.

Despite the popularity of teasers, there is little research on whether they sell papers or increase readership of the inside stories that are promoted. Media General, in fact, found that three-fourths of the people who bought a newspaper from a rack did so out of habit, rather than for what was in the paper that day (Mauro 1986). And the Poynter Institute color study found that if there is color below the flag but none on the teasers above the flag, few people see the teasers (Garcia and Fry 1986).

Still, teasers persist. Until there is adequate research to say they do not work, many editors will continue to use them, and not without reason. Teasers are a variant of a table of contents, which in proprietary studies some magazines have found to have high readership. As long as teasers are so prevalent, designers need to learn to deal with them. The following are guidelines (not rules):

1. Be careful not to let the teaser feature get too deep. Two inches from top rule to bottom rule is normal. If the teaser feature is at the top of the page, a depth of more than two inches will push the flag and the lead story too deep into the page and counteract whatever advantage the teaser might provide on the newsstand (Fig. 15.18).

2. Teasers appearing above the flag should be boxed to provide a visual border at the top and set them off from the flag.

3. Do not try to jam too many items into the space available. Keep it simple. This is essentially a billboard.

15.18. Teasers must not go so deep that the lead story cannot be seen in the newsrack. Readers would be able to see the two lead headlines on this page.

4. Do not overuse special effects. Photography and artwork should be used, but silhouettes and special screens for photographs can be overdone. This is a quick-check reader feature, not a freak show.

5. Bold, extrabold, and bold condensed type are effective for titles because they can be downsized and still retain impact. Use lighter faces for the details.

6. Do not get too predictable. The format should not be so static that the teasers look the same every day, or the readers will soon regard them as a reference point instead of a reader feature (Fig. 15.19).

7. Say something. Too many teasers consist of a two- or three-word title with a refer to the page. That is a waste of space. Use smaller type to set the hook in a snappy copy block.

The *Seattle Times* runs a typical over-the-top promotion box (Fig. 15.20). It is uniquely theirs because of the AM logo and fold at the left. Bold and light type provide contrast. The AM logo and 14-pt. rule at the bottom, which gives a shadow box effect because it does not extend to either end of the box, is run in color.

15.20. The *Seattle Times* uses a copy block to help sell the story beyond the headline.

Sometimes the tease is not just to stories appearing that day but to future stories or a series. This requires a series logo and imagination. That is what the *Columbia* (Mo.) *Daily Tribune* had when it opened a four-day report on children who have cancer (Fig. 15.21). The first picture in this teaser is the major illustration from the series, which started inside that day. The rest of the pictures show the four children to be profiled. The promotion remained on Page 1 for the rest of the series; one by one, as each case was covered, that child's picture was dropped.

15.21. The *Columbia Daily Tribune* used an imaginative series promotion above Page 1. Each day of the series, one of the children's pictures was dropped.

TEASER STYLE DAY_____ DATE _____

SUNDAY FORMAT 1

Sports
Major league baseball fans saw plenty of homeruns today   *Page* **1C**

BayLife
High-tech toys use words and imagination instead of joysticks   *Page* **1D**

Sports
The Golden Bear, Jack Niclaus comes out of hibernation   *Page* **1C**

BayLife
Marabel Morgan, author of "The Total Woman," talks with Bob Ross   *Page* **1D**

Business
Lincoln Property Co. will weather the market's financial storms   *Page* **1E**

SUNDAY   **FLORIDA EDITION**

Check Appropriate Box

☐

FORMAT 2 (SUNRISE EDITION)

BayLife
A new breed of computer game, high-tech toys are using words and imagination instead of joysticks   *Page* **12**

Sports   Major league fans saw plenty of homeruns   *Page* **1C**

Sports   Mike Ditka skeptic about new season   *Page* **12C**

BayLife   Marabel Morgan talks with Bob Ross   *Page* **1D**

Business   Lincoln Property will weather stormy market   *Page* **1E**

WEDNESDAY   **FLORIDA EDITION**

☐

FORMAT 3

BayLife
A new breed of computer game, high-tech toys are using words and imagination instead of joysticks   *Page* **12**

Sports
Mike Ditka skeptic about new season   *Page* **12C**

Sports
Major league fans saw plenty of homeruns   *Page* **1C**

Business
Lincoln Property Co. will weather stormy market   *Page* **1E**

WEDNESDAY   **FLORIDA EDITION**

☐

FORMAT 4 (SUNRISE EDITION)

Sports
The Golden Bear comes out of hibernation after five winless years   *Page* **1C**

Sports   High-tech toys use words and imagination   *Page* **12**

Sports   Mike Ditka skeptic about new season

BayLife   Marabel Morgan talks with Bob Ross   *Page* **1D**

Business   Lincoln Property will weather stormy market   *Page* **1E**

SATURDAY   **FINAL SUNRISE EDITION**

☐

FORMAT 5

friday extra
A new breed of computer game, high-tech toys are using words and imagination   *Page* **12**

Sports
Mike Ditka skeptic about new season   *Page* **12C**

Sports
Major league fans saw plenty of homeruns   *Page* **1C**

Business
Lincoln Property Co. will weather stormy market   *Page* **1E**

FRIDAY   **METRO EDITION**

☐

FORMAT 6 (SUNRISE EDITION)

friday extra
High-tech toys use words and imagination   *Page* **12**

BayLife
Marabel Morgan talks with Bob Ross   *Page* **1D**

Schoolfk|sj 29 Schoolwkuy 18
Schooh:th:sjl 29 ...School 18
School 29 ...Schoolskos 18
Schoolsk|s 29 School.kjs 18
Schoolpsos:k 29 .Schools 18
Schoolsk |29 . Schoolsj 18
School 29 ....Schools.lkj 18   *Page* **1C**

Business
Lincoln Property Co. will weather stormy market   *Page* **1E**

FRIDAY   **FINAL SUNRISE EDITION**

☐

FORMAT 7

Sports
Major league fans saw plenty of homeruns   *Page* **1C**

friday extra
High-tech toys use words and imagination   *Page* **12**

Sports
Mike Ditka skeptic about new season   *Page* **12C**

BayLife
Marabel Morgan talks with Bob Ross   *Page* **1D**

Business
Lincoln Property Co. will weather stormy market   *Page* **1E**

WEDNESDAY   **METRO EDITION**

☐

FORMAT 8

friday extra
High-tech toys use imagination   *Page* **1C**

Business
Lincoln Property Co. will weather the market's financial storms   *Page* **1E**

BayLife
Marabel Morgan talks with Ross   *Page* **1D**

TUESDAY   **METRO EDITION**

☐

15.19. Variations of teaser designs can be formatted as the *Tampa Tribune* has done. Readers may ignore the same format every day.

Bylines

Bylines help readers make the transition from the headline type to the text. There are several possibilities, some of which are shown here. The byline style that is selected should be harmonious with the overall style of the paper. Do not, for example, use a thick and thin line over and under a byline unless the overall design is black and white. Unity is the controlling principle.

There are two general guidelines for all bylines:

1. Flush left is best because we read from left to right. A style that runs bylines flush right is an affectation done without regard for readership patterns. However, if headlines are centered, it would make sense to center bylines.

2. Bylines normally are larger than text type. The size differentiation provides contrast and eases the transition from headline to text. Contrast can also be achieved by using a different form such as sans serif if the text is serif. In that instance, size differentiation is not necessary. The examples in Figure 15.22 illustrate several possibilities.

Logos

If you opened your local paper every day and saw a variety of column logos like those at the top of Figure 15.23, you would probably wonder if anybody at the newspaper was reading it. Designers rely on column logos (also known as sigs and standing sigs) to achieve unity, create a personality for writers, and help readers locate standing features. Because these three functions are critical to the success of a newspaper, designers spend a lot of time working on logos.

Good logos reflect the marketing philosophy of the newspaper. If the newspaper is trying to develop and sell personalities, the logos should contain a picture of the writer. If the newspaper is not trying to establish a personal relationship between reader and writer, a logo of type only is sufficient.

By GARY ROETS
Staff writer

BY GARY ROETS
Staff Writer

By Gary Roets
Staff Writer

By Gary Roets
Staff writer

By Gary Roets
Staff Writer

By Gary Roets
Staff Writer

by Gary Roets
staff writer

15.22.   There are numerous possibilities for bylines, but they should not draw too much attention to themselves.

15.23.   Compare the eclectic collection of column logos one newspaper ran across the top of a page with those below from the Fort Lauderdale *Sun-Sentinel,* which look as if they belong to the same newspaper.

Good logos that are used correctly help guide the reader through the newspaper. They should be used as locators, not headlines. Headlines attract the casual and infrequent reader to the content of a specific column; logos identify the feature for the faithful readers. The phenomenon is not unlike highway travelers who look for the billboard of a specific hotel chain. For some, the billboard is sufficient; others take a look at the motel itself before they decide whether to stay.

Logos also unify the newspaper. A consistent logo style identifies the paper to subscribers no matter which section they pick up. This consistency is one more indication that the editors are in control of the product. Inconsistency, whether in writing, editing, or graphics style, damages credibility. Some newspapers, particularly large ones, have different logo styles in different sections. Variation on a logo theme is a better approach than completely changing the style.

When designing column logos, five considerations should be kept in mind:

1. Size. Logos should be compact. They have more in common with the Izod alligator than a neon sign.

2. Flexibility. Are they proportioned so they can be set in 1, 1½, and 2 columns? Normally, 1-column logos are slightly wider than they are deep, and larger ones should be horizontal rectangles.

3. Marketing. If you are trying to sell the name of the column, emphasize it. If you are trying to sell the author, use a photograph. Column logos without pictures are not as warm or personal as those with them. Even artists' renderings of authors are less personal than pictures. Caricatures convey humor and informality.

4. Reproduction. Because most newspapers are offset, reproduction is less of a problem, but even offset newspapers must produce fresh logos on a regular schedule. Most pictures in column logos are Veloxes, a screened photograph that is pasted on the page. Eventually, they get muddy and must be replaced. Some newspapers use special-effect screens, often to produce high-contrast pictures. At most large newspapers, column logos are produced through the video display terminal system, which provides new copies easily.

5. Personality. Design of the column logos should be consistent with the design of other standing elements (such as the nameplate and sectional logos) and the tone of the publication. A bold publication, one that emphasizes blacks and whites, would use bold type and bold rules in the logos. A grayer publication would use lighter type and rules.

The column logos shown in Figures 15.24 through 15.28 illustrate the variety of marketing approaches and personalities that can be created.

If logos for columnists are run vertically, they should appear above the headline and be the same width as the type underneath. If run horizontally, columnist logos should be tucked under the headline in the second leg of type.

FOREIGN NEWS EDITOR

WILBUR G. LANDREY

15.24. Bold type and rules are combined with a photo in a space-efficient logo from the *St. Petersburg Times*.

Sylvia Porter

15.25. The *Star Tribune* uses a three-sided box in all its graphic elements. This gives editors unlimited flexibility in changing column widths. The photo is a line shot.

WILMA RANDLE
MARKETING

15.26. The *St. Paul Pioneer Press Dispatch* uses a halftone and rules for its space-efficient logo.

PHOTOGRAPHY
BY IRVING PASTARNACK

15.27. The Gannett Westchester papers use a popout and two colors of type.

"Just as hope was fading, Ol' Diz would arrive, pick up a rock or a ball or a bottle and throw it unerringly at the bad guy's head."

Cecil Williams
The Town Talk

15.28. The *Alexandria* (La.) *Daily Town Talk* has built-in space for a pullout quote in its column logo.

Story logos

Any story that runs more than one day should have a graphic identifying element to remind readers that it is a continuing story. Graphic logos help editors get around the problem of series, which readers generally avoid unless the content is gripping. Do not scare off readers, who do not want to make a long-term commitment or may have missed one or more parts, by labeling related stories as a series (Fig. 15.29). Each story should stand alone, while the graphic logo provides the continuity. Space for a teaser line for the next day's story can be built into the logo.

nked to good race relations

Atlanta. It's two hours drive from Washington, D.C. The James River, which flows west to east through Richmond, gives the city a port and, in the spring, whitewater rafting in Class 4 rapids.

There are three universities in Richmond: Virginia Commonwealth University, a public school; the University of Richmond, a private, predominantly white school; and Virginia Union University, a private, predominantly black school. Because of its schools, as well as because it is the state capital, Richmond is the center of Virginia fine arts and culture.

It also is the financial center of Virginia, headquarters for most of Virginia's big banks and for the Federal Reserve's 5th District. Because of the Federal Reserve designation, Richmond is the financial focal point for a region that includes Maryland, the District of Columbia, West Virginia, North Carolina and South Carolina.

At least 20 major corporations are headquartered in the Richmond area, 13 of which are Fortune 500 companies.

Unemployment in the metro area hovers around 5 percent.

There is a solid, built-in history on which to build a tourism industry. Besides the Civil War connection, Richmond is where the Marquis de Lafayette set up headquarters; where Patrick Henry gave his

famous "give me liberty or give me death" speech; where Thomas Jefferson outlined plans for democracy; where Edgar Allen Poe wrote "The Raven."

By definition, "booms" happen quickly. Richmond in the '60s and '70s was reeling from a mass exodus of whites from the city to the suburbs, a growing and impoverished black population, an eroding tax base, the tensions of school desegregation, the disintegration of the downtown business core. And, ultimately, in the early '80s it was not so much altruism as it was money — the prospect of losing money — and an acute image consciousness that drove the white economic leaders to try to work with the new black political leaders.

Ten years after the minority became the majority in Richmond, there still is racial animosity in city politics. Some of it stems from fundamental philosophical differences among social-issues-oriented blacks and economic-issues-oriented whites. Some of it stems from blacks' failure to translate newfound political power into economic power. And there still is the tendency for racism to creep into a wide range of city policy issues.

But black and white Richmonders have learned that they must work together, however uneasily at times, to move the city forward. During interviews with Richmond business

Cities in Transition
THE RICHMOND EXPERIENCE

Part one of a series
Related story, 7A

Richmond, Va.

☐ Established: 1742.
☐ City population: 220,000 in 63 square miles.
☐ Metropolitan area population: 800,000 in 2,200 square miles.
☐ State capital.
☐ Leading manufactured products include chemicals, tobacco products, food products, paper products, clothing, textiles, lumber, metals. More than 20 major corporations headquartered, including 13 Fortune 500s.

and political leaders, the word most cited was "partnership."

That partnership must continue and strengthen. Now, blacks make up 52 percent of the city's population. It is estimated that their majority will increase to 60 percent by the turn of the century.

15.29. Series should have logos so readers can recognize them from day to day, but the word "series" should be avoided. It signals a commitment many readers are unwilling to make.

Logos for continuing stories are common, but logos that pick up an element of the coverage itself are relatively uncommon. When the *Columbia Missourian* opened its coverage of the race for the board of education, it began with a portrait of the three candidates running for two available positions. That portrait was reduced and used as a logo for campaign coverage (Fig. 15.30). The logo appeared for a final time with the results of the election.

Page 14A — COLUMBIA MISSOURIAN, Friday, March 28, 1980

The
School Board
Race

Joel Harris: Teachers key

By Valerie Battle
Missourian staff

Joel Harris regards himself as a good judge of educational systems. He knows what composes a strong, successful system and a poor one. He has experienced both the good and the bad in education.

"Columbia has an excellent education system — and I'd like to keep it that way," he says.

He is seeking the chance to do that as a candidate for one of two positions on the Columbia Board of Education in the April 1 election.

Harris grew up in Piedmont, a small town about 40 miles (64 kilometers) from Poplar Bluff in the southeast section of the state. He attended the public schools there for 12 years and received a "very basic" education. He decided to continue his education, receiving his bachelor's degree from Central Methodist College in Fayette and his medical degree from the University. He then completed pediatrics special training at the University Hospital and Clinics.

Today, he is one of a five-man pediatric group that ministers to the health needs of "between 6,000 and 7,000 children" in the Columbia area.

Harris says he realizes that his pre-medical educational background was weak.

"I'm amazed that I was able to successfully complete a pre-medical college course, coming from the high school and curriculum that I had, seeing it in comparison with the school system Columbia has," he says. "A lot of the courses that I took in college my son is taking in high school."

Harris, who is involved with the PTA organizations at Jefferson Junior High School and at Ridgeway Elementary School, has been interested in Columbia's educational system since his children began attending school. However, he says his work and daily contact with children and their needs led to a deeper interest in educational matters and, ultimately, to his decision to run for the school board. He says his experience with children has given him insights into their educational, emotional and health needs, and he thinks this could be an asset to the school board.

"I see kids every day who aren't getting any help at home; they don't have any good, stong background coming into the school, and the person that then becomes most influential in their life, besides their peer group, is the teacher," Harris says. "And this is especially true with kids who come from single-parent homes. I think I see this a little bit more on a daily basis than the average citizen. Some average citizens think teachers are overpaid. I just don't see it that way."

He believes dedicated, well-qualified teachers are the key to Columbia's education system. If elected to the school board, Harris hopes to keep dedicated teachers in the system and attract others by raising base salaries.

"If elected to the school board, I think one of the first things I want to look at is the budget and see if there are areas in the budget that can be transferred to the teachers' fund," he says. "And as I've said before, I'd like to see an increase in the tax base, perhaps by attracting light, clean industry to a co-operative group that works with the city, the Columbia Chamber of Commerce. We need a real strong lobby group that works together.

"This is not a pro or con for Flat Branch, but I think definitely there should be no tax abatement for those structures. If the mall is built, obviously I'd like to see it built in the Columbia school district because that would mean an increase in the tax base. On the other hand, the other area I think we need to really keep pressuring is the state allocation and appropriations. I think there can be a similar type state lobby group working to increase state education appropriations."

Harris would like to change the sex-ratio imbalance of male to female teachers in the Columbia school system.

"I think there should be more male teachers at the kindergarten, primary, upper grade levels," he says. "I think with boys it is extremely important that they have some male figure to relate to. I've seen a couple of patients of mine who have been influenced positively in their lives by their association with some of their teachers."

Harris also plans to evaluate school health and safety programs. He is particularly interested in establishing a cardio-pulmonary resuscitation training program in the public schools.

Unlike many doctors, Harris is not on duty 24 hours a day. The group practice requires each doctor to work only one night a week and every fifth weekend. This gives Harris time to do the things he enjoys, like golfing with his son and jogging. In addition, he is a member of the medical advisory staff for the Missouri Crippled Children's Service. In April, he will become chairman of the School Health Committee for the Missouri Academy of Pediatrics. Harris, his wife, Jerry, a former teacher, and their two children, Jeff and Julie, live at 2501 E. Broadway.

15.30.   Logos can serve both as a display element and as a symbol.

16

Communicating with color

NEWSPAPERS ought to distinguish themselves, not just by how well they produce the color, not just by how much color, but also by what the color says.

N. Christian Anderson
EDITOR
Orange County Register

N. CHRISTIAN ANDERSON is editor of the *Orange County Register* in Santa Ana, Calif., which is often said to have the best color reproduction of all U.S. newspapers (Plate 16.1). "The response that we've had from readers tells us very, very clearly that [color] means something to them," he told the *Los Angeles Times*'s David Shaw. "You . . . think about all the terrific work that newspapers do in terms of content . . . and what do people respond to most? 'Gee, that was a great color picture.' And they tell us that time and time again. 'Man, I really like the color in your paper.' "

In the *Register,* there is plenty of color to like. It won a Pulitzer Prize for its photo coverage of the 1984 Olympics in Los Angeles. During the 16 days of the competition, the *Register* printed 187 Olympics-related pictures in color and another 113 color photos of other news and features. It was able to process up to 16 color pictures each evening compared to its normal average of 5.

The transformation of the *Register* from a black-and-white to color newspaper occurred in 1980 and was accompanied by a significant commitment of money for equipment and staff. The publisher, Anderson said, wanted to know how to get the best color, not how much it cost. The example of the *Register,* combined with new attention focused on the *St. Petersburg Times,* which had printed daily color for several years, and finally, the birth of *USA Today* in 1982, combined to show editors and publishers everywhere that quality color was possible and that it helps sell newspapers. Before that, editors and publishers generally accepted that newspapers could not produce quality color photographs and that, in most

THE ORANGE COUNTY Register

MONDAY   September 1, 1986   25 CENTS

Air disaster in Cerritos

At least 70 left dead after Aeromexico jet, small plane collide over residential area

By Maria Cone
The Register

A DC-9 jet bound for Los Angeles and a light plane collided Sunday over a residential area of Cerritos, killing at least 70 people and torching at least 20 houses in the worst crash in the history of Los Angeles International Airport.

Aeromexico Flight 498 smashed into two houses, leveling them, and triggered a fireball that ignited at least 18 other houses. The smaller plane, identified as a single-engine Piper Cherokee Archer II, crashed in an empty baseball diamond at Cerritos Elementary School.

All 64 passengers and crew aboard the jet apparently were killed, including at least three Orange County residents. The three people aboard the small plane died immediately, said William Cleveland, a battalion chief at Buena Park Fire Department.

"There were just parts of bodies everywhere," said Paul Schultz, 25, a neighborhood resident. "One lady was still strapped in her seat, and her Aeromexico booklet was still in her hand."

Officials could only speculate on the number of people killed on the ground, but three members of one family died when the jet smashed into their home. Some witnesses and other officials said they believe that perhaps 10 or more might people have been killed on the ground.

At least nine people on the ground were injured, including three firefighters and one sheriff's deputy who was shocked by an electrical line. Nine houses were destroyed, five suffered major damage, and two suffered minor damage from blown-out windows to gutted garages, said Los Angeles County Sheriff's office spokesman Drew Busey.

Jay Wright, an emergency nurse at nearby Pioneer Hospital, said about six people were treated there for minor burns and one for shortness of breath.

"The people involved were either killed or got out very well," he said.

The orange and silver jet owned by Aeromexico, which is operated by the Mexican government, had departed from Mexico City bound to Los Angeles. Fifty-two adults, one infant, six children between 1 and 12 years of age, and six crew members were aboard the jet. Aeromexico officials said.

The small plane was demolished but did not catch fire or explode.

The two women and one man killed aboard the Piper plane had not been positively identified by late Sunday. Investigators believed the three were from the Torrance area and had taken off at a small airport in Torrance, said Sgt. John Yarbrough from Los Angeles sheriff's office homicide bureau.

Please see CRASH A3

Aeromexico Flight 498 smashed into a Cerritos neighborhood and triggered a fireball that damaged or destroyed 20 homes.   Chris Crovetto The Register

Those who survived: They watched helplessly

By Edward Humes
The Register

CERRITOS — Edward Real was lying on his living-room couch watching the Dodgers on television when he heard it coming — a streak of jet engines followed by a sudden, sickening impact.

He and his family had just enough time to get outside, just enough time to see the flames engulf his new home. And they had just enough time to feel the heat of sudden, violent combustion reach them — almost, but not quite, burning them as it consumed their neighbors.

A crippled Aeromexico jetliner with 64 passengers and crew members had cut a terrible swath of destruction through the Reals' quiet suburban neighborhood Sunday, killing all aboard and at least three other people on the ground.

Some, like Real, were spared in turn only to stand helplessly behind police barriers as firefighters hosed the flaming homes — seven were destroyed and 13 others damaged — and rescue workers searched in vain for survivors. The randomness of the disaster, leaving some homes untouched, others gutted, had Real wondering why he was so lucky.

"I guess I can't complain. The wife is OK. My two kids are OK," he said. "Others weren't so lucky.

"First we thought it was thunder," the 35-year-old Rockwell International mechanic said. "But I know what jet engines sound like. I heard it getting louder, then the explosion ... Then I realized what was going on, and we just picked up the kids and split. There was a jet of fallout, debris everywhere. The fire was intense, all over. It was like a war."

An hour after the crash, he leaned against a fence and stared at the smoking ruin that had been his house at 17902 Holmes St., just over the Orange County line. He wore only a pair of blue shorts. His wife's purse, snatched from the fire at the last minute, hung over his shoulder, forgotten.

As he stood, a firefighter, sooty and wet, approached with a bedraggled, brown dog in his hand, pulled miraculously from the flaming rubble.

"Rocko! It's you. You made it!" Real exclaimed, grabbing the terrified dog. A friend took the animal, cradling it, the only known survivor from the destroyed homes of this neighborhood.

"It's all gone, isn't it?" Real mused, returning to his home. "It was close. So close. We've only lived here a year."

Next door, at 17908 Holmes, the destruction was far greater. Real's home, though badly burned, was still recognizable as a home. The place next door, where a family had been in the process of moving in with the help of friends, was a leveled pile of smoldering wood, twisted metal and murky water from the tangle of fire hoses snaking down the street.

Two fathers had lost their families in that home, Real pointed them out, two dazed, blank-eyed

Please see SURVIVORS A3

Plate 16.1. The *Orange County Register* made a commitment to print high-quality color, whatever the cost. That investment has paid dividends with increased circulation.

Plate 16.2.

Plate 16.3.

Plate 16.4.

Plate 16.2. Of the five front pages tested in the Poynter study, this one rated most important, easiest to read, loudest, and most modern.

Plate 16.3. In the Poynter study, this page from the *Daily Times* was the second most popular. A black-and-white page rated the lowest of the five pages in the study on the semantic differential scale.

Plate 16.4. As soon as it had built a new printing facility, the *Chicago Tribune* entered the world of color. The blue on the flag and on the teaser labels is the same each day.

Plate 16.5. The complete picture.

Plate 16.6.
The yellow separation.

Plate 16.7.
The red (magenta) separation.

Plate 16.8.
The blue (cyan) separation.

Plate 16.9.
The black separation.

Plate 16.10.

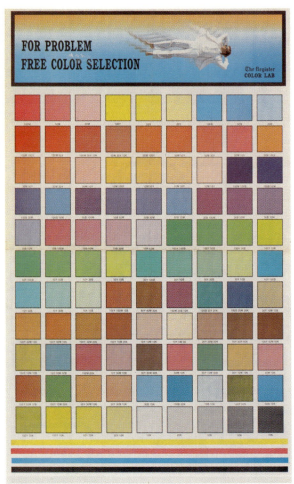

Plate 16.11.

Plate 16.12.

Plate 16.13.

Plate 16.10. With proper equipment and the proper training for its people, newspapers can produce excellent color.

Plate 16.11. Newspapers must learn how to choose colors that work in harmony as the *Memphis Commercial Appeal* did on this page.

Plate 16.12. The dramatic interplay of colors and composition in this photo was typical of the *Orange County Register*'s coverage of the Los Angeles Olympics. The *Register* won a Pulitzer Prize for its work.

Plate 16.13. Every newspaper running color should produce a color chart such as this. It shows exactly what colors are produced on one press at specific percentages.

instances, the time constraints precluded most uses of color photography in the news section.

The examples of these newspapers and fast-developing technology, which was improving the quality and decreasing the time needed to produce color photographs, excited newspaper managers. By 1979, the American Newspaper Publishers Association was able to report that the number of newspapers that had increased use of color had risen by 57 percent between 1978 and 1979. By 1983, 53 percent of all daily papers had color. A higher percentage of papers under 75,000 circulation use color more frequently than found in the higher-circulation categories because it is less costly for the smaller papers to buy the necessary equipment.

One of the reasons for the increasing use of color is that readers (subscribers and nonsubscribers alike) are telling newspapers that they like color. Click and Stempel (1976) reported that they had given each of 136 people front pages from four newspapers; two had black-and-white photos, and two had color photos. None of the papers were published near the city where the test was conducted. Respondents were asked to rate the papers on a number of factors by using a semantic differential scale. The pages with color were rated higher on 19 of 20 scales. The differences, the authors concluded, "are large enough that they can't be ignored."

Ten years later, Garcia and Bohle conducted a study of reader reactions to newspaper color for the Poynter Institute (Garcia and Fry 1986). In the most ambitious study of the editorial uses of color to date, they tested a series of pages with readers in four cities (Plates 16.2, 16.3). They sought to replicate the Click and Stempel study, determine how color affects reader eye movement, and get reader opinion about color in newspapers. They reported the following:

1. Reader attraction to color was at least as high as reported in the 1976 study. A full-color page was rated as more interesting than a black-and-white page by 2 points on a 7-point scale, "an astonishing difference," according to the researchers.

2. Color, as had been feared by many journalists, did not damage the perception of the paper on credibility and ethical scales. In fact, color improved reader perceptions on these scales.

3. Pages with color were rated more modern, louder, and easier to read than pages in black and white.

4. Although the dominant photo attracted attention first, color significantly affected eye movement. After looking at the photograph, readers usually were drawn to color at the bottom of the page. By contrast, if there was no color, they usually went from the photo to the lead story.

5. The more educated the subjects, the less they seemed to like color.

6. The subjects in the test markets where the local papers used color frequently seemed to like color better than those in other markets.

7. Older subjects seemed to like color better than did younger subjects.

The last finding contradicts other research showing young readers want and appreciate color. That contradiction highlights the industry's lack of knowledge about color. The research to date is just a start; much more is needed.

That is one reason the *Record* in Hackensack, N.J., contracted with a research firm to test reader reaction to color before it converted to offset printing and started using color daily. The researchers interviewed 785 persons by telephone and in person. Although the *Record* has kept most of the results private, they have reported, according to *Editor and Publisher,* these findings:

1. When converting from black and white to color, it is best to phase in color use and let readers get comfortable with it. (The *Record* considered this information its most valuable finding.) Color was more accepted in food, sports, and lifestyle sections.

2. About half the respondents preferred color as shown in the *Record* prototype, but about 30 percent preferred the black-and-white version.

3. Younger adults, groups from the low end of the economic scale, and males were more likely to prefer color.

4. Color appealed more to single-copy buyers than to home subscribers.

5. Color was perceived to have more impact on the newspaper's personality than did quality.

6. Among those who preferred color, it was considered more lively and interesting.

7. Readers who initially were negative about color use showed evidence they could be won over.

Woven through these three studies is a desire for color photography in newspapers, though not necessarily a demand from all demographic groups. Color is not regarded as a serious negative in terms of credibility and ethics, and, as with so many things in newspapers, color becomes a habit. If it suddenly appears, there will be a break-in period before there is widespread acceptance.

Yet another force is bringing color to American newspapers. That force is advertising. Advertisers know that more readers usually are attracted to their color ads than black-and-white ads. They want the ability to use color; newspapers like to sell color ads because they can charge more for the same space. Advertisers, according to Charles Kinsolving, Jr., vice president of the Newspaper Advertising Bureau, "are moving to color as fast as [newspapers] will let them." Between 1983 and 1985, color in newspaper advertising increased 8 percent while black-and-white linage was down 5 percent.

If the arguments for color are so strong, why aren't some of the nation's largest papers using it? The answer is that most of them believe that "if it ain't broke, don't fix it." They are successful without color; why change? But there are other reasons. Use of color would require them to make huge investments in more or different presses, and they would have difficulty printing the number of copies without pushing news deadlines back. Offset presses generally are slower than letterpress. The *New York Times,* for instance, has nine presses in New York City and seven in New Jersey running at near capacity without color. Still, color will eventually arrive at the *New York Times* and the *Los Angeles Times,* which has already started studying how it should be used. The *Los Angeles Times* demonstrated that it was capable of excellent color photography reproduction during the Los Angeles Olympics. The *Times* produced a daily special section full of color photos.

The large papers, like all the others, would do well to remember what a circulation director of a Dallas paper said when asked about the value of color. We should consider, he suggested, which attracts more attention, the red bird or the sparrow. The corollary of that is also true; in a flock of red birds, the sparrow stands out.

Vocabulary of color

Before discussing how to use color, we must first know the vocabulary. The basic terms are:

1. Process color—full- or four-color reproduction achieved by separating each color on individual pieces of film and burning them on separate printing plates.

2. Process colors—yellow, magenta (process red), cyan (process blue), and black.

3. Color separation—the product of a method of separating a color print or transparency into its three primary colors and black. Each separation contains the proportional amount of cyan, magenta, yellow, or black contained in the original.

4. Duotone—one color plus black, achieved by shooting two halftone negatives of the picture and producing two plates for the page. A duotone look can be produced by using a color screen tint behind the black halftone. This merely tints the reproduction.

5. Transparency—a color photograph on slide film. A transparency has excellent detail and is viewed by passing light through it.

6. Color print—a color photograph produced from negative film and commonly referred to as reflection copy because it is viewed by reflected light.

7. Spot color—a single color other than black on paper.

8. Key plate—the printing plate that puts the first image on the paper. To print process color, an image is printed on the page four times, once with each of the process colors. All the printing must be in register (each image must be in exactly the right place), or parts of the picture will overlap.

9. Scanner—a machine that reads visuals and transfers the information into impulses. Scanners read one color of a photograph at a time and transfer the image to a negative called a separation. Scanners are either electronic or laser.

10. Color filter—a filter that absorbs all but one color. Violet filters permit only yellow to pass through, green filters permit only red, and orange filters permit only blue. To make the black separation, a special filter is used to screen the primary colors.

In addition to the production terms, there are these basic color terms:

1. Pure colors—hues, such as red, yellow, green, and blue.
2. Tints—formed by mixing pure colors with white.

3. Shades—formed by mixing pure colors with black.
4. Tones—formed by mixing pure colors and white and black.
5. Value—the degree of lightness or darkness of a color.

Producing color

Before May 1980, the *Detroit Free Press* had never published color photography in its news section. Since then, the newspaper has published it nearly every day. Like the *Free Press,* Long Island's *Newsday* did not run color until 1980. The *Chicago Tribune* ran spot color often, but it was not until the 1980s that it suddenly started reporting the news in color. Instead of just a black-and-white nameplate with a tiny red, white, and blue American flag, the paper now also has a blue nameplate with red border and white reversed letters. Below the flag, color photographs are used almost daily (Plate 16.4). At all three papers, the installation of offset presses preceded the frequent use of color photographs. The industry's gradual acceptance of color photography was due less to lack of enthusiasm than to the mechanical requirements to produce it.

The *Tribune,* for instance, invested several million dollars in a new plant with new presses and new prepress systems to print color. Photos are scanned at the editorial offices and sent by microwave to the printing center two miles away. Four-color negatives are then produced by laser devices. One benefit of the investment in new technology is the ability to report the news in color on deadline. In the April 1987 mayoral election, a *Tribune* photographer shot a photo of the mayor giving his acceptance speech on the night of the election. Just 55 minutes later, separations were ready.

Rapidly developing technology has cut the time needed to produce color, and that is a critical reason why more newspapers are running color photography on Page 1. The same technology is also allowing newspapers to produce good quality color. That technology begins with the film and extends through the presses.

Film is getting faster and truer. But the industry is still undecided whether color negatives or transparencies (slides) produce better quality color. *USA Today* and the *St. Petersburg Times,* among many others, use transparencies. The *San Diego Union* and the Baltimore *Sun,* among others, use negatives. *Presstime,* the magazine of the American Newspaper Publishers Association, reported that negatives appear to be winning. Kenneth Paik, director of photography at the Baltimore *Sun,* lists the following advantages of color negatives (Paik 1985):

1. Several color prints can be scanned simultaneously; transparencies have to be separated one at a time.
2. Color can be corrected during both the printing and scanning process.
3. Color of the negative is edited from contact sheets, while transparencies have to be edited from the originals. The negative color original is preserved.
4. Color film and processing for negatives is less expensive.

While many photographers will agree that the quality of color produced from transparencies is probably better, the quality of negative color is not far behind. Probably critical to the rapidly increasing use of negative color is the ability to produce a black-and-white print from it. That means that a photographer does not have to shoot the assignment with two cameras or the newspaper does not have to send two photographers. Many assignments are made before it is known whether the photos will run in color. It is much more difficult to produce a black-and-white print from a transparency than from a color negative. That is why the Associated Press now shoots all of its assignments using color print film. Most of the photos are distributed as black and whites, but any member who wishes a color print can order one.

The print or transparency goes to the camera room or the scanner to be separated into the primary colors and black. Separations can be made by using filters on the process camera. However, the process takes longer, the operator has no way of correcting color, and the separations produced are susceptible to uneven shrinkage. If they shrink unevenly, it becomes impossible for the press to print the colors in register. That is when the photograph looks like three or four photos slightly off kilter.

Scanners, which range in cost from $50,000 to $400,000, can produce the four separations in 15 minutes to an hour, depending on the model of scanner and the size of the image. Newspapers are rapidly acquiring scanners. In 1985, only 17 percent had scanners; by 1987, 26 percent had one or more. Scanners have cut the time required to make separations and increased their quality. Any newspaper serious about the quality of its color photos must have a scanner.

After the scanner separates the print, negative, or transparency into the four versions of the same picture, each representing a process color and black (Plates 16.5 through 16.9), a plate is made to place on the press. A plate must be made for each process color and black. That is why printing color requires so much press capacity. Instead of the entire page requiring one plate position on the press, a page with process color requires four plate positions. Newspapers such as the *New York Times,* which is at press capacity running black and white, cannot print color without substantial investment in new presses.

For many of the largest newspapers, it is not only a matter of additional press capacity but also of the right kind of presses. All presses technically can print color, but only those built with color decks, or units whose rollers can be adjusted horizontally and vertically, can print color well (Plate 16.10). In addition, many of the largest newspapers are still using letterpress units. The best color is being produced on offset and flexographic presses. Instead of replacing all their letterpress units, some of the large newspapers have added offset presses. They then try to schedule that part of the paper with process color to run on the offset presses. They are not always able to accomplish that scheduling; thus some newspapers' color quality varies greatly.

Using spot color

Newspapers need to articulate a color philosophy just as they articulate a typographic philosophy. And just as few, if any, newspapers would permit a designer to change the headline type from day to day, newspapers should not permit a designer to use a different color scheme each day. There should be a rationale and a consistency. There is another good reason for specifying color use: a significant percentage of the people who decide which colors to use are color blind. Eight percent of North American white males are color blind compared to only 1 percent of North American white females. The inability to distinguish between red and green is even more prevalent among men; some estimates are as high as 25 percent. Color blindness shows up in about 4 percent of black males and in only 2 percent of Mexican males. Few females in any category are color-blind (Sharpe 1974). This kind of statistics leads to the first rule of newspaper color usage: test staff members who are handling color decisions for color blindness.

A sound color philosophy should define when you will use color, where you will use it, and which colors you will use.

The market and your production facilities and staff capabilities help define when you will use color. Both papers in Dallas and Detroit use color photos and spot colors in profusion, not only on Page 1 but also on section fronts. A paper such as the *Los Angeles Times,* which has such a dominant market position, will decide on its own terms when it will use color. The *Chicago Tribune* attributes part of its dominance in its market over the *Sun-Times* to the fact that it went to color. In their rush to embrace color, however, many newspapers adopted a policy that there would be a process color photo on Page 1 every day. That type of policy ensures that mediocre color pictures sometimes will be selected over good black and whites and that on many days the front page will have a nonnews or soft picture. James Squires, editor of the *Chicago Tribune,* calls the soft pictures the "Florida-frost-on-your-oranges pic." It is also the kids-at-the-beach, kids-at-the-lemonade stand and pets-at-the-playground picture. Most newspapers would be better off running black-and-white news pictures than feature pictures. Often papers running the soft pictures are doing so because of the time it takes to process the film and produce the separations. As those newspapers buy scanners, there will be one less reason to run soft pictures.

One reason the *Tribune* chose to run color in the flag, according to Squires, was that it would ensure that the paper would have color on Page 1 every day, even when there was not a color photo (Hunter 1986). It also leads its vertical teaser package with a color photo and uses blue color bars as labels in the teaser package. That is how the *Tribune* designed for color. Each newspaper that uses spot color should do the same; locate color on the page and use it consistently. The *Alexandria* (La.) *Daily Town Talk* uses a green color bar across the bottom as a label on its briefs and teasers. The bar is always green, the company's corporate color. In Chicago or Alexandria, in Hackensack or Santa Ana, the principle is the same. Anchor your color locations and restrict the color choices.

Why restrict them? One reason is so that your paper does not look, as the *Tribune*'s Squires puts it, like a Hawaiian shirt. Of the journalists who know which colors harmonize, few have realized that the principles ought to be applied to the newspaper page. A sound color philosophy is built upon knowledge of the emotional and visual qualities of color. It also must take into account the way color influences reader eye movement, helps to organize and show relationships, and influences legibility.

Qualities of color

Scientists at the Institute of Biosocial Research in Tacoma, Wash., found that pink reduces anger, aggression, and physical strength. As a result, holding cells in the U.S. Naval Correctional Center in Seattle were painted pink. Red is a favorite color at restaurants because it is supposed to make you hungry. Red is also associated with anger and love. Even without research, we know that instinctively we associate certain colors with certain emotions. The research shows us that many of us react to colors in the same ways. Bernard Aaronson asked 33 females and 33 males to rate certain hues and black and white according to a list of adjectives. Both red and orange were rated as assertive; yellow was active but did not draw a negative response; yellow-green was regarded as aggressive; blue-green was adventurous but calm; blue was the calmest; purple was regarded as antisocial; white was associated with obedience, gray with depression, and black with official or somber moods (Aaronson 1970).

Red is hot; blue is not. Yellow is active; gray is passive. Designers must think of the impact of the package, not just one element. A reader looking at a page full of active colors would be bouncing all over. Every color would be screaming for attention. Yellow is the first color we see among other colors; a small patch of yellow could detract from a large picture or the headline on the lead story. Red and orange are also aggressive; they pop off the page. Green is a calming influence on yellow; yellow-green and green tend to sit on the page. Green is static. Blue is calm because it has a tendency to recede. Blue-green attracts you. Gray is neutral, a rest stop. It is a good buffer between other colors or between colors and the white of the newsprint. Black is the farthest away. These are the emotional qualities of color. Designers should try to match these qualities with the content of the article.

There is another consideration, of course. That is the harmony of the colors (Plate 16.11). Of the many theories of color harmony, the two most applicable to the journalist are analogous and complementary harmonies.

Analogous colors are next to each other on the color circle (Fig. 16.1). The circle shows that yellow-orange and yellow-green would go with yellow; that red-violet or blue-violet would go with violet; that is, the colors on either side of a color match each other. Working with that philosophy, a designer who had a color picture with a dominant color of blue could pick a blue-violet or blue-green as a color for a title or other accessories in the package. One advantage of adjacent colors, Birren (1961) points out, is that they define a precise mood, "active where the arrangement is warm, passive where it is cool."

However, the harmony of complementary colors is based on contrasting colors. It is perhaps more popular with artists and should be more popular with journalists. As we see on the color wheel (Fig. 16.2), red and green complement each other. So do red-orange and blue-green; orange and blue; yellow-orange and blue-violet; yellow and violet; and yellow-green and red-violet. Designers who are choosing colors should remember not only the emotional values of colors but also the mix on the page. Birren recommends using warm colors as the feature color because they are aggressive. Cool hues are useful as background colors because they are passive. Tints, shades, and tones are also retiring. The stronger the color, the less is needed.

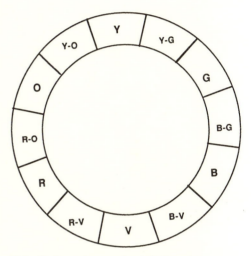

16.1. On the analogous color circle, the colors on either side of a color are compatible. Thus red-orange and yellow-orange are compatible with orange.

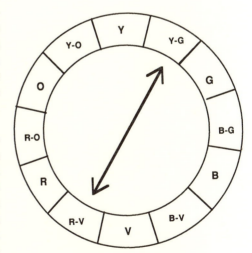

16.2. The complementary color chart matches colors by placing them opposite one another. Thus yellow-green and red-violet are complementary colors. So are yellow and violet.

Against active colors, the designer uses a peach tint and a tan tone or gray as a neutral buffer. When the *Orange County Register* ran a huge picture of an Olympic athlete stretching up to the stands to touch fans' hands, the athlete was leaning against a giant American flag. The photo, as a result, was full of bright red. The paper used a beige screen for the rest of the page (Plate 16.12). Gray would work as a color in any set of teaser boxes that contained color; peach would work in most. That is why the peach has become such a popular color in newspapers. It works. It is the product of different percentages of colors at different newspapers. The percentage depends on each newspaper's production system. The *Orange County Register* uses a beige of 10 percent magenta and 10 percent yellow. That would be shown as 10R, 10Y. That means that the color is produced by using a 10 percent screen on each color, the same effect you get by calling for a 10 percent gray screen. Another way of saying this is that you want 90 percent of the color withheld. Thus, a 10 percent gray screen means you screen away 90 percent of the black. A 100 percent gray screen, if there were such a thing, would produce white.

Each newspaper that runs color regularly should have a color chart showing exactly what the color combinations will look like on your press (Plate 16.13). The designer can then specify the color by citing the percentages of each color needed to make it.

If the designer is making an effort to harmonize colors, it is important to be able to get as close as possible to the actual color that will be produced. Choosing colors for maps and other information graphics should be done within the context of the other colors in the graphic and of the other colors on the page on which they appear. A design stylebook can help by specifying that cool (darker) colors are to be the primary colors on information graphics and that tints are to be used as borders for framing. That type of philosophy would preclude the appearance one day of a map or chart that had yellows and oranges, colors that would draw attention to themselves rather than the information in the graphic. It should also ensure the publication of a consistent personality.

Impact of color

The Poynter study (Garcia and Fry 1986) indicated that color has the power to affect the reader's path around a page. The designer knows that a small color photo competes with a larger black-and-white photo. The size differential and placement also determine where the reader will look. In building colors into the basic format of the page, the designer chooses cool or neutral colors, which help organize but do not detract from the news or features.

A design stylebook should also specify limits on the use of color tints and shades over text because color can damage legibility quickly. The *Orange County Register,* for instance, does not permit color over text in the news section. That immediately differentiates it from *USA Today,* where color over copy is common. The *Register*'s news philosophy is to surround its color photos with crisp blacks, whites, and grays. In feature sections, the *Register*'s stylebook specifies that tints over copy should be no heavier than 10 percent for primary colors or black or specifies yellow at any percentage with "no more than 10 percent of magenta, cyan or black. Any combination of magenta and cyan should not exceed 20 percent. Do *not* combine magenta and black or cyan and black and expect to print readable body copy over it."

Other legibility guidelines include:

1. Avoid running tints over stories 15 inches or longer unless you increase the size of type.

2. Screen everything back to 10 percent to protect the type.

3. Black on white is the most legible combination. Black type against a yellow background is also legible.

4. Do not use text type in color against any background.

5. Do not reverse white text type out of a color background.

Spot color is a powerful organizing factor. Rules, if they are at least 4 points, not only can define story modules but also can help establish relationships. The opposite is also true. If the dominant color in a photo is blue, blue should not be used on an unrelated element on the page or the reader will try to connect the two. One researcher found that given a mixed set of triangles, circles, and squares people will arrange them by shapes. That is, for example, they will put all the triangles together. However, if you color one triangle, one circle, and one square the same color, people will arrange them by colors. Designers should use that knowledge in using colors to show relationships on the page.

Color is best when it is used to communicate. That includes not only using it to show relationships but also using colors on maps because color helps distinguish one country from another and separates water from land. It means using color illustrations just as we use color photographs because the people and scenes that illustrations depict are in color. It means using color consistently in hue and location to establish an identity. It means knowing not only how to use color but also why you are doing it.

Producing quality color

Producing quality color on newsprint requires the combined talents of everyone from the photographer to the person operating the press. Many newspapers expect the actual printing process to make up for any inadequacies in preparation, but papers with the most experience in producing color place the least amount of responsibility in the pressroom. "Too many newspapers just produce color and then expect the pressmen to print it when it is beyond the equipment's capability," says Bill Howard, color lab supervisor of the *St. Petersburg Times.* "We take an entirely different approach. We don't try to make the press make color. As color separators, we try to give the press good color to print."

Of all the people involved in color production, the press operators are the least able to adjust for poor quality transparencies or separations or to compensate for plates that are not in register. Color can be adjusted on the press, but any adjustment affects the entire picture or page, not just an area of the picture. Press operators should be primarily concerned about getting the press in register once the basic color is adjusted. At the *St. Petersburg Times,* where color is produced daily, the responsibility starts with the photographers. Because they use transparencies, photographers must fill in shadow areas, which usually means using flash and flash fill. *Times* staff photographer Ricardo Ferro says that the original quality of the photograph is the most important determinant. "If you start your color reproduction with an inferior product . . . and process it through the world's best production system, the end result will be a perfectly reproduced poor quality photo." The scanner operators know that the press gains on blue and loses on red, and they make the separations accordingly. The platemakers must reproduce the separations dot for dot and place the material in exactly the right position on the plate to reduce registration problems. "If this commitment [to quality] is missing from just one department," Howard says, "quality color cannot be achieved." At the Fort Myers (Fla.) *News-Press,* production director Don Miller also believes in the team approach: "It takes everybody to do good color—photographers, the separation process, pressmen and good equipment." Miller, who believes in specialization, added, "I hire the experts and the experts do the job. When I know as much as the guy who's working for me, he doesn't last long. There's no way you can keep track personally of all the skills needed of the people in these jobs." Neither can the journalist. But just as editors must understand how to combine type, photographs, and artwork, they must also understand the potential and limitations of using high-speed web presses to produce color on newsprint.

17

The process of redesign

THE kind of environment you are giving us to present our story, I think, is way out of date. I think newspapers are way back in the twenties some time.

Lee M. Dubow
ADVERTISING/MARKETING EXECUTIVE
DEPARTMENT STORE CHAIN

THE *Ledger-Star* of Norfolk, Va., according to executive editor Sandy Rowe, was going to be a better newspaper, not just a different one. Her note to the staff introducing the new design stylebook was written nearly a year after the newspaper conducted a readership study. During that year, the management had digested the study results and articulated marketing goals. Then design director Alan Jacobson translated the goals into mock-ups.

Redesigns are not done overnight or even in a month. Tinkering with the type, changing the nameplate, and creating new logos can be done quickly, though not necessarily well. But tinkering is not designing, and the people at the *Ledger-Star* knew that. That is why they started by asking readers such things as what they read and when they read it. The process of redesign starts with an examination of content. What should stay, what should go, and what should be added? The designer does not answer those questions alone; answers should come from management, staff, and readers. Thus a redesign should start with the formation of a committee representing all segments of the newspaper.

Getting others involved

Just as tapping the creative resources of people in the newsroom results in a better product, so will tapping the resources of a wide variety of the newspaper's employees. The person who has final authority to accept or reject the plans, whether it is the editor or the publisher, should be on the committee. In addition, the committee should include the staff member primarily responsible for graphics; departmental editors and representatives of the copy desk; reporters; and personnel from the production, advertising, and circulation or marketing departments.

233

Why should nonnews people be on the committee? The news or editorial department may be responsible for content and form, but the marketing or circulation department has to sell it. Unfortunate as it may be, the people in marketing often talk to more customers than editors do. No design is going to be successful unless the production department has the opportunity to point out mechanical possibilities and limitations. At the same time, the production department representative communicates the goals to fellow department employees.

Advertising representatives are equally important. Column widths cannot be changed in any publication without involving advertising and management. Other policies that may come out of a redesign, such as restrictions on reverse ads and on small editorial holes at the top of inside pages, also require involvement of the advertising department.

There is yet another important reason to include all these people: it is good management. A broadly based committee offers a variety of perspectives and experiences, and because the members are responsible for the formulation of the plan, they will be more enthusiastic about implementing it. A design cannot be done by committee; that must be the work of one or two people. The committee establishes goals, and the designer translates those goals to paper.

Predesign questions

Design, as we have seen, involves both content and form. Because form follows content, questions about content are very important and must be answered before a redesign is ordered. Susan Clark, editor and publisher of the *Niagara* (Niagara Falls, N.Y.) *Gazette,* emphasized this point in a report on her paper's redesign. "The reader survey has not meant just a redesign of our newspaper. It has meant, most importantly, an examination of what we write and how we write it."

Every publication must answer the following questions before undergoing a redesign:

1. *What content changes should be made?* The *Ledger-Star* reports in its stylebook the questions it asked itself: What are the strengths of an afternoon newspaper? Who are the potential readers of the *Ledger-Star?* How can we attract new readers without alienating present ones?

The answers to these questions are all based on content. For the *Ledger-Star,* those answers included paying more attention to military news and to news from other parts of the country. For other newspapers, the answers range from increasing coverage of courts, police, and fire records to creating new beats to support new sections. Sometimes the fresh look at content results in taking things out.

Readers can help make those decisions, and newspapers can determine relatively cheaply what they think. Some newspapers use focus-group sessions. The newspaper invites groups of readers and nonreaders (perhaps to separate sessions) to a roundtable discussion. If possible, the editors watch through one-way windows. Otherwise, they can listen to a tape recording or watch a videotape. Another approach, sometimes used in addition to focus groups, is to survey a scientifically selected group of subscribers and possibly nonsubscribers. What you ask depends upon what you have identified as potential problem areas: content, personality, organization, credibility, usefulness. A semantic differential scale such as that used by Click and Stempel (1974) to test readers' reactions to front pages is useful to check their perceptions of personality and credibility factors. Respondents are asked to rate the newspaper on a 1 to 10 scale with word pairs at either end. You can see from the categories and word choices below that the scale is also useful for testing design prototypes and the redesign after it is published:

Evaluative: pleasant, unpleasant; valuable, worthless; important, unimportant; interesting, boring.

Ethical: fair, unfair; truthful, untruthful; accurate, inaccurate; unbiased, biased; responsible, irresponsible.

Stylistic: exciting, dull; fresh, stale; easy, difficult; neat, messy; colorful, colorless.

Potency: bold, timid; powerful, weak; loud, soft.

Activity: tense, relaxed; active, passive; modern, old-fashioned.

It is enlightening to have readers, editors, and staff rank the present paper on these factors. The staff often has a perception quite different from management, and the readers may respond differently than either the staff or management. The scale provides guidelines, not answers. Important questions about content and organization are not answered with this kind of test.

2. *What are your marketing goals?* How many editions do you have and who are the audiences of each? How many newspapers are sold in vending machines? What is the potential for growth? Who subscribes to your paper and why? Who does not and why not?

3. *What are the characteristics of your market?* Is it highly competitive? Does the competition come from other newspapers, shoppers, and broadcast or home delivery information systems? What is the white-collar, blue-collar mix? What time do people go to work and get home? What kind of a mass transportation system exists? Are you near lakes, mountains, or forests where people spend hours in recreation? Are you in an urban area where movies, theater, dining out, and sports are important recreational activities? Is there a mix of religions or does one denomination dominate? How would you describe the community—retirement? financial? agribusiness?

4. *How will the paper be organized?* In survey after survey, market after market, readers repeat that their primary design concern is with the organization of the paper. Beyond the basic divisions for news (which should be subdivided)—features, sports, and business—what additional sections do you have for your particular audience? For instance, Dallas is a fashion center, and both newspapers have big fashion sections. The *St. Petersburg Times* has a successful religion section. The *Miami Herald* prints a Spanish-language edition. The *New York Times* has an outstanding books section. Each market has its own peculiarities, and each newspaper ought to reflect them. When answering these questions before a redesign, some newspaper managements, especially if they are consulting with the advertising and marketing departments, may find potential sections that will broaden the newspaper's appeal. Organization also means anchoring all regularly appearing features, ranging from advice columns to editorial columns, in the same place in every issue. Everything in the paper—obi-

tuaries, record copy, and weather—should be anchored.

5. *What personality do you want to project?* Type used in combination with other devices creates a personality. Ask key management personnel to describe the personality they want the paper to have and compare the responses. If they agree, the management team has a common goal. However, there will probably be severe differences of opinion. Also ask staff members and readers to describe the newspaper's personality. Chances are, there will be differences between the intent of the staff and the perception of the readers. Agreement must be reached on the personality desired before the designer can select the elements to achieve the desired result. Although readers get their first impression from the typography of a newspaper, the content must be consistent with the rest of the message. If the graphics are modern and lively and the copy is dull, the reader soon realizes that something is amiss.

6. *What are your personnel limitations?* Is the newspaper large enough to have a design editor? How many staff members will be responsible for the daily implementation of the design? Who are they? Is the staff capable of carrying out the design? Will someone watch for slippage and make the necessary adjustments as problems arise? Does the staff have an artist to do the illustrations, maps, and charts? If the staff is limited, should you consider a formatted design?

7. *What are the limitations of the management system?* If the editorial management does not include a strong graphics voice, the design cannot be executed no matter how well-intentioned the editor may be. The format can change, but lack of visual thinking will not produce good word and picture combinations or a paper that explains with graphs, maps, and charts.

8. *What are the limitations of the production system?* If color is wanted every day, is there a photo staff capable of producing it, a production staff capable of processing it, and enough press capacity to print it? Are the deadlines so restrictive that screens and double burns are impractical? Is the paper cold type and offset? What limitations does the production process impose on the design?

The content and organization of the newspaper can largely be determined by the answers to these questions. That is important because design is the proper organization of the content in an artistically pleasing and technically legible package. The only way to reach the point of design is through planning—long-term to establish the newspaper's goals and short-term to produce the stories and illustrations that appear in the newspaper daily.

Implementation

Using the responses to the questions, the designer can begin to organize and label the content and select the elements to achieve the personality desired. If a modern functional look is desired, the popular Helvetica, Univers, or Franklin Gothic faces may be appropriate. If management wants to emphasize the newspaper's tradition, one of the classic faces such as Caslon or Century may be useful. If the newspaper wants to build a reputation for local coverage, the second section, clearly labeled, could lead off with local news. However, the front-page story selection is also vital to that image. Decisions about the packaging, placement, and playing of columnists must be determined by how hard the editors want to sell them. If the paper has large amounts of record copy (real estate transactions, court news, and police blotter material), decisions are necessary so that the material is gathered efficiently and presented coherently. If sections are involved, special requirements must be outlined. Localized weather packages must be constructed.

As the designer tries to solve each of these problems, the redesign committee, or a smaller group representing it, needs to see and respond to proposed changes. Incorporating some of the committee suggestions into the redesign will be helpful in getting their support and will save the designer a great deal of time. Problems or disagreements that surface early in the process can be solved much more easily than those that surface at the last minute. A designer who is deeply involved in the project may find it difficult to compromise or separate ego from practicality. If the committee members have seen the various parts of the redesign, they are more likely to approve the whole.

Once the committee has approved the project, it must be sold to both staff and readers. If the staff has been kept informed during the course of the project, the results will not be a surprise. However, the committee and the designer must have enough flexibility to adjust the plan when staff members find weaknesses. Because staff members must work with the plan daily, their support is essential. In addition to the meetings where the philosophy and technical points of the plan are discussed, it is necessary to write a design stylebook. Before its redesign was implemented, the *Alexandria* (La.) *Daily Town Talk* held workshops with department heads and all editorial employees, developed a design stylebook, and went through a dry run to familiarize the desk people with the new formats.

Reader acceptance is also critical. How the redesign is implemented depends on the condition of the newspaper. If the newspaper is operating from a position of strength in the market and has a reasonably high degree of acceptance from readers, the design should be phased in. If a newspaper is failing, management may have to make the changes overnight. That obviously is the last resort. A failing newspaper will not be saved by a redesign. Peter Palazzo redesigned the *New York Herald Tribune* and the *Chicago Daily News* as they lay on their deathbeds. The diagnosis was terminal before the transfusion. The time to redesign is when things are going well. A newspaper that is constantly updating is responding to changing market conditions.

A close look at the *New York Times* behind its traditional news pages reveals a surprisingly well-designed variety of sections. The *Times* changed a section at a time, quietly and steadily. Its readers, like those of the *Wall Street Journal,* are consumers of the newspaper's tradition, credibility, and authority. Any dramatic change in format or content could have been disastrous.

The *Town Talk* prepared its readers by publishing full-page explanations of the redesign twice. Newspaper reading is a habit. A dramatic change in the content, organization, and appearance of the paper is more acceptable to the staff than the readers. When the Long Beach papers were redesigned, the changes were phased in over a year's time. Depending on the depth and variety of changes, a gradual phase-in, accompanied by promotional advertising and columns explaining the changes, will reassure present readers and attract the attention of new ones. A phase-in is likely to result in some unpleasant typographic effects as both the old and the new appear on the same page, but that will be more bothersome to journalists than readers in the short run. The readers will be affected, however, if the clash of materials continues for an extended period.

The results

Ledger-Star. Readers told the editors that most of them buy the afternoon paper instead of the morning because they go to work early in the day. Nonreaders said they did not have time to read the paper. The solution encompassed the following.

17.1. After researching the market, the Norfolk (Va.) *Ledger-Star* editors decided to publish a scanner's paper—one that could be read quickly—and emphasized news that appealed to their marketplace.

A scanner's paper is shown in Figure 17.1. It differs from its predecessor (Fig. 17.2) in that it has a higher element count, more focused marketing, shorter stories, more labeling, bolder typography, and the same format on Page 1 and section fronts each day. As part of the education process for the staff, designer Alan Jacobson remade old *Ledger*s by using the format and philosophy of the new *Ledger*. The before-and-after comparisons are shown in the stylebook (Fig. 17.3). The redesign was promoted for six weeks on television, radio, and billboards and in house ads. Circulation added new delivery districts and set penetration goals. Carriers were offered prizes for new subscriptions, and professional sales crews helped sell the paper.

17.2. Before the redesign of the *Ledger-Star*, there were fewer elements and less focused editing.

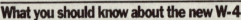

17.3.   As part of the staff education process,
the *Ledger-Star* put before-and-after examples in
its design stylebook.

Daily Town Talk. In Alexandria, La., management's primary goal was to clean up the typographic clutter and to organize the product better. Over the years, various department editors had designed their own logos and added typefaces without regard to what other sections were doing. As a result, there were 10 headline faces and nearly a dozen logo formats. The paper's primary headline face was Futura medium (Fig. 17.4). Because Futura is a light type, the newspaper lacked contrast and typographic vigor. Futura also has a small *x*-height. Futura bold and extrabold, rather than looking modern and dignified, looks short and squat. Working from the typefaces already in the typesetter, Daryl Moen replaced Futura with Royal Bold and used the lighter Royal as the subordinate head. Labels are set in Gothic. He also standardized logos and pullout quotes, increased the front page element count by building several short stories in the horizontal module at the bottom, and stretched a green bar, the corporate color, across the module (Fig. 17.5). The paper runs front page color photos daily. The order in which regular features and sections are run was standardized. More effort was made to get readers into stories by increasing the use of pullouts, including design of column logos that had pullout quotes in them and design of a 1-column headshot cutline format that requires the editor to write a tease for the story.

17.4. Before its redesign, the *Alexandria Daily Town Talk* had a mix of typefaces throughout the paper and was not organized consistently.

17.5. After the redesign, the *Daily Town Talk* was bolder, more consistent, and better organized. The front page also had a higher element count because of the built-in frame at the bottom.

Colorado Springs Gazette Telegraph. Just as significant as Robert Lockwood's redesign, which was a dramatic facelift, was the change in the management structure of the newsroom. Long before the redesign was implemented, a deputy managing editor of design and graphics was appointed. Previously, the graphics editor was on the same level as other department editors such as Sports and City. At the deputy managing editor level, the design director has authority to influence how the information is presented in all departments. The design director now manages the photo, design, and art departments, which were greatly expanded to handle the demand of the new product. Someone from the design department works at each copy desk.

Like the *Ledger-Star,* the redesigned *Gazette Telegraph* is strictly formatted (Fig. 17.6). The nameplate features a color photo with scenic Pike's Peak, an area landmark. The photo changes with the seasons. Below the nameplate are shorts, such as teasers for a popular television show or a reference to a story on Page 1. The briefs can stand alone or refer to the inside story. Most of the photos are in color; on pages where color is available, the labels are also in color. Page 2 (Fig. 17.7) is dedicated to a table of contents of text and visuals and the weather package.

17.6.   The redesigned *Colorado Springs Gazette Telegraph* features color, strict organization, and labeling.

17.7.   Page 2 has a magazinelike table of contents in addition to the familiar weather package.

Headlines are in Franklin Gothic Bold Condensed, Demibold Condensed, and Century. The labels are in different weights of Franklin Gothic. Text type is 9.5-pt. Century Schoolbook set on a 10-pt. slug. The product is quite a change from the old *Gazette Telegraph* (Fig. 17.8).

The stylebook

Like the editing stylebook, the purpose of the design stylebook is to enforce consistency and arbitrate disputes. It should not restrict creativity. Stylebooks should concentrate on what is, not what should not be. The book should be written with the minimum of "nevers."

The length and detail of a stylebook varies according to the size of the newspaper and the staff. Small newspapers, which do not have many sections, may get by with a few pages; papers with several sections and several people doing layouts need a stylebook that will probably run 50 or more pages. Formats alone often take another 10 to 20 pages.

Every stylebook should include information on how the paper is to be organized, the grid (Fig. 17.9); typography; spacing; rules; photography; color; and design accessories such as logos, cutlines, jump lines, etc. By the time the staff receives the stylebook, members should be well briefed on the contents. Some excerpts from two typical stylebooks follow. One is for the Copley Los Angeles newspapers, which were redesigned by Mario Garcia of the Poynter Institute; the other is from the *Alexandria Daily Town Talk,* which was redesigned by Moen.

17.8. The former *Gazette Telegraph* nameplate and the format of the teasers gave the paper a dated 1960s look.

Copley Stylebook. "A key goal of the redesign is to create a series of 'handles' for the reader to grasp enabling him/her to scan the paper easily and find stories or fixed features of interest. Indexing has another benefit: highlighted items can catch the reader's eye and lure them into stories they might otherwise have passed by. . . .

"Our 1986 focus group studies showed many of our readers are scanners who spend anywhere from 10–45 minutes reading our newspapers. It is our job to get them where they want to be as quickly and effectively as possible; the less time readers spend searching, the more time they can spend reading. . . .

"The basic color scheme for a page is a combination of light and dark tones, chosen from a limited number of options. . . . The following circumstances are appropriate for color screens: miniposter packages; art elements (index, bars, at-a-glance boxes, promo boxes); art-directed pages under the direction of graphic designer or photo editor."

Daily Town Talk **Stylebook.** "Contrast in weight and form is built into basic *Town Talk* typography. You will rely on two weights, or colors, of type in the serif headline display faces. Additional contrast is achieved by using sans serif type in cutlines, labels and page headers. Because contrast in weight and form are built into the basic typography, there is little need to deviate from the basic faces. The exception is when you are matching the typeface with the content of the story on a special design package.

"Standard spacing is built into the formats in the pagination system.

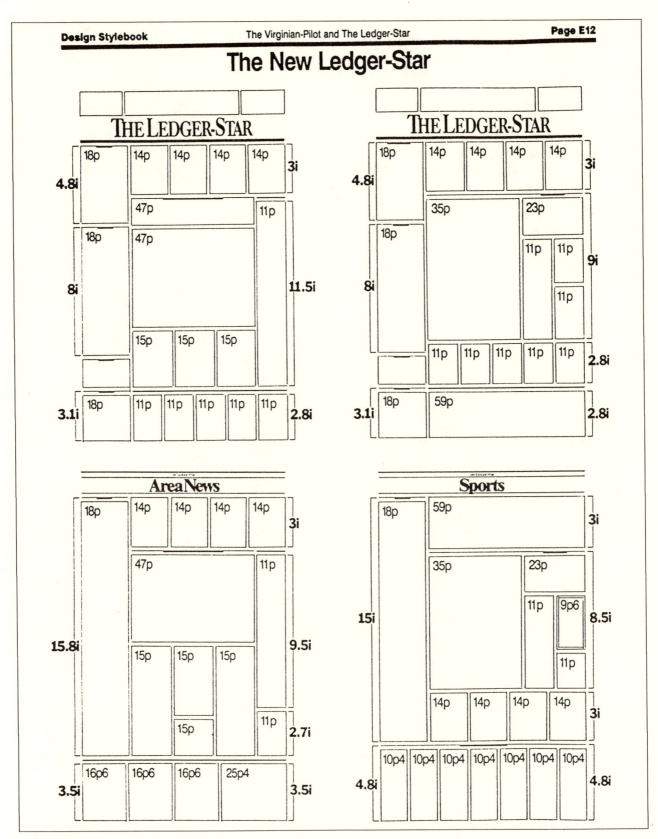

17.9. Because the *Ledger-Star* formatted its newspaper, the grid options are shown in the stylebook.

Leading is based on the principle that there should be more space between unrelated material than between related material.

"For instance, there is more leading between body copy and the subhead below it than there is between the subhead and the body copy below it. . . . "

Education and promotion

A good newspaper belongs to the readers, not the publisher. That is why it is important to talk to the readers when you are about ready to introduce the redesign. You are changing *their* newspaper; they at least deserve the courtesy of knowing ahead of time what is coming and why.

The newspaper can communicate through stories or advertisements. The Alexandria paper ran two full-page stories and graphics to explain the redesign. One appeared just before the new look was introduced; the other page appeared the day the redesign was introduced (Fig. 17.10). Those kinds of efforts are educational. The *Chicago Sun-Times* underwent a modest change and promoted it by showing the evolution of the newspaper's nameplate (Fig. 17.11).

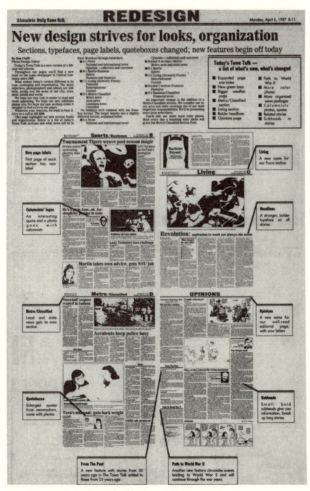

17.10. Readers of the *Daily Town Talk* were introduced to the redesign through a full-page information graphic.

17.11. The *Chicago Sun-Times* teased the design changes by showing the evolution of the nameplate.

Then get ready for the negative reaction. Regardless of how good or bad the newspaper was before the redesign, some readers will not like the change. The primary complaint usually is that they cannot find what they were looking for. That complaint is a reflection of the importance most readers place on consistency of organization. Those complaints fade quickly as readers become accustomed to the new format. When the *Colorado Springs Gazette Telegraph* unveiled its new design, it had five people manning the phones for two days. All calls were logged; callers were even asked some demographic information. The number one complaint? They did not want the comic strip Gasoline Alley taken out of the paper. The editors got the message; it was quickly returned.

When is the design work done? For some, like J. Ford Huffman, formerly of the Rochester *Times-Union,* the answer is, "never and that's the best part about our new format. Each time we try to package the news of the day, we discover different ways to use the typographic elements we have." A dynamic publication is one that is constantly finding better ways to report and explain the world to its readers. Progress should not come in five-year intervals.

GLOSSARY

Agate – Traditionally, 5½-pt. type, though now commonly used for type up to 7 points; agate line is an advertising space measurement ¹⁄₁₄ of an inch deep.

Ascender – That part of the letter that extends above the body of the type.

Balance – Placement of elements to produce a harmoniously integrated page.

Banner – A large headline that extends across the top of the front page above the most important story of the day.

Bar – In type, a horizontal or slanted line connected at both ends.

Baseline – Line on which the center body of type rests.

Bastard type – Type set a different width than the standard column setting.

Black letter – *See* Text letter.

Bleed – An illustration filling one or more margins and running to the edge of the page.

Blurb – A quote or a small part of a story displayed in type larger than text, usually 14 to 18 points.

Body type – *See* Text type.

Boldface – Type that has thicker, darker lines than the medium or lighter weights of the same face.

Border – An ornamental rule.

Bowl – In type, the line enclosing a space.

Burn – To transfer type and images to a sensitized plate.

Byline – Line crediting the writer, photographer, or designer. Most commonly, it refers to the writer's credit at the top of the story.

Cathode ray tube (CRT) – An electronic tube used to transmit words and pictures onto paper or film.

Characters per pica (CPP) – Measurement of the width of a typeface, computed by counting the average number of letters that will fit in a given horizontal space and dividing by the number of picas.

Cold type – Type produced by a photographic or digitized process rather than by pressing inked metal forms against paper.

Color filter – Filter that absorbs all but one color.

Color separation – The product of a method of separating a color print or transparency into its three primary colors and black.

Concord – Blending of typographical elements to form a uniform impression.

Contrast – Effect achieved by varying shapes, sizes, and weights of the elements on the page.

Contrast and balance – Layout technique in which a page is balanced by using contrasting shapes and weights.

Counter – White space within the letter.

Cursive – Race of type that is a stylized reproduction of formal handwriting. Also known as script.

Cutline – Information under a picture or artwork; also called a caption.

Cutoff rule – A line used to separate elements on a page.

Deck – One or more lines of display type that are smaller than the main headline.

Descender – That part of the letter that extends below the body of the type.

Design – A system of planning in which the person who arranges the elements on the page has some influence over the collection and selection of those elements.

Display type – Type larger than that used for text. In newspapers, display type ranges upward from 14 points.

Double truck – Facing pages in which the space between the pages is also used.

Dummy – The page, usually half the size of the page being produced, on which the editor shows where all the elements are to be arranged; the blueprint of the page.

Duotone — One color plus black, achieved by shooting two halftone negatives of the picture and producing two plates for the page.

Dutch wrap — Extending copy beyond the headline; also called a raw wrap.

Ear — The distinctive stroke at the top right of the letters *g* and *r*.

Em — A unit of space equal to the space taken by the capital *M* of the type size being used.

En — Half an em, or half the size of the capital *M* of the type size being used.

Family — In type classification, typefaces that are closely related in design and share a common name. They differ in width, weight, and form.

Flag — *See* Nameplate.

Flush left — Type that begins at the left-hand edge or border of the column.

Flush right — Type that ends at the right-hand edge or border of the column.

Focus — Starting point on the page, achieved by selecting a dominant element or elements.

Font — A complete set of type of one style and size.

Frame — Those elements of the page that are the same each issue. Teasers or a column are often part of a page frame.

Gutter — The vertical white space between columns of type.

Hairline — The thin stroke of a letter.

Halftone — Reproduction in which tones have been photographed through a screen to break up the areas into dots whose size determines the dark and light areas.

Hammer — One- or two-word headline in large type, usually over a deck.

Hues — Pure colors such as red, yellow, green and blue.

Inset — Photograph or copy contained within the borders of a photograph.

Italic — Serif type sloped to the right.

Jim dash — Cutoff rule that does not cross the entire column.

Justified type — Type set so that the lines are all of equal length by hyphenating words and placing more or less space between words.

Kenaf — A fibrous plant that is being tested as a substitute for wood pulp as a raw material in making newsprint.

Kerning — Touching the letters of type.

Key plate — Printing plate that puts the first image on the paper.

Kicker — Three or four words that are set about half the size of the main headline and usually appear flush left above the main headline.

Layout — Arrangement of elements of the page, usually done without any voice in the preparation or selection of those elements.

Leading — Sometimes written "ledding," this is the space between lines of type.

Leg — A column or wrap of type in a story.

Legibility — Measurement of the speed and accuracy with which type can be read and understood.

Letterpress — Method of printing in which raised letters are inked and pressed against paper.

Logo — An insignia of type, art, or both that ties together stories in a series or identifies a regular feature such as a columnist.

Loop — The curved part of letters such as *o, c,* and *e,* which is often drawn distinctively.

Masthead — A listing of the publication's managers and editors, name of the paper, date, volume, and sometimes the publication's creed.

Modern — Sometimes used to differentiate among types in the roman race. The type is geometric and symmetrical.

Module — A rectangular or square shape. To run a story in modules means that each column of type is the same depth.

Mortise — Overlapping of two or more photographs or of a headline and a photograph.

Nameplate — The newspaper's name as it appears at the top of Page 1; also known as the flag.

Novelty — *See* Ornamental.

Nut graph — A conversational headline deck; it includes subject, verb, and articles.

Oblique — Sans serif type slanted to the right.

Offset — A printing method in which the inked image transfers from plate to rubber blanket to paper. It is based on the principle that grease and water do not mix.

Old style — Sometimes used to differentiate among types in the roman race. The type is asymmetrical and less formal looking than other roman faces.

Optimum format—The layout in which columns are set at the most legible line length. For broadsheet newspapers, this has been six columns, but with pages becoming narrower, five columns is becoming more legible.

Ornamental—Race of type specially designed to create such a specific mood or emotion that it is not useful for other uses; also known as novelty.

Pagination—System of producing pages from a typesetting machine, thus eliminating the need for a composing room.

Photocomposition—Method of producing type by exposing negatives of the characters on film or paper or reproducing them digitally.

Pica—A unit of measurement; 6 picas equal 1 inch.

Plate—The metal on which the photographic image of a page is developed by exposing it to a negative. The plate is then placed on the press.

Point—A unit of measurement; 12 points equal 1 pica. Headlines are measured vertically in points.

Poster—The space on the page left after framing to be used for display. A poster or billboard page is one devoted to a single subject. A miniposter is a small space, about tabloid size, devoted to a display.

Process color—Full- or four-color reproduction achieved by separating each color on individual pieces of film and burning them on separate printing plates. The process colors are yellow, magenta, cyan, and black.

Proportion—Proper size and spacing relationships among the elements on the page.

Pullouts—Any typographic devices pulled out of a story and displayed in form other than text. Pullouts include blurbs, summary boxes, fact boxes, quotes, etc.

Pyramid format—Arrangement of advertisements in a stack up the right or left side of the page.

Quad—An empty printing unit for spacing. An em quad is the square of the type size.

Race—The broadest category of type classification. Type is divided into six categories; roman, square serif, sans serif, text letter, cursive, and ornamental.

Ragged right type—Type set with a fixed left starting point but with an irregular ending point at the right of the line.

Readability—Measurement of the difficulty of the content.

Readin—Type subordinate in size to the main head and placed above it. The main head completes the thought started in the readin.

Readout—A deck that reads directly out of the main head. Unlike the main head, it is written in a conversational tone.

Roman—A race of type characterized by serifs and thick and thin strokes; also used to mean straight-up-and-down type as opposed to italic or oblique.

Rule—A plain line that ranges upward in width from ½ point. *See* Border.

Sans serif.—Race of type without serifs and with uniform strokes. Also referred to as gothic.

Scanner—Electronic or laser machine that reads one color of a photograph at a time and transfers the image to a separation.

Screen—Glass or film used in cameras to break copy into halftone dots. The number of lines per linear inch of the screen determines the fineness of the reproduction; the higher the number, the better the reproduction.

Script—*See* Cursive.

Segmenting—Dividing a story into smaller bites.

Separation—A negative containing elements to be printed in one of the process colors. A full-color picture normally requires four separations.

Series—The range of sizes in a typeface. With photocomposition and digital typesetting, the range of sizes includes fractions of points.

Serif—The cross-stroke at the end of the main stroke of a letter.

Shades—Color formed by mixing pure colors with black (*See* Hues).

Sidebar—A secondary story intended to be run with a major story on the same subject.

Side-saddle—Placement of type to the left side of the story rather than over it; also called side head.

Slug—One-word designation for a story as it moves through the production system.

Spot color—Any color printing other than process.

Square serif—Race of type with monotone strokes and squared-off or blocked serifs.

Stereotype—A flat or curved metal plate cast from a papier-mâché mold; the process.

Stress—The thickness of a curved stroke; the shading of the letter.

Stroke—The primary line of the letter.

Tabloid—A publication whose pages are approximately half the size of a broadsheet of full-sized newspaper and usually printed on newsprint.

Teaser—A graphic written and designed to draw readers' attention to something in the publication, usually on an inside page.

Terminal—The distinctive finish to the stroke on sans serif type.

Text letter—Face of type that has a medieval appearance of early European hand lettering. Also known as black letter.

Text type—Also referred to as body type; used in the stories and editorials.

Tints—Color formed by mixing pure colors with white.

Tombstoning—Bumping of two or more headlines or unrelated graphic elements.

Tones—Color formed by mixing pure colors and white and black.

Transitional—Sometimes used to differentiate among types in the roman race. The type has characteristics of both old style and modern faces.

Transparency—A color photograph on slide film.

Typography—The arrangement and effect of type.

Unity—Harmony among the elements on a page and among the parts of the publication.

Value—The degree of lightness or darkness of a color.

Video display terminal (VDT)—Electronic typewriter with a televisionlike screen.

Well format—Arrangement of advertisements in the shape of a U on a page.

W format—A layout in which one column is run about 50 percent wider than the others.

Wrap—A column or leg of type. Type set over six columns would have six wraps.

X-height—Height of the lowercase x, the standard for measuring type.

REFERENCES CITED

Aaronson, Bernard. 1970. Some affective stereotypes of color. *Int. J. Symb.* 2(2):15–27.

Bain, Chic. 1980. Newspaper design and newspaper readership: A series of four experiments. Center for News Communications Res. Rep. 10, School of Journalism, Indiana University, Bloomington.

Bain, Chic, and Weaver, David H. 1979. Newspaper design and newspaper readership. Paper presented to the Graphics Division, Association for Education in Journalism, Houston.

Becker, D., Heinrich, J., Von Sichowky, R., and Wendt, D. 1970. Reader preferences for typeface and leading. *J. Typogr. Res.* 1(Winter):61–66.

Benton, Camille. 1979. The connotative dimensions of selected display typefaces. Paper presented to the Association for Education in Journalism, Houston.

Birren, Faber. 1961. *Creative Color.* New York: Reinhold, p. 48.

Clark, Ruth. 1979. Changing needs of changing readers. American Society of Newspaper Editors Newspaper Readership Project, May, p. 30.

Clarke, Rory. 1986. A study of the *Tampa Tribune* headline format. Unpublished master's professional project. Columbia, Mo.: University of Missouri.

Click, J. W., and Stempel, Guido H. III. 1974. Reader response to modern and traditional front page make-up. American Newspaper Publishers Association News Research Bull. 4, June.

———. 1976. Reader response to front pages with four-color halftones. *Journalism Q.* 53:736–38.

Curley, John. 1979. PILOT research tailored to unique needs of each newspaper. *Gannetteer* March:8.

Curley, Thomas. 1979. Readers want latest news, consistent and complete newspapers. *Gannetteer* March:6–8.

———. 1980. What the readers want—And how newspapers can give it to them. Editorially speaking. *Gannetteer* May:2–4.

Dowding, G. 1957. *Factors in the Choice of Typefaces.* London: Wace.

Emery, Edwin, and Emery, Michael. 1978. *The Press and America,* 4th ed. New Jersey: Prentice-Hall, p. 236.

Fabrizio, R., Kaplan, L., and Teal, G. 1967. Readability as a function of the straightness of right-hand margins. *J. Typogr. Res.* January:90–95.

Garcia, Mario, and Fry, Don, eds. 1986. *Color in American Newspapers.* St. Petersburg, Fla.: Poynter Institute for Media Studies.

Gersh, Debra. 1987. Reaching the younger generation. *Editor and Publisher,* June 13, pp. 34, 50.

Hartley, James, and Barnhill, Peter. 1971. Experiments with unjustified text. *Visible Language* 5(3):265–78.

Haskins, Jack. 1958. Testing suitability of typefaces for editorial subject matter. *Journalism Q.* 35:186–94.

Haskins, Jack P., and Flynne, Lois P. 1974. Effect of headline typeface variation on reading interest. *Journalism Q.* 51:677–82.

Hays, Harold T. P. 1977. The Push Pin conspiracy. *New York Times Magazine.* March 6, pp. 19–22.

Holmes, Grace. 1931. The relative legibility of black print and white print. *J. Appl. Psychol.* 15(June):248–51.

Hubbard, Tom. 1987. AP photo chief, AEJMC, professors discuss ethics, electronic pictures at convention. *News Photographer* January:23–33.

Hunter, Carol. 1986. How can you make it look good? APME Media Competition Committee, Earl Maucker, Fort Lauderdale *Sun-Sentinel,* chairman, pp. 20–23.

Hurlburt, Allen, 1976. *Publication Design.* New York: Van Nostrand Reinhold, p. 7.

Hurley, Gerald D., and McDougall, Angus.

1971. *Visual Impact in Print*. Chicago: American Publishers Press, p. 45

Hvistendahl, J. K., and Kahl, Mary R. 1975. Roman v. sans serif body type: Readability and reader preference. ANPA News Res. Bull. 2, January.

Itten, Johannes. 1964. *Design and Form*. New York: Reinhold, p. 98.

Kobre, Kenneth. 1980. *Photojournalism, the Professionals' Approach*. Somerville, Mass.: Curtin and London, p. 9.

Mauro, John. 1986. *Survey of Front Page Color vs. Black and White*. Richmond, Va.: Media General.

Mott, Frank Luther. 1945. *American Journalism*. New York: Macmillan. (Most of the dates contained in this discussion of evolution of design are taken from Mott's book.)

Orlando Sentinel Research Department. 1984. Attitudes toward the Orlando *Sentinel* in the central Florida market.

Paik, Kenneth. 1985. How the versatile negative color approach works. Chapter in A White Paper on Newspaper Color. National Press Photographers Association, Durham, N.C., pp. 30–31.

Pipps, Val Steven. 1985. Measuring the effects of newspaper graphic elements on reader satisfaction with a redesigned newspaper using two methodologies. Doctoral diss., Newhouse School of Mass Communications, Syracuse, N.Y.

Pitnof, Barbara Bell. 1980. The front page. *Nieman Reports* Summer:46–49.

Poindexter, Paula M. 1978. Non-readers: Why they don't read. ANPA News Res. Rep. 9, January.

Polansky, Sharon. 1988. Address to the Pittsburgh Design Conference.

Poulton, E. C. 1955. Letter differentiation and rate of comprehension of reading. *J. Appl. Psychol.* 49:358–62.

Puncekar, Sandra. 1980. Presses: Technology is catching up. *Presstime* June:4–6.

Reaves, Shiela. 1987. Digital retouching. Is there a place for it in newspaper photography? An examination of the ethics. *News Photographer,* January:23–33.

Robinson, David O., Abbamonte, Michael, and Evans, Selby. 1971. Why serifs are important: The perception of small print. *Visible Language* 5(Autumn):353–59.

Roethlein, B. E. 1912. The relative legibility of different faces of printing type. *Am. J. Psychol.* 23(January):1–36.

Rowe, Sandra. 1986. Reports from seven editors who chose to run difficult photos. APME Photo and Graphics Committee report, James Vesely, *Detroit News,* chairman, pp. 2–3.

Sharpe, Deborah T. 1974. *The Psychology of Color and Design*. Chicago: Nelson-Hall, pp. 91–92.

Siskind, Theresa G. 1979. The effect of newspaper design on reader preferences. *Journalism Q.* 56:54–61.

Sissors, Jack Z. 1974. Do youthful, college-educated readers prefer contemporary newspaper designs? *Journalism Q.* 51:307–13.

Stanton, James C. 1986. Newspaper design preferences among students revisited. *Journalism Q.* 63:633–36.

Tannenbaum, Percy, Jacobson, Harvey K., and Norris, Eleanor L. 1964. An experimental investigation of typeface connotations. *Journalism Q.* 41:65-73.

Terry, Art. 1980. Photography for editors. Unpublished master's thesis, University of Missouri, Columbia.

Thornburg, Ron. 1986. The ethics of the controversial photo. APME Photo and Graphics Committee Report, James Vesely, *Detroit News,* chairman, pp. 2–11.

Tinker, Miles A. 1963. *Legibility of Print*. Ames: Iowa State University Press, pp. 88–107.

Tinker, Miles A., and Paterson, D. G. 1929. Studies of typographical factors influencing speed of reading: III. Length of line. *J. Appl. Psychol.* June:205–19.

Tipton, Leonard, 1978. ANPA newspaper readership studies. ANPA News Res. Rep. 13, July, p. 4.

Tufte, Edward R. 1983. *The Visual Display of Quantitative Information*. Cheshire, Conn.: Graphics Press.

U & lc. What's new from ITC. 1983. August:27–33.

ADDITIONAL READING

Arnold, Edmond C. 1969. *Modern Newspaper Design.* New York: Harper and Row.

———. 1981. *Designing the Total Newspaper.* New York: Harper and Row.

Bain, Eric K. 1970. *The Theory and Practice of Typographic Design.* New York: Hastings House.

Baird, Russell N., Turnbull, Arthur T., and McDonald, Duncan. 1987. *The Graphics of Communication,* 5th ed. New York: Holt, Rinehart and Winston.

Berry, W. Turner, and Johnson, A. F. 1953. *Encyclopedia of Type Faces.* London: Blandford Press.

Birren, Faber. 1969. *Principles of Color.* New York: Van Nostrand Reinhold.

Bohle, Robert. 1984. *From News to Newsprint: Producing a Student Newspaper.* Englewood Cliffs, N.J.: Prentice-Hall.

Burt, Sir Cyril. 1959. *A Psychological Study of Typography.* London: Cambridge University Press.

Conover, Theodore E. 1985. *Graphic Communications Today.* St. Paul: West.

Craig, James. 1981. *Designing with Type.* New York: Watson-Guptill.

Dair, Carl. 1982. *Design with Type.* Toronto: University of Toronto Press.

Dorn, Raymond. 1983. *Tabloid Design for the Organizational Press: A Compendium of Designs.* Chicago: Lawrence Ragan Communications.

Ernst, Sandra B. 1977. *The ABC's of Typography.* New York: Art Direction Book Co.

Evans, Harold. 1973. *Newspaper Design, Book Five.* New York: Rinehart and Winston.

Garcia, Mario, R. 1987. *Contemporary Newspaper Design, a Structural Approach,* 2d ed. Englewood Cliffs, N.J.: Prentice-Hall.

Gregory, D. L. 1970. *The Intelligent Eye.* New York: McGraw-Hill.

Holmes, Nigel. 1984. *Designer's Guide to Creating Charts and Diagrams.* New York: Watson-Guptill.

———. 1985. *Designing Pictorial Symbols.* New York: Watson-Guptill.

Hurlburt, Allen, 1977. *Layout: The Design of the Printed Page.* New York: Watson-Guptill.

———. 1982. *The Grid.* New York: Van Nostrand Reinhold.

Johnson, A. F. 1966. *Type Designs.* Norwich, England: Jarrold and Sons.

Lieberman, J. Ben. 1978. *Type and Typefaces,* 2d ed. New Rochelle, N.Y.: Myriade Press.

Merrinian, Frank. 1965. *A.T.A. Type Comparison Book.* Advertising Association of America.

Muller-Brockman, Josef. 1981. *Grid Systems in Graphic Design.* New York: Hastings House.

Nelson, Roy Paul. 1983. *Publication Design,* 3rd ed. Dubuque, Iowa: William C. Brown.

Ovink, G. W. 1938. *Legibility, Atmosphere—Value and Forms of Printing Types.* Leiden: A. W. Sijfhoff.

Polk, Ralph W., and Gage, Harry L. 1953. *A Composition Manual.* Washington, D.C.: Printing Industry of America.

Rehe, Rolf. 1979. *Typography: How to Make It Most Legible.* Carmel, Ind: Design Research International.

———. 1985. *Typography and Design for Newspapers.* Carmel, Ind.: Design Research International.

Rookledge, Gordon, and Perfect, Christopher. 1983. *Rookledge's International Typefinder: The Essential Handbook of Typeface Recognition and Selection.* New York: Beil.

Rosen, Ben. 1967. *Type and Typography,* 2d ed. New York: Van Nostrand Reinhold.

Seybold, John. 1979. *Fundamentals of Modern Photocomposition.* Media, Pa.: Seybold Publications.

———. 1984. *The World of Digital Typesetting.* Media, Pa.: Seybold Publications.

Smith, Charles. 1965. *Color—Study and*

Teaching. New York: Van Nostrand Reinhold.

Solomon, Martin, 1986. *The Art of Typography.* New York: Watson-Guptill.

Spencer, Herbert. 1969. *The Visible Word.* New York: Hastings House.

Wheatley, W. E. 1985. *Typeface Analogue.* Arlington, Va.: National Composition Assoc.

White, Jan V. 1974. *Editing by Design: Word and Picture Communication for Editors and Designers.* New York: R. R. Bowker.

Zachrisson, Bror. 1965. *Studies in the Legibility of Printed Text.* Stockholm, Sweden: Almquist and Wiskel.

PERIODICALS

Advertising Age, 740 Rush St., Chicago, IL 60611.

AdWeek, 49 East 21st St., New York, NY 10010

American Photographer, 1225 Portland Place, P.O. Box 2833, Boulder, CO 80302.

APME News, The Associated Press, 50 Rockefeller Plaza, New York, NY 10020.

Art Direction, 10 E. 39th St., New York, NY 10016.

Bulletin, American Society of Newspaper Editors, 11600 Sunrise Valley Dr., Reston, VA 22091.

Communication Arts Magazine, P.O. Box 10300, Palo Alto, CA 94303.

Design: The Journal of the Society of Newspaper Design. The Newspaper Center, Box 17290, Dulles International Airport, Washington, DC 20041.

Design Graphics World, 6255 Barfield Rd., Atlanta, GA 30328.

Editor & Publisher, 11 West 19th St., New York, NY 10011.

Folio, 125 Elm St., Box 4006, New Canaan, CT 06840.

Graphic Arts Monthly, 875 Third Ave., New York, NY 10022.

Graphic Design: USA, 120 E. 56th St., New York, NY 10022.

How: The Magazine of Ideas and Techniques, 355 Lexington Ave., New York, NY 10017.

Ligature, 145 East 32nd St., New York, NY 10016 (free).

News Photographer, National Press Photographers Assoc., Inc., Box 1146, Durham, NC 22702.

Photographer's Forum, 614 Santa Barbara St., Santa Barbara, CA 93101.

Presstime, American Newspaper Publishers Association, 11600 Sunrise Valley Dr., Reston, VA 22091.

Professional Photographer, 1090 Executive Way, Des Plaines, IL 60018.

Step-By-Step Graphics, 6000 N. Forest Park Dr., Peoria, IL 61614.

U & lc, 2 Hammarskjöld Plaza, New York, NY 10017 (free).

Credits

The author and publisher wish to thank the following publications and individuals for permission to reprint their material as well as others who graciously granted permission but did not request a credit citation.

Figs. 1.6, 4.1, 5.11, 9.2, 9.3, 10.13, 13.26: Reprinted with permission from the *Seattle Times.*

Figs. 1.7, 8.26, 8.27, 10.6, 10.12, 10.16: Copyright © 1987 *Los Angeles Times.*

Figs. 1.8, 3.4, 13.23, 17.1, 17.2: Norfolk (Va.) *Ledger-Star.*

Figs. 1.9, 3.3, 10.7, 14.20, 14.46: Reprinted courtesy of the *Boston Globe.*

Figs. 2.7, 2.8, 7.4, 7.14, 10.17, 14.29, 14.36, 14.39, 14.49: Reprinted courtesy of the Fort Lauderdale (Fla.) *News/Sun-Sentinel*

Figs. 3.11, 14.9, 14.18, 14.52: *Los Angeles Herald Examiner.*

Figs. 3.13, 10.18, 10.19, 10.20, 14.51, 16.10: Reprinted with permission from the Memphis (Tenn.) *Commercial Appeal.*

Figs. 3.5, 7.2, 7.9: Lakeland (Fla.) *Ledger.*

Fig. 3.6: *Pittsburgh Post-Gazette.*

Fig. 4.4: Reprinted by permission; Albany (N.Y.) *Times-Union.*

Figs. 4.5, 14.54: *Reston* (Va.) *Times.*

Figs. 4.10, 14.21: *Philadelphia Inquirer.*

Figs. 4.12, 6.16, 14.25, 14.28: Reprinted with permission. Copyright © 1986–87, *Detroit News.* A Gannett newspaper.

Figs. 4.14, 4.15, 6.18, 13.12, 14.14, 14.38: Copyright © 1987, *USA Today.* Reprinted with permission.

Figs. 4.17, 6.13, 6.19: *Dallas Times Herald* graphics.

Figs. 5.7, 14.19: *Marin Independent Journal.*

Fig. 5.18: Photo credit—Steve Biehn, *Daily Ardmoreite.*

Figs. 5.21, 5.28, 6.24: Lexington (Ky.) *Herald-Leader.*

Fig. 5.26: New Orleans (La.) *Times-Picayune.*

Figs. 6.4, 6.5, 6.8, 6.25: Knight-Ridder Graphics Network. By Tribune Media Services, Inc., 1988.

Figs. 6.5, 6.7, 6.11, 6.20, 13.35, 16.4: *Chicago Tribune.*

Figs. 6.14, 13.18, 14.35: *Tampa Tribune.*

Fig. 6.15: Reprinted with permission from the *San Diego Union.*

Figs. 6.17, 12.8: *Virginian-Pilot.*

Figs. 6.23, 14.17: *Kansas City Times,* Copyright © 1987, all rights reserved.

Figs. 7.1, 10.8, 14.31, 14.44: *Hartford Courant.*

Fig. 7.8: *Daily Oklahoman.*

Figs. 7.13, 14.22: *Arkansas Gazette.*

Figs. 7.15, 15.21: *Columbia Daily Tribune.*

Figs. 7.16, 7.17, 7.18, 14.23: Copyright © 1987 *Washington Post.*

Fig. 8.1: *New York Amsterdam News.*

Figs. 8.4, 13.34: Copyright © 1986, Newsday, Inc. Reprinted with permission.

Figs. 8.6, 8.12, 8.21: Reprinted with permission from the *Christian Science Monitor.* Copyright © 1987 The Christian Science Publishing Society. All rights reserved.

Figs. 8.7, 8.13, 8.20: Copyright © 1986, 1987 New Times, Inc.

Figs. 8.8, 8.15, 8.19, 14.48: Copyright © 1986 *San Francisco Business Times.*

Fig. 8.9: Tom Helmick, production/art director, *New Orleans City Business.*

Figs. 8.10, 8.11: *Baton Rouge Business Report.*

Fig. 8.14: Denver (Colo.) *Rocky Mountain News.*

Fig. 8.16: Ted Wood, *Jackson Hole* (Wyo.) *News.*

Figs. 8.17, 8.18: Reprinted with permission from the Aug. 11, 1986, issue of *Crain's Chicago Business.* Copyright © 1986 by Crain Communications Inc.

Fig. 8.22: Layout and Design—Grover Gatewood, *Hamptons Newspaper/Magazine.*

Figs. 8.24, 10.10, 13.11: Copyright © 1987 *Kansas City Star,* all rights reserved.

Fig. 8.25: *Orlando Sentinel.*

Fig. 9.5: Reprinted with permission from the *San Jose Mercury News.*

Figs. 10.14, 14.12, 14.53: Reprinted with permission from the *Des Moines Register.*

Fig. 13.2: *St. Petersburg Times.*

Figs. 13.3, 13.9, 13.14: Reprinted courtesy of the *Fort Worth Star-Telegram.*

Fig. 13.4: *Baltimore Sun.* Copyright © 1987 the Baltimore Sun.

Figs. 13.6, 13.7, 17.6, 17.7, 17.8: Reprinted with permission from the *Colorado Springs Gazette Telegraph.*

Fig. 13.18: *Portland Oregonian.*

Figs. 13.19, 13.30, 14.33: *San Antonio Light.*

Figs. 13.22, 16.9: *Charleston* (W. Va.) *Gazette.*

Fig. 13.27: *Virginian-Pilot* and *Ledger-Star.*

Fig. 13.28: *Miami News.*

Fig. 14.2: Reprinted with permission from the Rochester (N.Y.) *Times-Union.*

Figs. 14.3, 14.4: Graphics editor, *Wichita Eagle-Beacon.*

Fig. 14.13: *Star and Tribune,* Minneapolis.

Fig. 14.24: Reprinted by permission from *Adweek.*

Fig. 14.26: *Fort Myers* (Fla.) *News-Press.*

Fig. 14.27: St. Paul *Pioneer Press Dispatch.*

Fig. 14.30: *Anchorage Daily News.*

Fig. 14.32: *Cincinnati Enquirer.*

Figs. 14.40, 14.42, 14.47: *Denver Post.*

Fig. 14.47: Los Angeles *Daily News.*

Fig. 14.57: Copyright © 1987 *St. Louis Post-Dispatch.* Reprinted with permission.

Figs. 16.2, 16.3: The Poynter Institute for Media Studies.